CW01207083

DIE WEHRMACHT IM KAMPF

PANZER TACTICS

Tank Operations in the East, 1941–42

OSKAR MUNZEL

Translated by
LINDEN LYONS

Series editor
MATTHIAS STROHN

CASEMATE
Philadelphia & Oxford

AN AUSA BOOK
Association of the United States Army
2425 Wilson Boulevard, Arlington, Virginia, 22201, USA

Published in the United States of America and Great Britain in 2021 by
CASEMATE PUBLISHERS
1950 Lawrence Road, Havertown, PA 19083, USA
and
The Old Music Hall, 106–108 Cowley Road, Oxford OX4 1JE, UK

© 2021 Association of the U.S. Army
English translation © Casemate Publishers

Originally published as Die Wehrmacht im Kampf 20: Oskar Munzel, *Panzer-Taktik: Raids gepanzerter Verbände im Ostfeldzug 1941/42* (Scharnhorst Buchkameradschaft GmbH, Neckargemünd, 1959)

Hardback Edition: ISBN 978-1-61200-989-6
Digital Edition: ISBN 978-1-61200-990-2

A CIP record for this book is available from the British Library

All rights reserved. No part of this book may be reproduced or transmitted in any form or by any means, electronic or mechanical including photocopying, recording or by any information storage and retrieval system, without permission from the publisher in writing.

Printed and bound in the United Kingdom by TJ Books

Typeset by Versatile PreMedia Service (P) Ltd

For a complete list of Casemate titles, please contact:

CASEMATE PUBLISHERS (US)
Telephone (610) 853-9131
Fax (610) 853-9146
Email: casemate@casematepublishers.com
www.casematepublishers.com

CASEMATE PUBLISHERS (UK)
Telephone (01865) 241249
Email: casemate-uk@casematepublishers.co.uk
www.casematepublishers.co.uk

Front cover: Bundesarchiv Bild 169 0116

Contents

Introduction	v
Translator's Note	ix
Foreword	xi
Offensive Operations	xiii
Translations of Place Names	xv
Maps	xix

Chapter 1	The XXXXVIII Panzer Corps Prepares for the Campaign in Russia	1
Chapter 2	The XXXXVIII Panzer Corps Thrusts to the Stalin Line	5
Chapter 3	The XXXXVIII Panzer Corps Penetrates the Stalin Line	31
Chapter 4	The XXXXVIII Panzer Corps in the Battle of Uman	59
Chapter 5	The XXXXVIII Panzer Corps Thrusts to the Black Sea	89
Chapter 6	The III Panzer Corps Drives Towards Kiev	103
Chapter 7	The XXIV and XXXXVIII Panzer Corps in the Battle of Kiev	107
Chapter 8	The XXIV Panzer Corps Drives Towards the Zusha and in the Direction of Tula	115
Chapter 9	The First Panzer Army Advances into the Caucasus	125
Chapter 10	Experiences with Panzer Attacks	135

Appendix 1	*Headquarters Staff*	145
Appendix 2	*Excerpts from the War Diary of the Commander of the 8th Company of the 6th Panzer Regiment*	148
Appendix 3	*A Selection of Orders Issued by the Units of the 11th Panzer Division*	153
References		162
Index		163

Introduction

The Eastern Front was the decisive theatre of operations during World War II. Approximately 80 per cent of all casualties were sustained here in the titanic clash between National Socialist Germany and the Communist Soviet Union. The first two years saw the occupation of large parts of the Soviet Union during the German summer offensives in 1941 and 1942, respectively. Even though the armoured units and formations formed only a small part of the German (and their allied) troops that fought on the Eastern Front, their mobility and panache was essential in making these gains possible, before the pendulum of war swung irretrievably from (perceived) German superiority to Soviet victory. This book analyses some of the armoured thrusts that occurred on the Eastern Front at that time.

The author of this book, Oskar Munzel, was born in 1899 and joined a cavalry regiment in 1917. His military abilities were spotted by his superiors and he was allowed to remain in the drastically reduced army after World War I. He rose through the ranks and, from June 1941 to September 1943, he served in the 6th Panzer Regiment, which formed part of 3rd Panzer Division that fought on the Eastern Front. In December 1941, Munzel became the commanding officer of this regiment. The division was part of the spear-heads that penetrated deep into Soviet territory, and it was involved in major battles, including the battles of Kiev and Moscow in 1941, and the German thrust towards the Caucasus in 1942. The remainder of the war saw Munzel move between staff positions (including the command of the tank school) and command roles (including divisional and corps command). On 1 December 1944 Munzel was promoted to the rank of Generalmajor. After the war and two years in Allied captivity, Munzel went to Egypt in 1951, where he worked as military advisor for four years. When the West German

Bundeswehr was founded in 1955 Munzel quickly re-joined the army. He served as the commandant of the tank school, clearly making use of his previous experience in this role during the war. Later, he became the *Inspekteur* of the tank forces, and he left the Bundeswehr in 1962 as a Generalmajor, becoming the head of the German military advisory group to Taiwan. He died in Bonn in 1992.

Munzel was thus well equipped to write the study that you, the reader, hold in your hands. He combined practical experience of the command of armoured units and formations with staff posts that had required a more theoretical analysis of this type of warfare. It is therefore not surprising that his writings presented the actual operations and the fighting, but also offered some deep analysis of the actions, their successes and the problems that the German armoured formations had encountered. As Munzel explains in his foreword, he used private or semi-official records for the book in order to 'express from the heart the thoughts and concerns of the combat troops.' Having said this, his writing style is still that of the staff officer who is somewhat detached from the action. This style can appear a little cold, but is necessary in order to move from the personal experiences and hardships to what Munzel regards as the main task of the book: drawing valuable lessons for the command of armoured units and formations.

Munzel wrote the book in 1959. At this time, the Cold War was in full swing and the operational expertise of the former Wehrmacht was highly sought after by NATO, which the Federal Republic of Germany had joined in 1955. The lessons of World War II and the alleged German operational brilliance and tactical superiority on the Eastern Front seemed to offer the solution for the numerically weaker NATO forces in a conventional conflict against the Warsaw Pact if the Cold War should ever turn hot. It is therefore perhaps to be expected that the analytical lessons and accounts from former German officers in this period tended to concentrate on German successes during the first half of the war. Munzel's study also falls into this category, although he hints at the eventual defeat in his conclusion when he says that 'no longer was our sword sharp.'

Within this context, the book remains valid even in the 21st century. It describes the successes of the German armoured formation in the early period of the war in the East, but it also provides insights into the unchanging nature of war and offers thoughts that are still relevant today. Last, but not least, it offers an indirect window into the thinking of the German Army and NATO in the early phase of the Cold War.

Prof. Matthias Strohn, M.St., DPhil., FRHistS
Head of Historical Analysis,
Centre for Historical Analysis and Conflict Research, Camberley
Visiting Professor of Military Studies,
University of Buckingham

Translator's Note

The original German-language text of Oskar Munzel's book makes frequent use of the word 'Raid', but I have rarely rendered it as 'raid' in my English-language translation. The use of this word by the German military, or at least by Munzel, is a little broader than its use in English. While the actions described by Munzel might encompass hit-and-run tactics, what he really refers to are offensive operations with panzer formations. I have therefore made use of whatever term I think best fits the context on a case-by-case basis – usually 'advance', 'attack', 'drive', 'offensive operation', 'strike', or 'thrust' – although there are of course other German words which have these meanings.

It is worth noting in this regard that Anthony G. Powell's translation of Erich von Manstein's memoirs, *Lost Victories* (London: Methuen, 1958), renders 'Panzer-Raid' as 'Panzer Drive'. While 'panzer raid' might occasionally be seen in English-language literature on the German military in World War II, it does not convey an accurate picture of what is meant.

The translation of place names in Eastern Europe is always challenging. Many cities, towns, and villages have names that have changed over time as borders have shifted; others, especially smaller localities, are obscure or have possibly disappeared. On top of that, the names used by German forces were not always consistent. Munzel predominantly uses a mixture of Polish spellings and German transliterations of Russian spellings. I have accordingly used Polish spellings and English transliterations of Russian spellings, except in those cases where there are generally well-known English-language names.

Foreword

'The main thing in war is speed. Take possession of what the enemy cannot reach. Make use of roads that he has not considered. Attack where he does not expect it.'

FROM *THE ART OF WAR* BY THE CHINESE GENERAL AND MILITARY PHILOSOPHER SUN TZU AT THE END OF THE 6TH CENTURY BC

This volume in the Wehrmacht im Kampf series describes the sequence of events of a number of panzer attacks that were carried out on the Eastern Front in 1941 and 1942.

The main part of the book deals with the offensive operations of the XXXXVIII Panzer Corps in the direction of the Black Sea. I have drawn upon a detailed combat report that had been prepared by the headquarters of the panzer corps immediately after the fighting it describes. Its observations on the development of the operation are particularly valuable. This has allowed me to portray the vividness of the frequently chaotic events and to clearly illustrate the problems that bombarded, and that had to be overcome by, the troops and their commanders. The maps in this book are closely based on photocopies of the original situation maps from that report.

I have mostly made use of private or semi-official records for the other operations presented in this book. The descriptions of these other operations are shorter so as to avoid the repetition of any events described in relation to the XXXXVIII Panzer Corps. The accompanying maps provide only a general overview of the situation.

All the records I have used were produced near the front. They capture the impressions of those who personally experienced the depicted events. They therefore achieve what a great soldierly teacher of the 19th century,

Prince Friedrich Karl, had sought to do in vain, namely, to express from the heart the thoughts and concerns of the combat troops.

German motorised and armoured formations stormed forward and brought about tremendous victories. This one day led to the creation of the term 'Blitzkrieg'. In World War II, this term referred only to swift movement and rapid successes, but, in the age of the atom, it could become reality in the true sense of the word. Survival might now only be possible if the soldier digs in deeply or moves quickly on the battlefield in armoured vehicles.

Despite the time that has passed since the end of World War II, the study of offensive operations from that time can still yield valuable lessons for the command of modern combat units. Most importantly, the events that are described in this book provide insight into the nature of the fighting conducted by the mobile troops. Their courage and exemplary performance during the fierce struggle in the East should be recorded for posterity.

Deserving of thanks for their support are General of Panzer Troops (ret.) Werner Kempf, commander of the XXXXVIII Panzer Corps; Lieutenant-General (ret.) Werner Friebe, chief of staff of the XXXXVIII Panzer Corps and my regimental comrade; and Lieutenant-General (ret.) Ernst-Felix Faeckenstedt, chief of staff of the III Panzer Corps in the autumn of 1941 and later of the First Panzer Army in the Caucasus.

Furthermore, I have Major Löffler to thank for lending me the combat report of the XXXXVIII Panzer Corps, Hans Müller-Witten for sourcing the orders cited in the appendix, and Captain (ret.) Becker for the excerpt from his private diary.

Oskar Munzel

Offensive Operations

In an offensive operation, an objective is pursued and must be reached quickly. The operation must take by surprise an unsuspecting or inattentive enemy, must rapidly exploit his known weaknesses, and must be boldly executed even if at a numerical disadvantage. History has shown that offensive operations have only been successful when the troops taking part in them have been well-equipped, properly trained, and daringly led.

In times past, attacks were carried out with what was for centuries the fastest means of transportation: the horse, the chariot, or the sleigh. In the coldest regions of the planet, skiers were typically employed to conduct offensive operations. In the Orient, the most tenacious of pack animals, the camel, was used. The best army commanders have always understood that mobile warfare demands the establishment of superiority at the most decisive location.

Alexander the Great, Hannibal, Scipio Africanus, and Caesar were renowned in antiquity for their ability to cover vast distances quickly when conducting military campaigns. In the Middle Ages, the push of Islam into the Near East, Africa, Spain, and southern Italy is noteworthy, as are the attacks carried out by the Mongolian ruler Genghis Khan. In the early modern period, there were the incursions of Charles XII of Sweden into the depths of Russia as well as the tactical achievements of Gustavus Adolphus of Sweden and of his opponents Johann Tserclaes, Count of Tilly, and Albrecht von Wallenstein. In the winter of 1678, the horse-drawn sleighs of Frederick William, the Great Elector of Brandenburg-Prussia, covered a distance of 540 kilometres in a period of 15 days so as to reach East Prussia and prevent a Swedish corps, at that time advancing from the Baltic region, from relieving Swedish-held areas in Pomerania. Frederick the Great could attribute his greatest victories to the rapid advance of his units and their concentration at the most decisive points. In the late modern period, the achievements of the imperial army commanded by Napoleon were astonishing. The division led by Pierre Dupont covered 834 kilometres in nine days. In 1806, the Imperial Guard advanced up to 100 kilometres per day by horse and cart in its rush from Paris to the Rhine.

In the envelopment manoeuvres that were carried out during the battle of Tannenberg in 1914, East Prussian cavalry regiments rode 80–100 kilometres a day for days on end. Also well-known from that first year of the First World War is the thrust of the Belgian 5th Cavalry Division into the rear of the German First Army in the battle of the Ourcq. Yet it was becoming ever more the case that neither the horse nor its armament could fully accomplish what was required of it. A new era with increasing firepower demanded a new means of conducting mobile warfare. The motor commenced its triumphal march. Its abilities were demonstrated in World War II, above all in armoured tracked vehicles with heavy armament. The panzer strikes launched by Erwin Rommel in Africa have already been written about extensively. Erich von Manstein wrote in his book, *Lost Victories*, about the panzer drive of his LVI Panzer Corps which struck from Tilsit as far as Dünaburg in the summer of 1941. The opposing side also conducted a number of offensive operations as the war neared its end. Those of the American General George S. Patton are particularly worthy of mention, as are those of the Russians as they pushed towards Germany in 1944 and 1945.

It was quickly recognised that success in modern warfare is dependent upon the ability to fight in three dimensions. This led to closer cooperation between ground, air, and naval forces during both world wars and in the years since. Foreign armies have even experimented with the transportation of light armoured vehicles by air. The era of three-dimensional warfare is clearly by no means past.

The objectives that are set, the forces that are employed, and the armament that is used for the purpose of carrying out offensive operations can all be expected to change over time, but there are fundamental principles that remain the same: the sudden push into enemy territory wherever possible, the rapid evacuation of an area if necessary, and the immediate exploitation of one's own successes or of the enemy's weaknesses. The primary task of an attack was and always will be to throw the enemy into a state of confusion and to strike him hard for the purpose of attaining victory.

Translations of Place Names

German	English
Belew	Belyov
(die) Bjelaja	Belaya River
Bol. Sserbulowka	Bolshaya Serbulovka
Bol. Wisska	Bolshaya Viska
Brazlaw	Bratslav
Chazyn	Khazhyn
Chersson	Kherson
Chizna	Khizhnya
Chmielno	Khmilno
Cholojew	Kholoyov
Choloniow	Kholonov
Chorolj	Khorol
Chorow	Khorov
Christoforowka	Khristoforovka
Cudnow	Chudnov
Cybulow	Tsybulov
Dacki	Datski
Dnjepropetrowsk	Dnepropetrovsk
Gaiszin/Hajsyn	Gaysin
Iwachny	Ivakhny
Jampol	Yampol
(der) Jegorslyk	Yegorlyk River
Jelanez	Yelanets
Kalmücken-Steppe	steppes of Kalmykia
Kamenetschje	Kamyaneche

Kisslin	Kislin
Kol. Mytnica	Mytnitsa
Kol. Rawszczynia	Rawszczynia
Kristinowka	Khristinovka
Krzemieniec	Kremenets
Laschtschewoje	Lashchova
Leschtschinowka	Leshchinovka
Leszniew	Leshnev
Lezelow	Lezhelov
Lipnjashka	Lipnyazhka
Lipowiec	Lipovets
Lochwiza	Lokhvitsa
Luck	Lutsk
Lyszaja Gora	Lysaya Gora
Maidanezkoje	Maidanetske
Maschurow	Mashurov
Michajlowka	Mikhailovka
Michnow	Mikhnov
Monastyrischtsche	Monastyryshche
Newinomyskaja	Nevinnomysskaya
Nowyj Bug	Novyi Bug
Now. Ukrainka	Novo Ukrainka
Ozenin	Ozhenin
Ozierna	Ozerna
Pesstschanyj Brod	Peschanyi Brod
Pjatki	Pyatki
Pletjanyj Taschlyk	Pletenyi Tashlyk
Podwyssokoje	Podvysokoye
Popushinzy	Popuzhintsy
Priwoljnoj	Privolnoye
Radziechow	Radekhov
Rowne	Rovno
Sasselje	Saselye
Selenkow	Zelenkov
Shitomir	Zhitomir
Sokalberg	Sokal Hills

Ssentscha	Sencha
(die) Ssinjucha	Sinyukha River
Ssnjatin	Snyatin
Ssuchoj-Jelanez	Sukhoi Yelanets
Ssuworowka	Suvorovka
Sswerdlinowo	Sverdlinovo
Stobiec	Stobyets
Stscherbany	Shcherbany
Swenigorodka	Zvenigorodka
Tetyjow	Tetiev
Troitzkoje	Troitskoye
Tscherkassy	Cherkassy
Tschjornaja Kamenka	Chernaya Kamenka
Werba	Verba
(die) Wilja	Viliya River
Wojtowka	Voytovka
Wolica	Volitsa
Wolodarka	Volodarka
Wolosowka	Volosovka
Woroschilowsk	Voroshilovsk
Wosneszensk	Voznesensk
(die) Susha	Zusha River
Zwiahel	Zvyahel

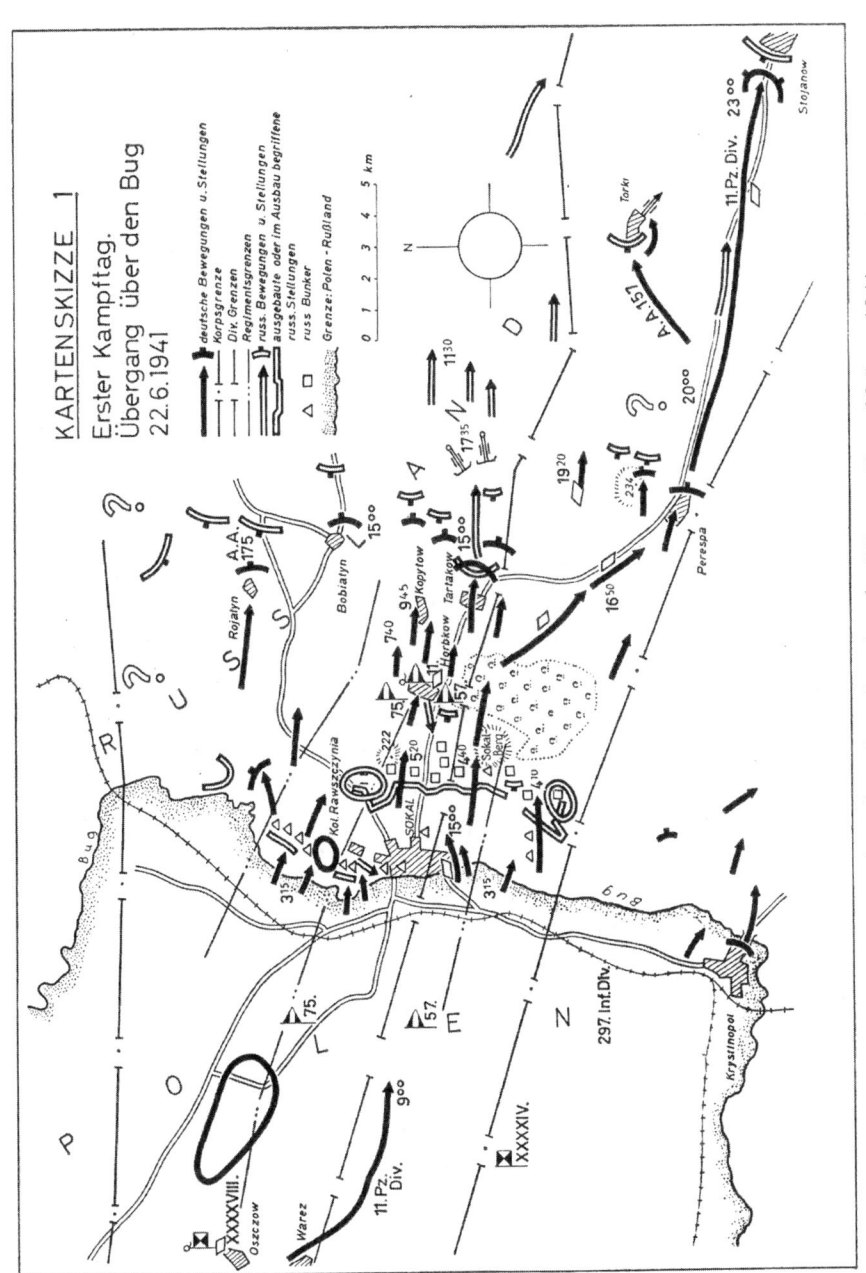

Map 1 – First day of combat. Crossing the Western Bug. 22 June 1941

xx • PANZER TACTICS

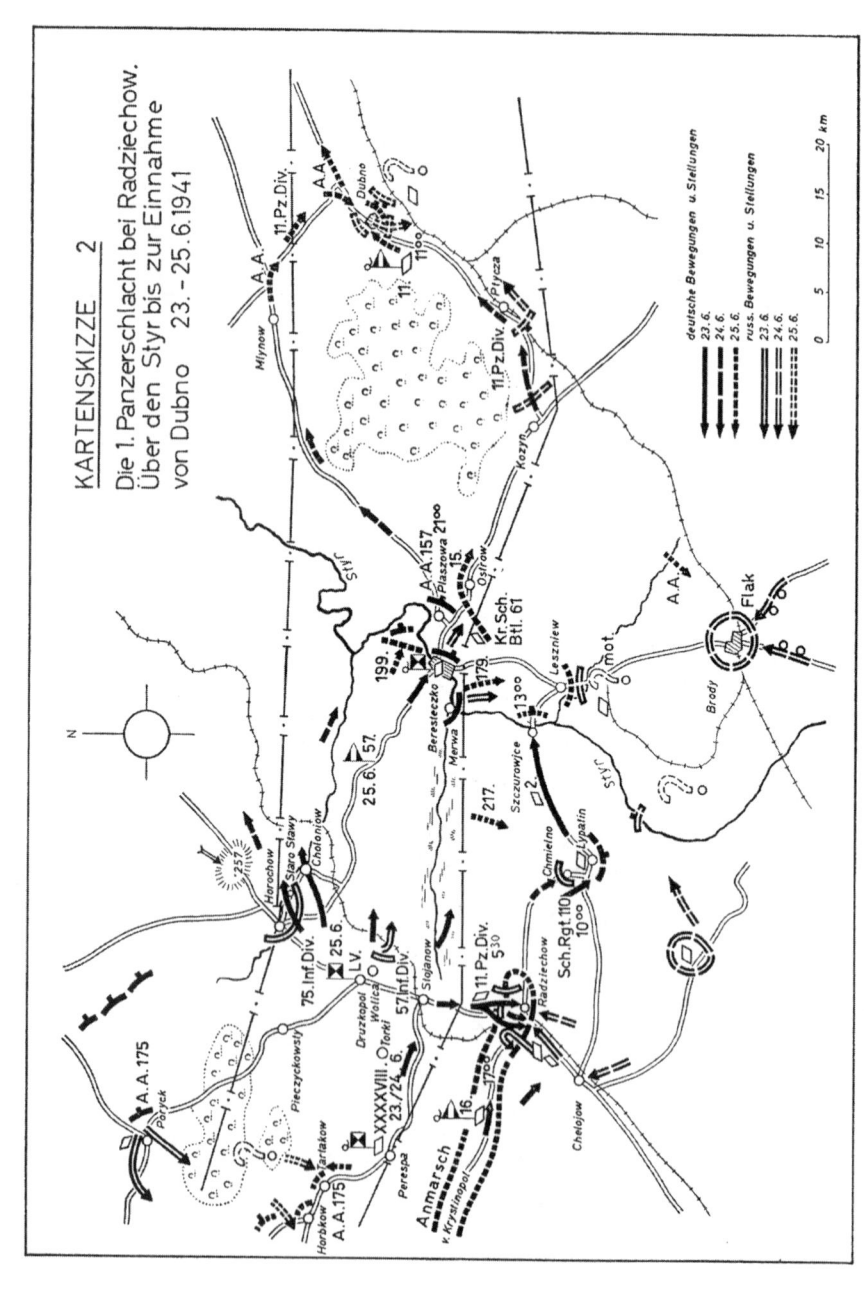

Map 2 – First tank battle near Radekhov. Over the Styr and the seizure of Dubno, 23–25 June 1941

MAPS • xxi

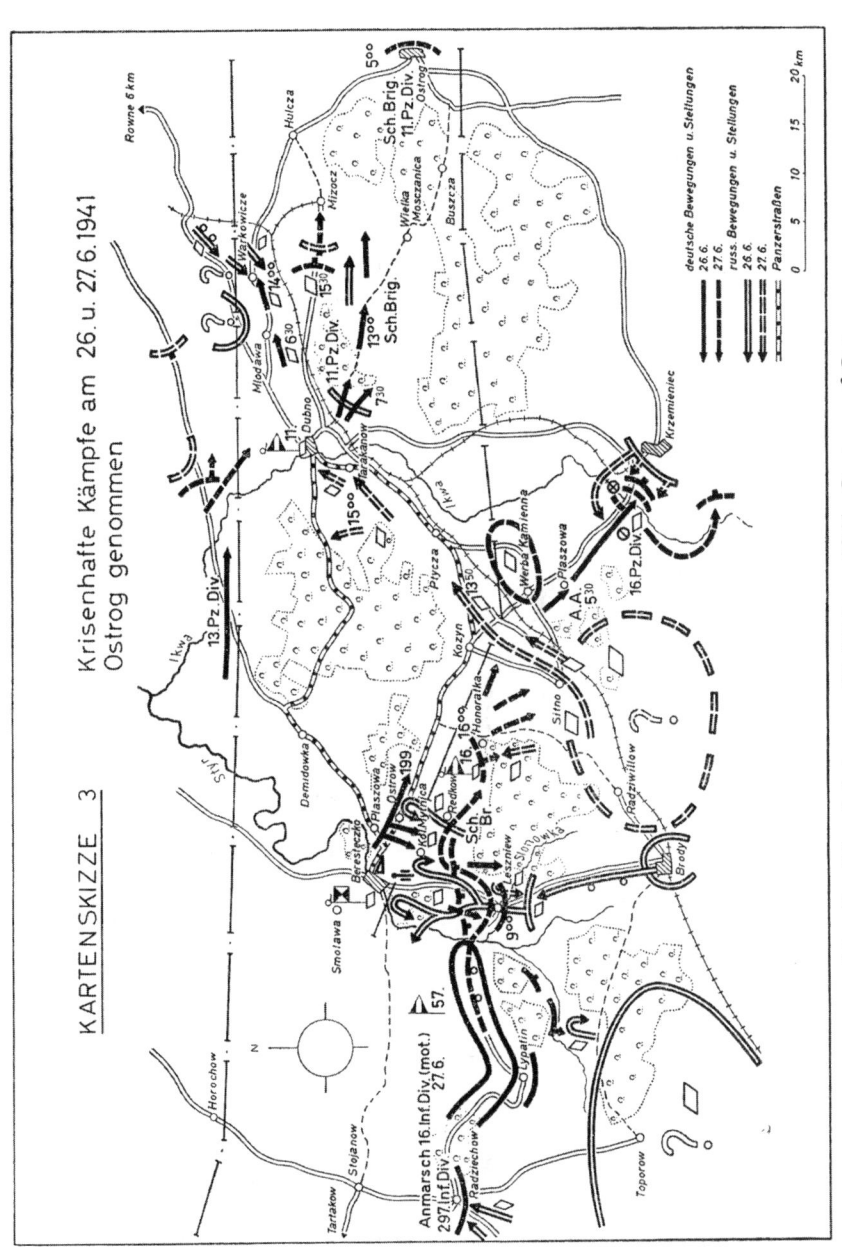

Map 3 – The fighting on 26–27 June 1941. Capture of Ostrog

xxii • PANZER TACTICS

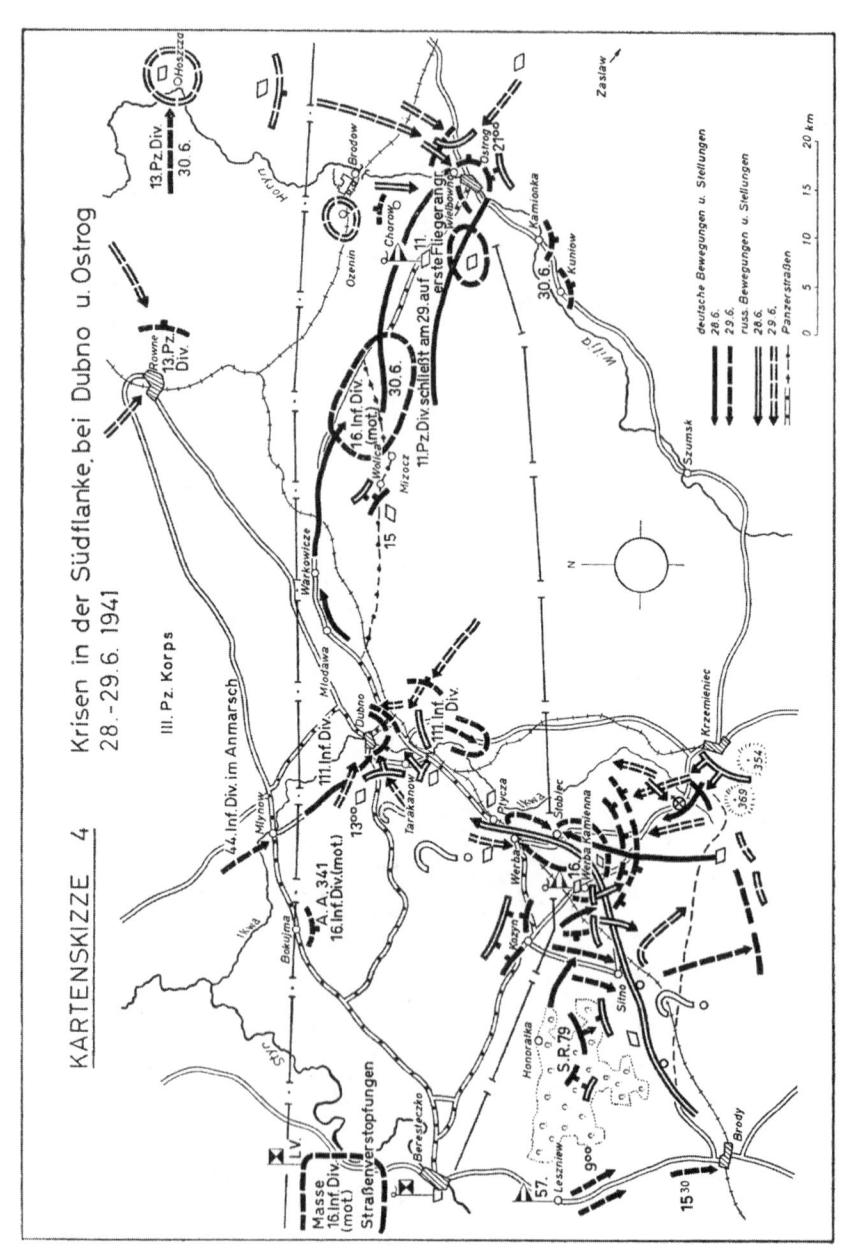

Map 4 – Crisis on the southern flank near Dubno and Ostrog, 28–29 June 1941

MAPS • xxiii

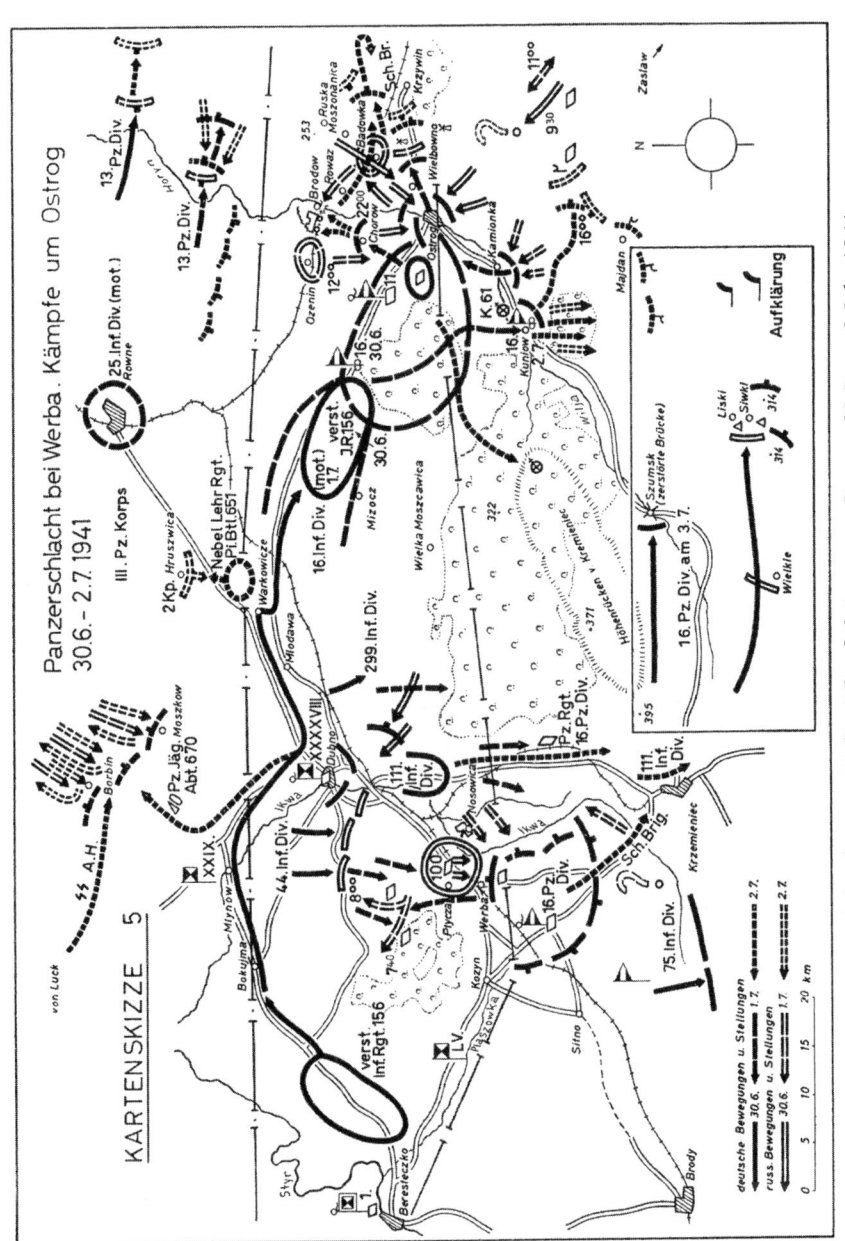

Map 5 – Tank battle near Verba. The fighting near Ostrog, 30 June–2 July 1941

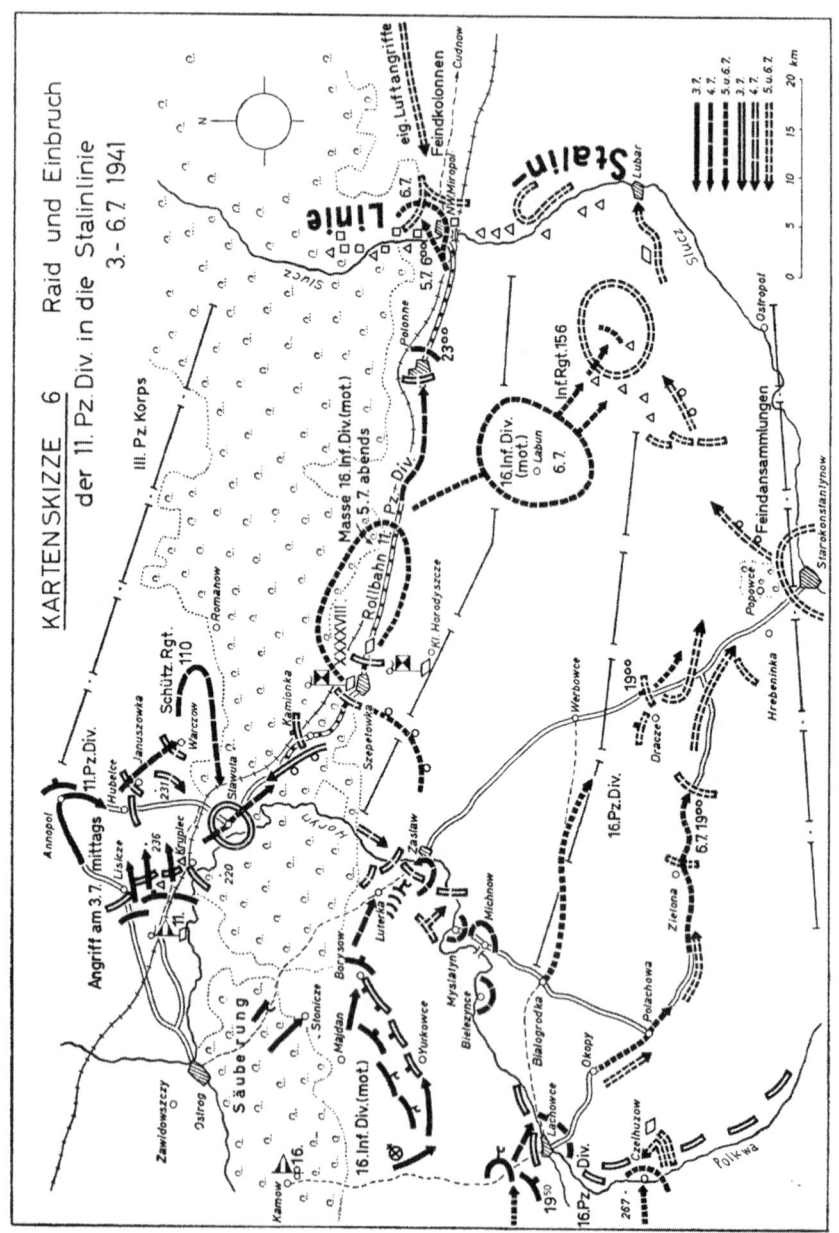

Map 6 – The 11th Panzer Division prises open the Stalin Line. 3–6 July 1941

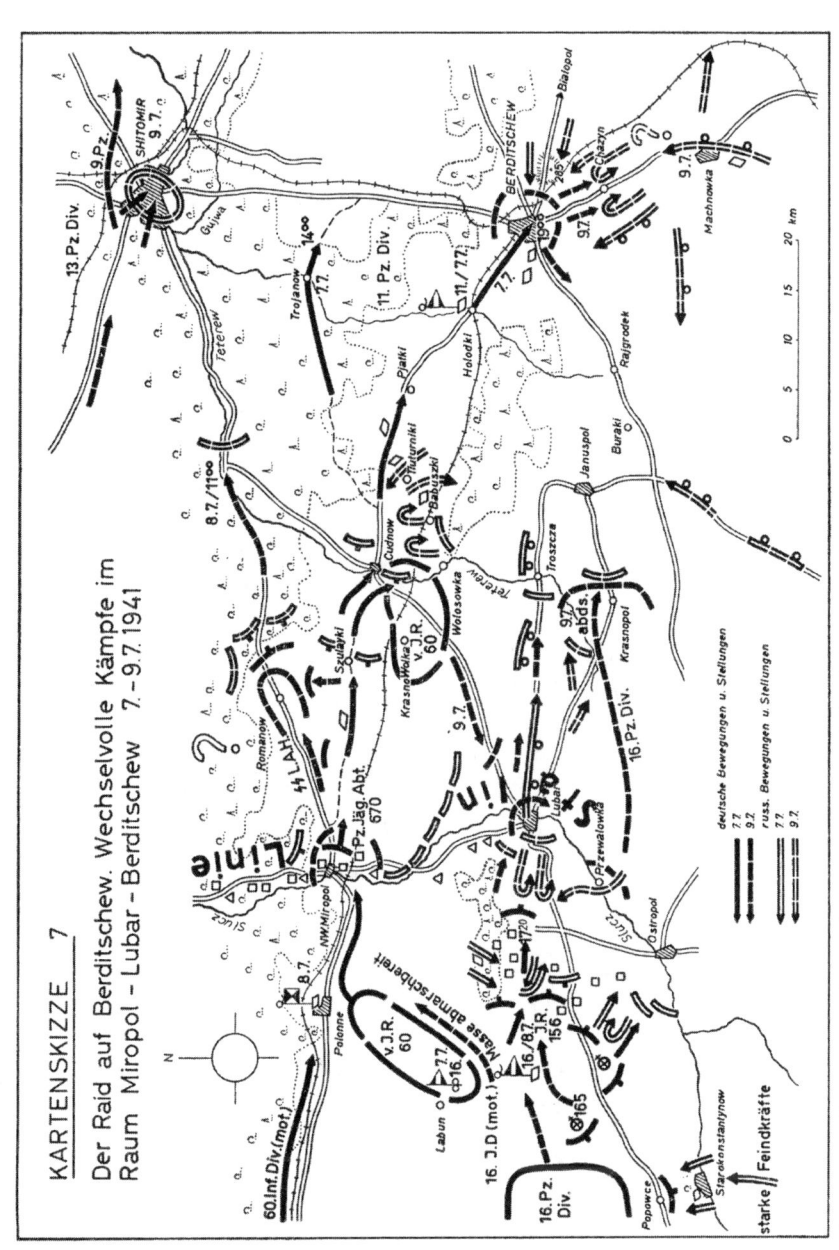

Map 7 – Thrust towards Berditchew. The to-and-fro fighting in the Miropol-Lubar-Berdichev area. 7–9 July 1941

xxvi • PANZER TACTICS

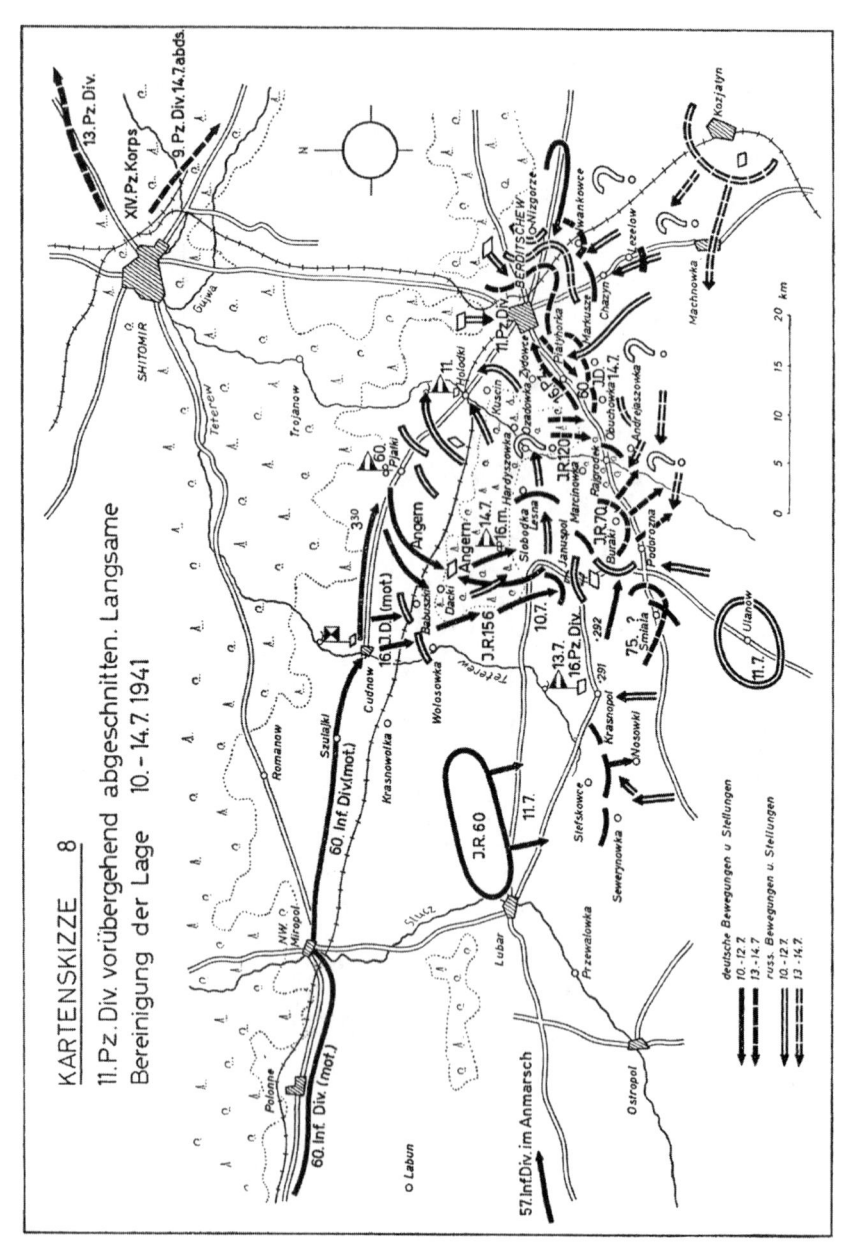

Map 8 – The 11th Panzer Division is temporarily cut off. Gradual resolution of the situation. 10–14 July 1941

MAPS • xxvii

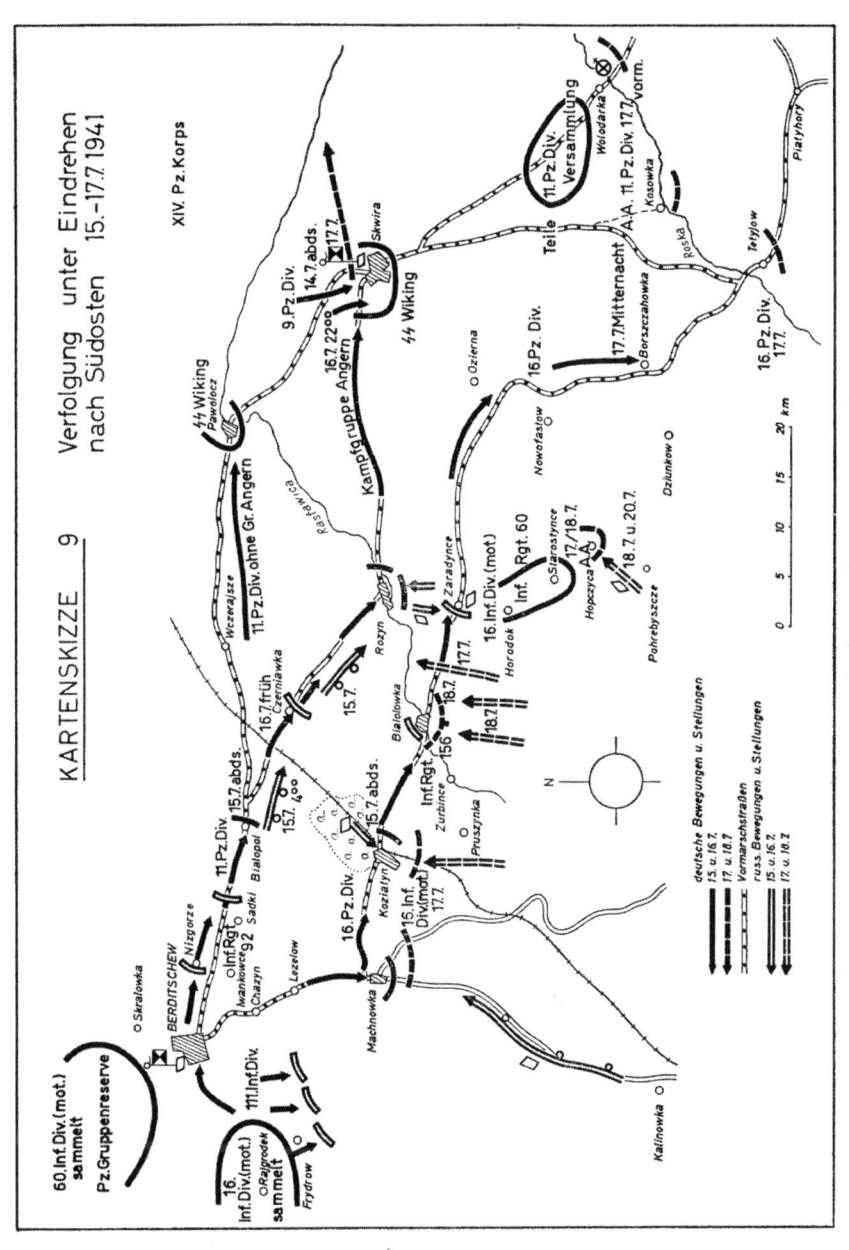

Map 9 – Pursuit towards the south-east, 15–17 July 1941

xxviii • PANZER TACTICS

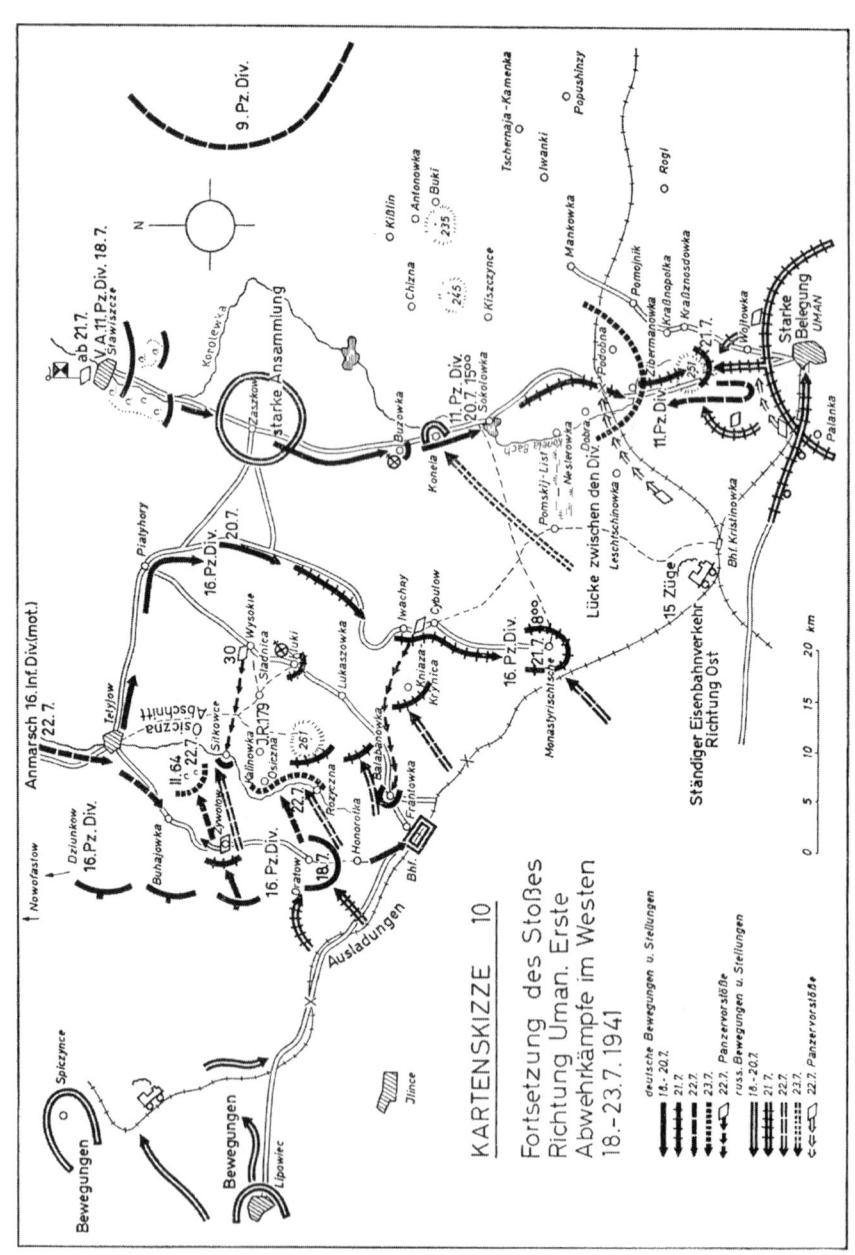

Map 10 – Continuation of the advance in the direction of Uman. First defensive fighting to the west. 18–23 July 1941

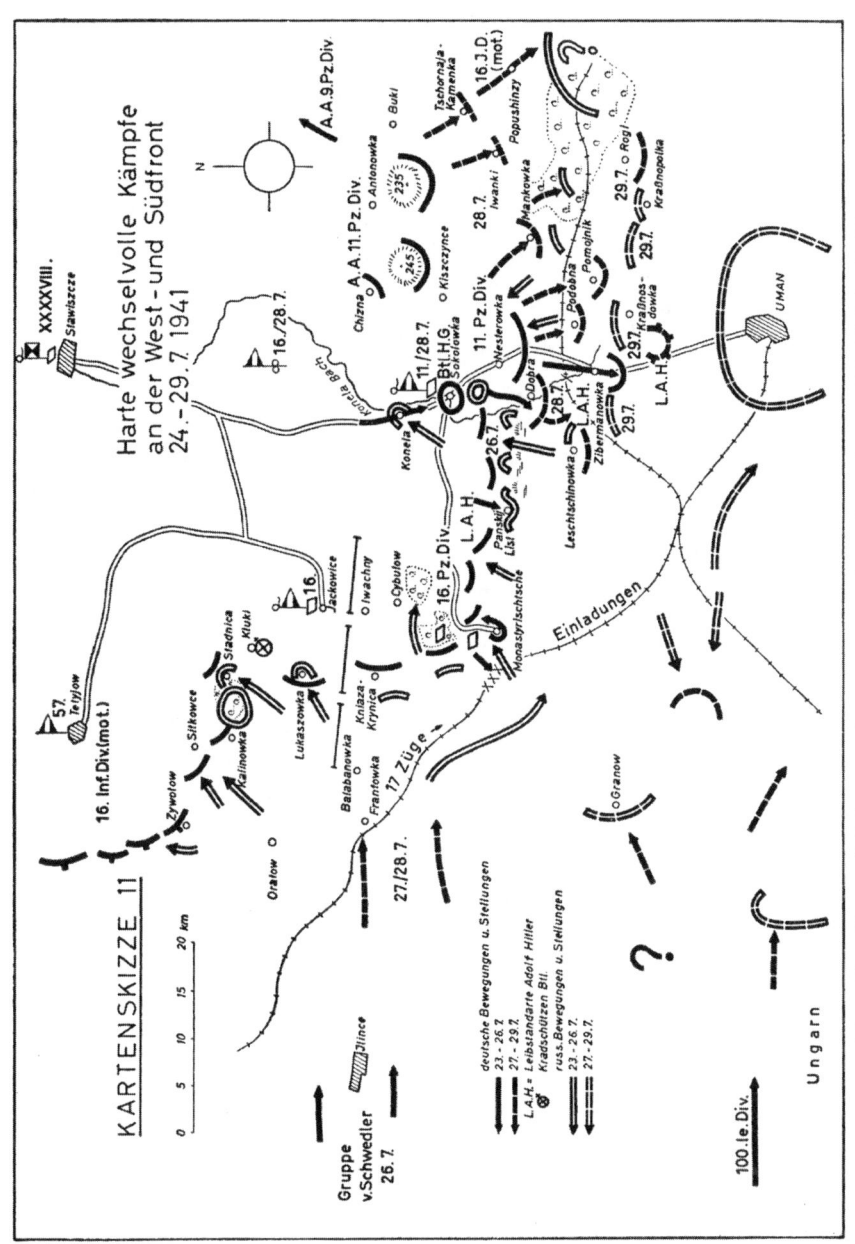

Map 11 – Fierce fighting on the western and southern fronts, 24–29 July 1941

xxx • PANZER TACTICS

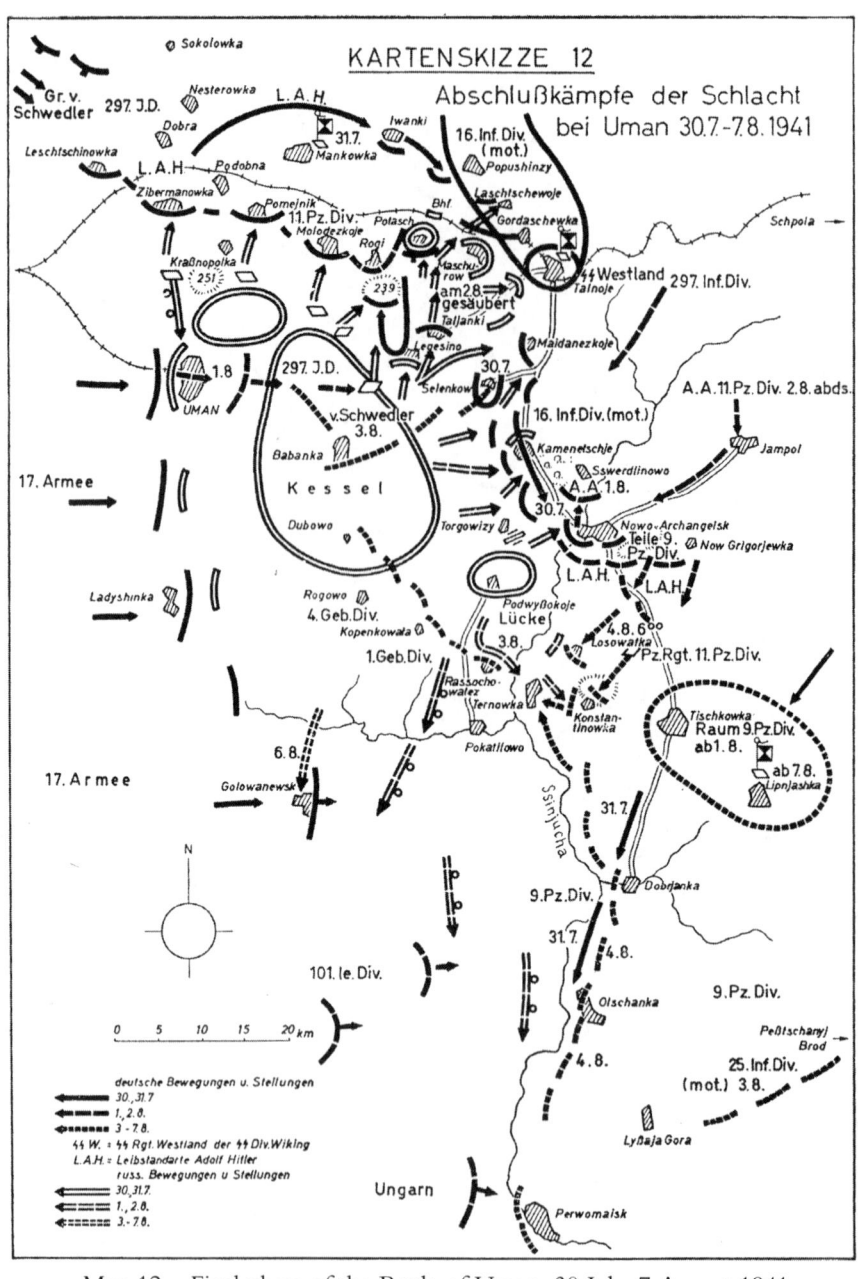

Map 12 – Final phase of the Battle of Uman. 30 July–7 August 1941

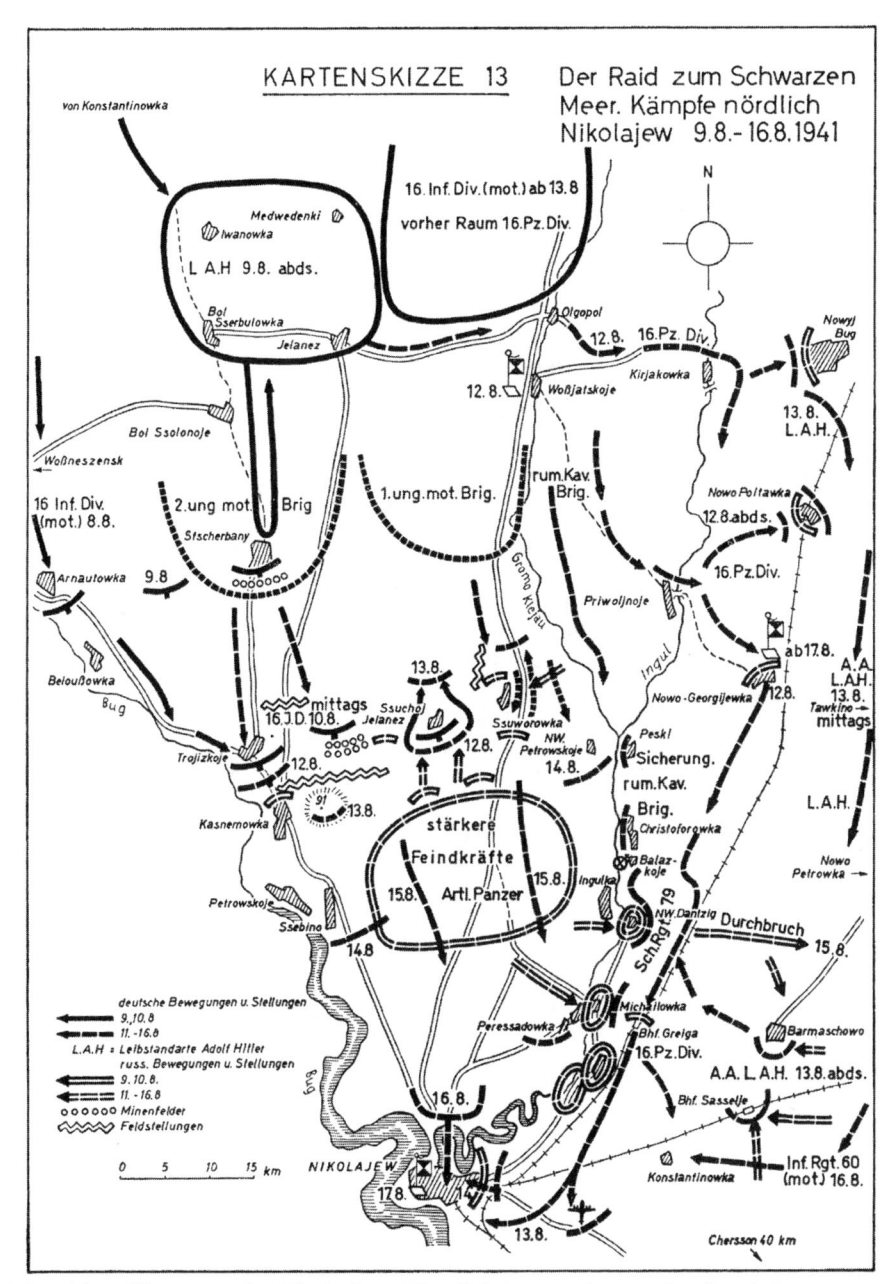

Map 13 – Thrust to the Black Sea. The fighting to the north of Nikolayev. 9–16 August 1941

xxxii • PANZER TACTICS

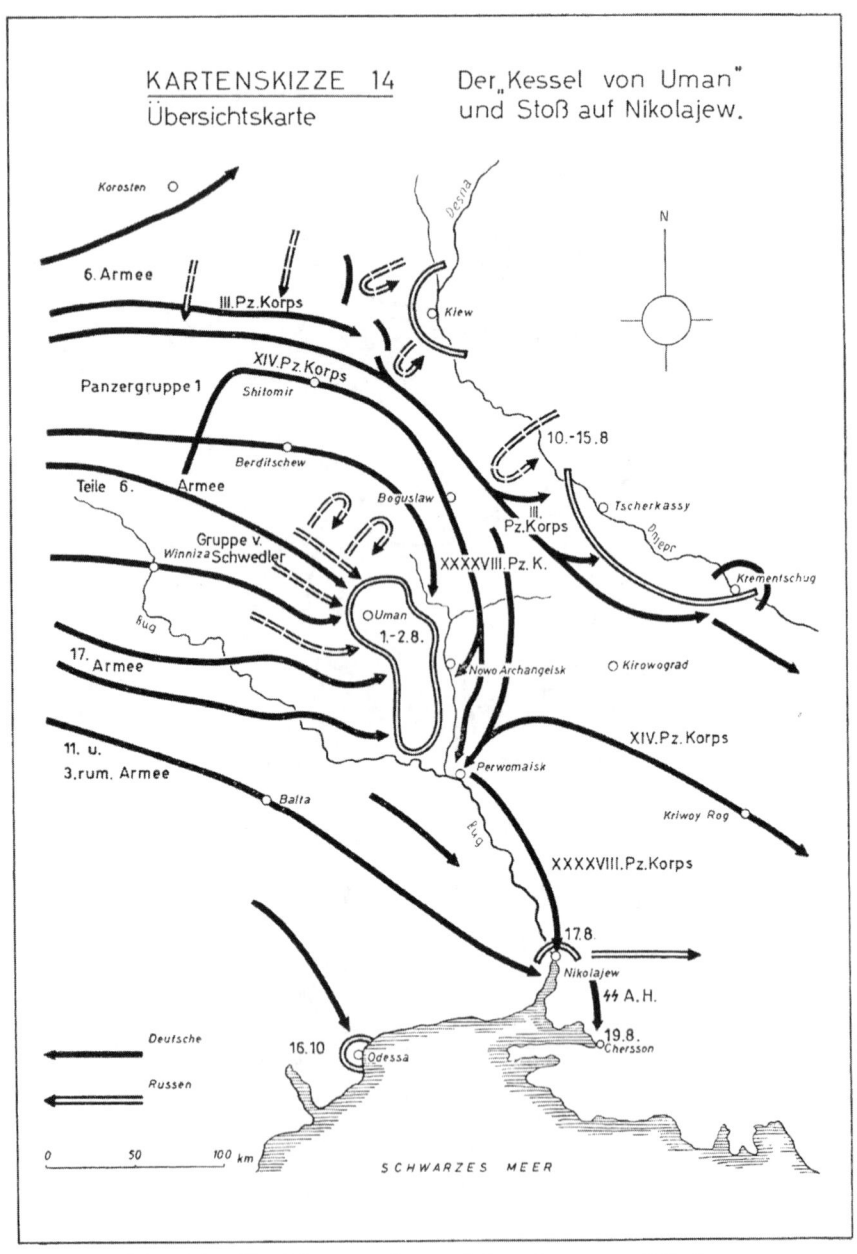

Map 14 – The Uman pocket and the advance on Nikolayev

MAPS • xxxiii

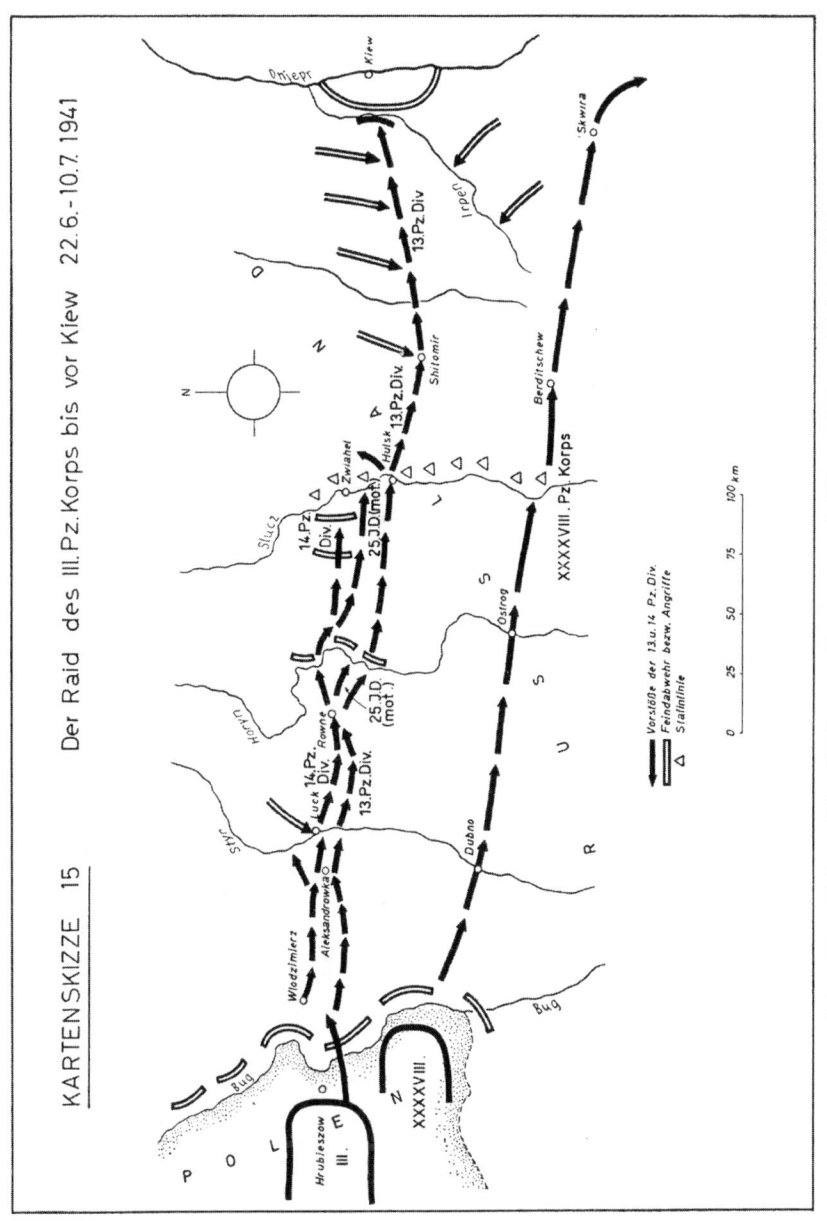

Map 15 – Drive of the III Panzer Corps towards Kiev. 22 June–10 July 1941

xxxiv • PANZER TACTICS

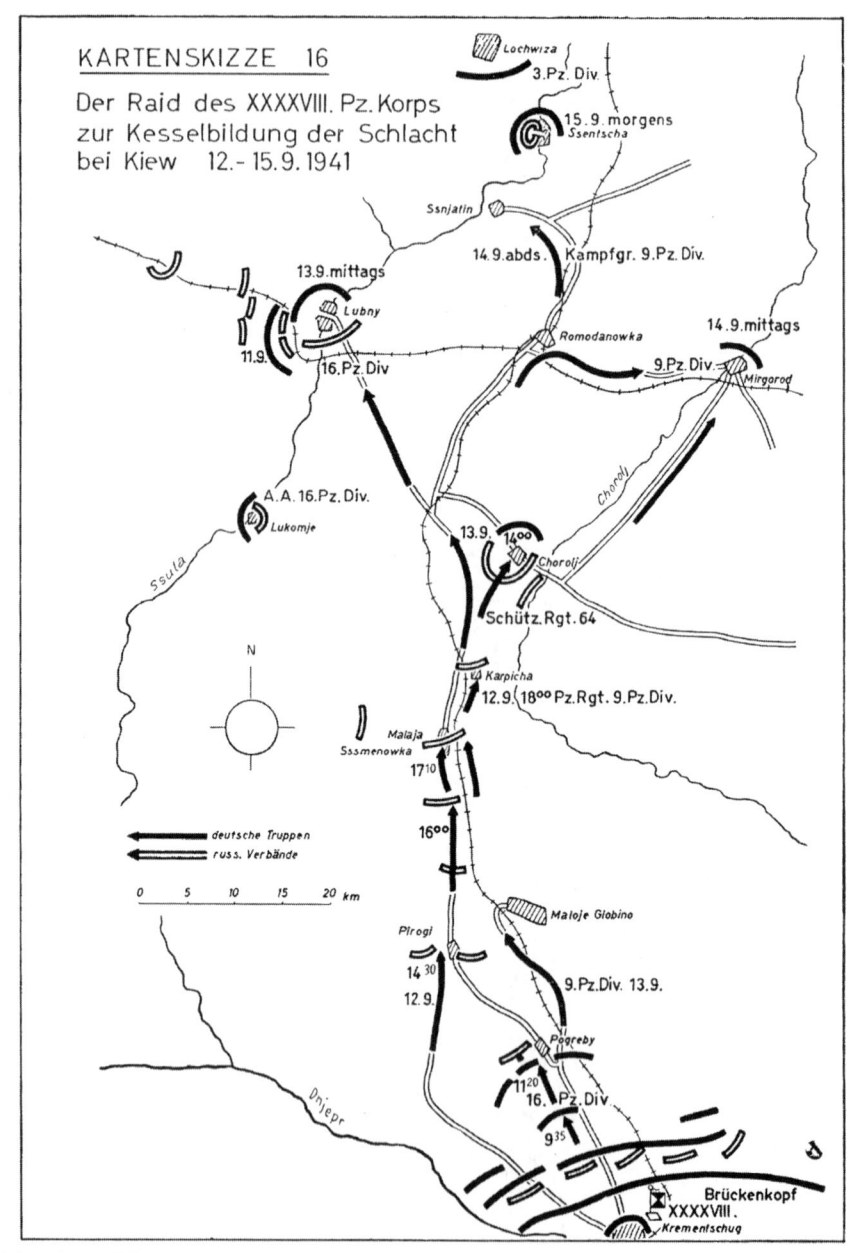

Map 16 – The XXXXVIII Panzer Corps helps to close the pocket in the Battle of Kiev. 12–15 September 1941

MAPS • XXXV

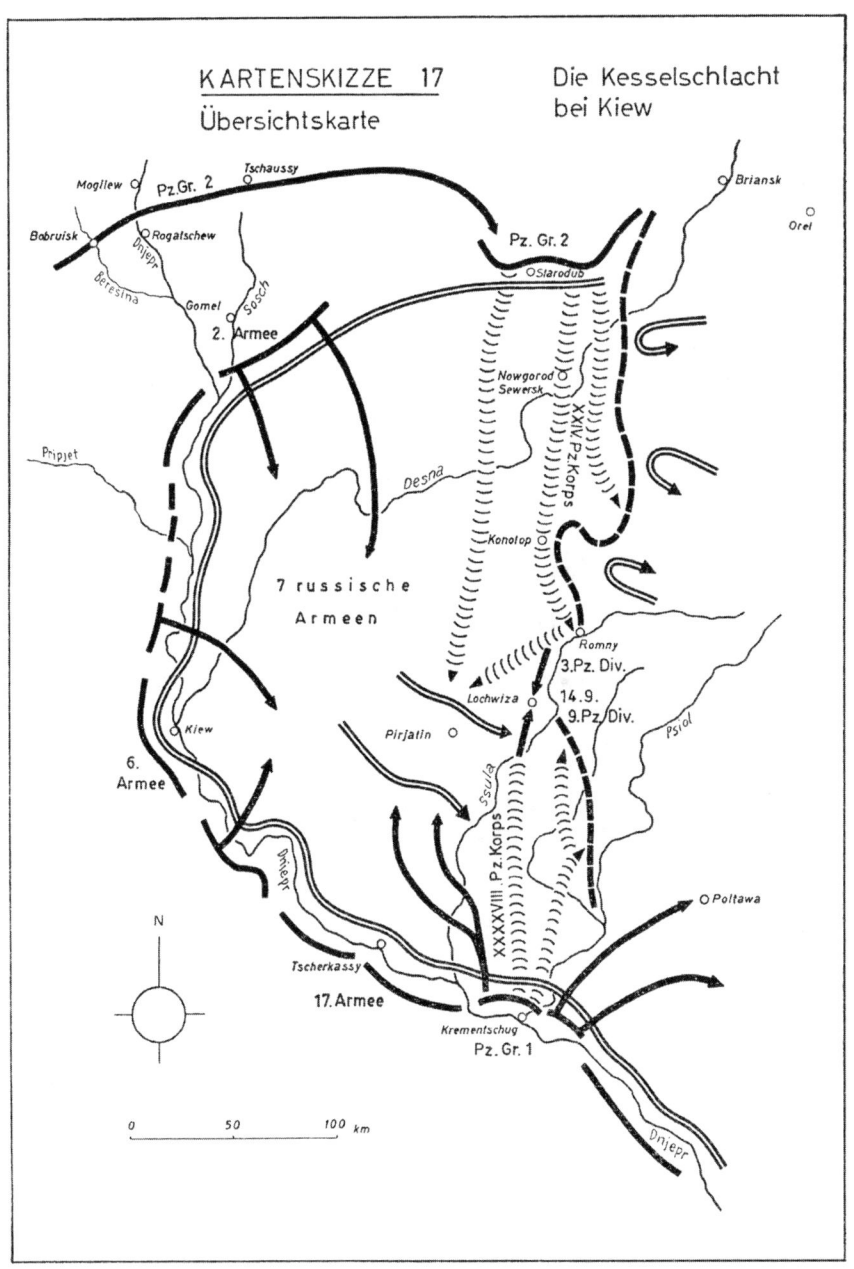

Map 17 – Outline of the Battle of Kiev

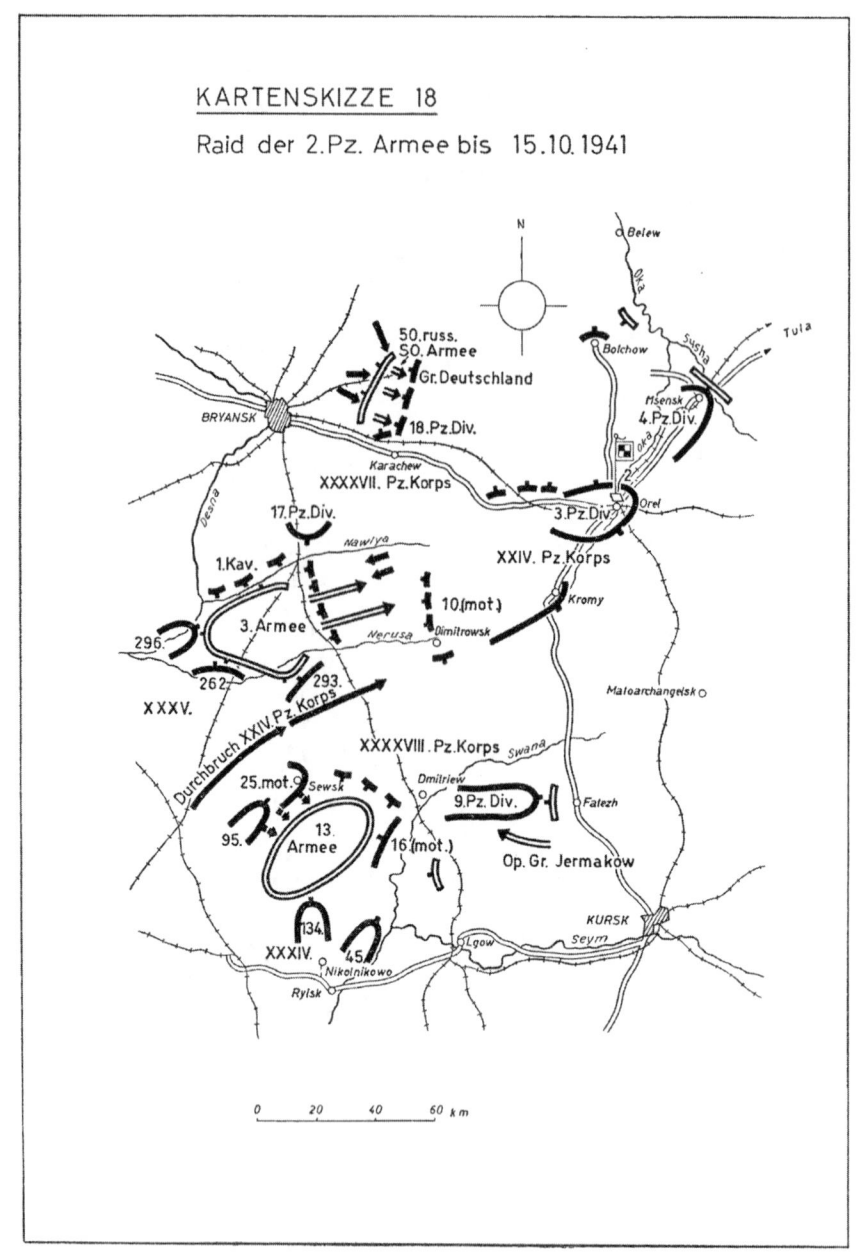

Map 18 – Advance of the Second Panzer Army up until 15 October 1941

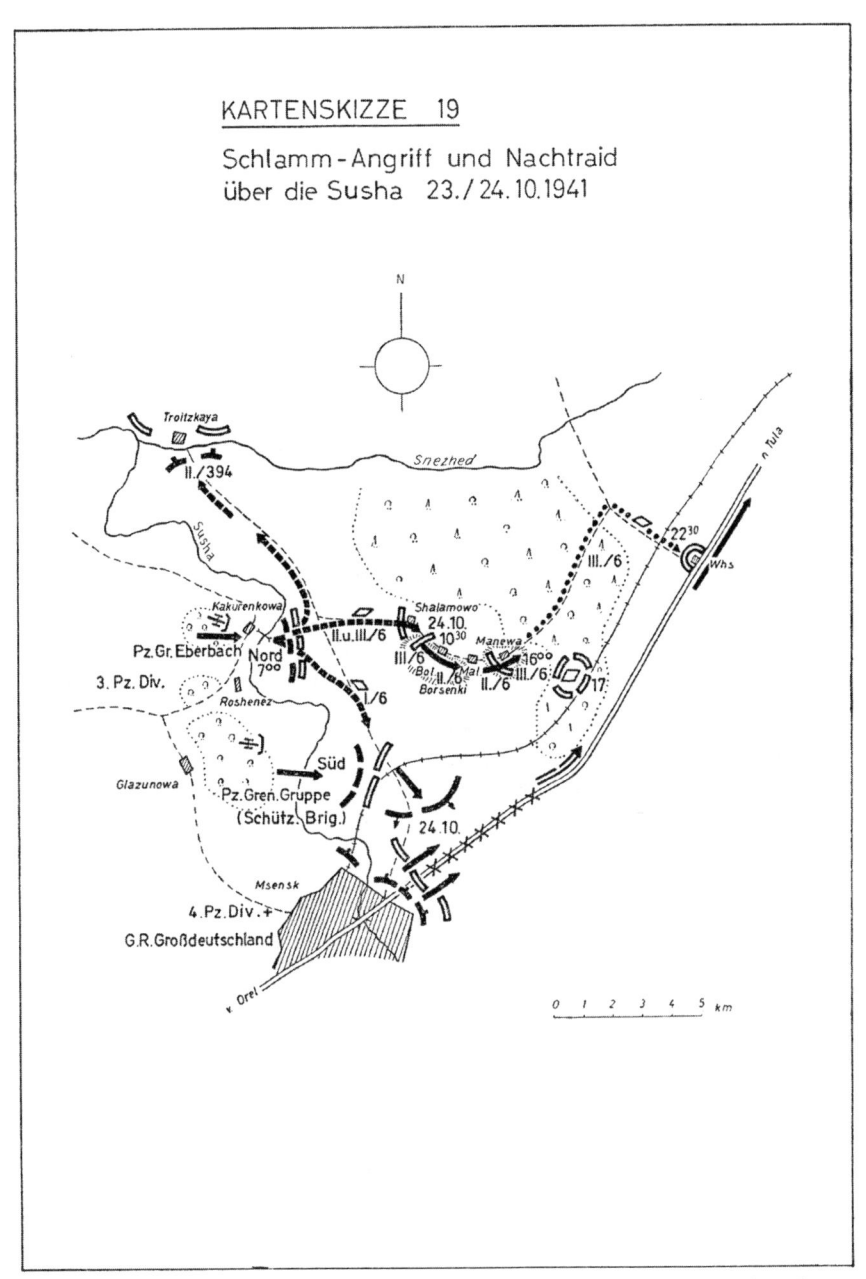

Map 19 – Attacking through the mud and over the Zusha on the night of 23/24 October 1941

xxxviii • PANZER TACTICS

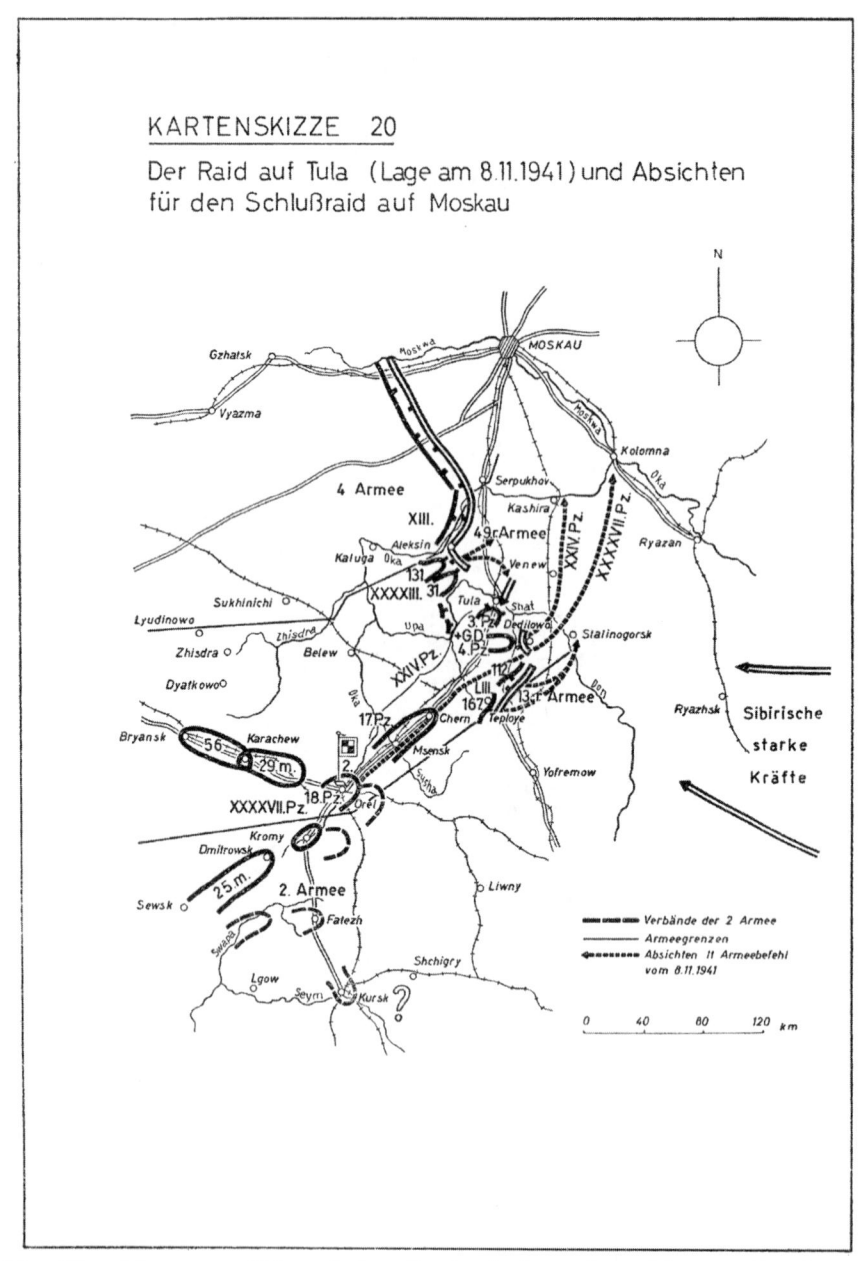

Map 20 – Advance on Tula and plans for the final assault on Moscow (situation on 8 November 1941)

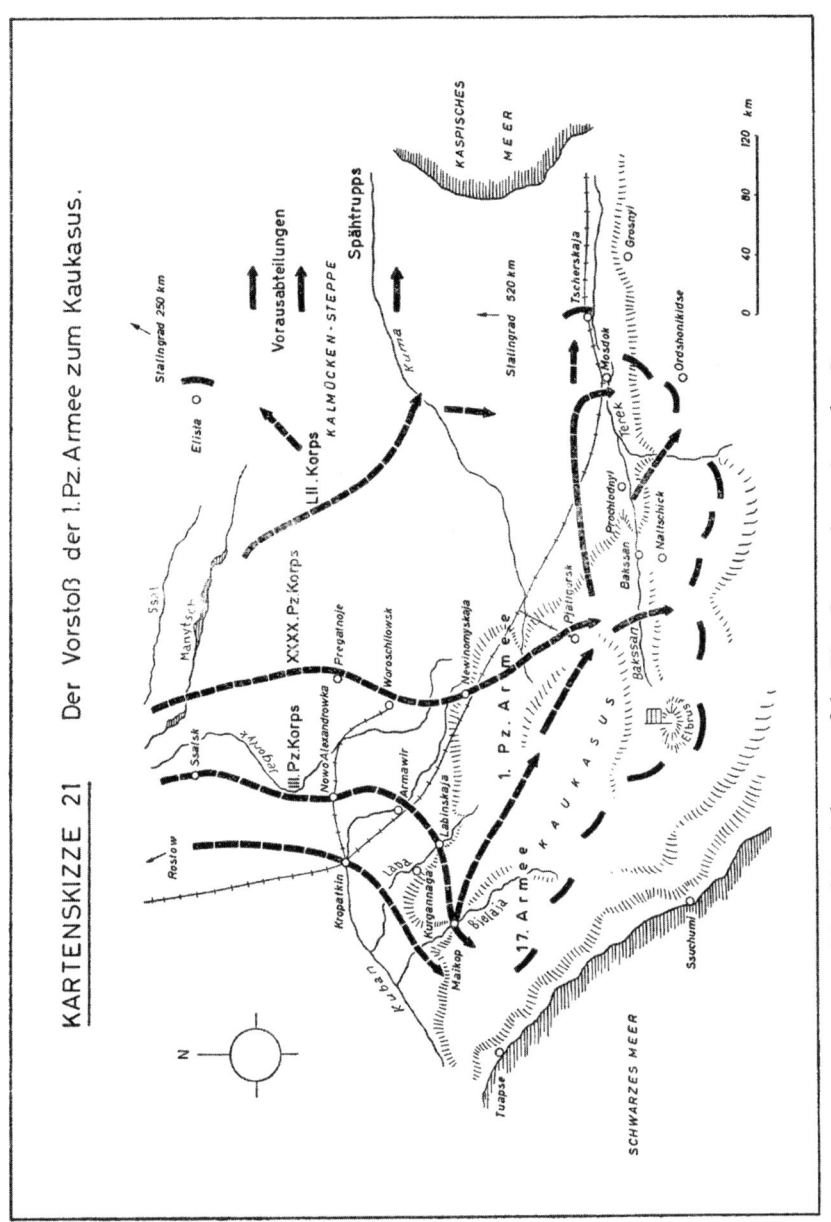

Map 21 – Advance of the First Panzer Army into the Caucasus

CHAPTER I

The XXXXVIII Panzer Corps Prepares for the Campaign in Russia

The situation at the beginning of the campaign in the East

The first major objective of the campaign in the east in 1941 was the annihilation of the enemy forces that stood in western Russia and thereby the prevention of the withdrawal of those forces into the depths of the country. The Pripet Marshes, which lie in the middle of western Russia, considerably influenced the operational plan. German forces, especially motorised units, would be unable to advance through such terrain. They would have to go around it instead.

The operational area was therefore split into two, and the inner wings of the army groups on either side would be separated from one another. This proved to be disadvantageous, as the strong Russian forces that remained behind in the gap eventually had to be dealt with. The bulk of both army groups had to pivot inwards, the result of which was the battle of Kiev.

The point of main effort of the entire campaign in the East lay to the north of the marshes. Two army groups were to be committed there. Their task was to gain ground to the east in the direction of Moscow as quickly as possible.

To the south of the marshes was Army Group South under the command of Field-Marshal Gerd von Rundstedt. With a strong northern wing, this army group would initially push towards and to the south of Kiev and then, advancing into the deep flank and rear of the enemy forces in Galicia and western Ukraine, would roll up the enemy along the

Dnieper. The first operational objective would be to take the economically important Donets Basin.

The task to be undertaken by the army group would be a great challenge. The terrain was vast, and the German forces, weakened as they were after the campaign in Greece, were few. The enemy was almost twice as strong. Rapid movement would be difficult. A 400-kilometre stretch of the Carpathians ran along the border, but it had to remain demilitarised on political grounds. The Pripet Marshes on the northern flank presented an element of uncertainty. It was possible that enemy forces would be lying in wait there. These circumstances essentially dictated that the army group place the emphasis of its advance on its northern wing. The formations on that wing were the Sixth Army, the Seventeenth Army, and Panzer Group 1. The last of these was commanded by Colonel-General Ewald von Kleist. With the infantry armies on either side, the task of the panzer group was to break through the Russian front between Rava-Ruska and Kovel, to advance through Berdichev and Zhitomir, and to reach the area near and to the south of Kiev as soon as possible so as to prevent the withdrawal of the enemy over the Dnieper.

The Sixth Army was to follow closely behind the panzer group, eliminate any Russian forces that remained behind the armoured spearhead, and prevent any threat to the flanks of that spearhead.

Facing the army group and on standby were two strong enemy formations under the command of Marshal Semyon Budyonny. These formations were distributed in depth between Kiev and the headwaters of the Western Bug.

At the beginning of the campaign, Panzer Group 1 consisted of the XXXXVIII Panzer Corps and the III Panzer Corps. It was also allocated the XXIX Army Corps to help with the penetration of the border fortifications. The success of the entire operation in the southern sector of the Eastern Front would depend on whether the panzer formations could swiftly dislodge and destroy the enemy forces near the frontier.

The main thrust would be carried out by the XXXXVIII Panzer Corps. Although it was at that time still known as a motorised army corps, it would be redesignated as a panzer corps as early as August. Its commander was General of Panzer Troops Werner Kempf.

Preparations for the operation

The XXXXVIII Motorised Army Corps was formed in Wiesbaden on 15 December 1940 from the deputy headquarters of the XII Army Corps. The new motorised army corps was fully operational by 15 January 1941. It was transferred to Bad Schandau on 19 and 20 February, making its way there by road via Erfurt. On 15 March, the 14th Motorised Infantry Division (from the vicinity of Leipzig) and the 18th Panzer Division (from the military base in Milowitz) were subordinated to the motorised army corps.

The motorised army corps was ready to march on 6 April. Between 20 and 23 April, it was transported by rail to Kielce via Breslau and Czenstochau. After a short stay in Kielce, it proceeded by road through Oratow, Sandomierz, Nisko, Janow, and Bilgoraj to Zamosc, with the last unit arriving at its destination on the night of 25/26 April. The II Battalion of the 64th Motorised Heavy Artillery Regiment was placed under the command of the motorised army corps on 24 April, and the same was done with the 520th Motorised Pioneer Regiment on 29 April.

Coming under the command of the Sixth Army, the motorised army corps was assigned the codename '48th Fortress Construction Headquarters'.

The motorised army corps was to advance through Sokal, but the roads in its vicinity were in poor condition. The headquarters of the Sixth Army therefore created a special Construction Headquarters Puttkammer so that a useable and partly cemented road could be built for the motorised army corps.

On 10 June, the motorised army corps was allocated the 57th and 75th Infantry Divisions.

The commander in chief of the German Army, Field-Marshal Walther von Brauchitsch, visited Zamosc on 11 June. He met with the commander of the Sixth Army and the commander of Panzer Group 1 and then drove to the German position near Sokal, where General Kempf showed him the terrain into which the motorised army corps would advance.

Early on 16 June, the commander of the motorised army corps held a conference at which the upcoming operation was discussed. In attendance were the divisional, regimental, and even battalion commanders from the 57th Infantry Division, the 75th Infantry Division, and the 11th Panzer Division. At noon, Field-Marshal von Rundstedt arrived at the headquarters of the motorised army corps near Sokal so that General Kempf could present to him his plans for the operation.

Another conference took place on 18 June. This one was held by the commander of Panzer Group 1 with the commanders of the III, XIV, and XXXXVIII Panzer Corps, as well as with the commanders of the panzer divisions.

It was very busy at the command post of the XXXXVIII Panzer Corps, which was shifted to Usmierz (north of Waręz) on 19 June. Many commanders came and went in order to partake in last-minute discussions.

On 21 June, the XXXXVIII Panzer Corps was placed under the command of Panzer Group 1. And at 1645 hours, the panzer corps received the following message from the first general staff officer of the panzer group: 'Heroic Saga, Odin, Neckar 15.' With that, the commencement of the campaign against Bolshevism had been ordered for 22 June at 0315 hours. The panzer corps correspondingly issued its own orders to the units under its command.

Despite the difficulties presented by the bad roads and the concentration of large numbers of troops in the narrow assembly zone, the preparations of the panzer corps were thorough and proceeded according to plan. The last elements of the artillery and heavy weapons were brought into position on the night of 21/22 June. The infantry units made themselves ready without making a noise.

Sokal was not blacked out. The Russian troops could be seen quite easily in their bunkers. They seemed to have no idea what was about to occur.

The XXXXVIII Panzer Corps was fully prepared for the attack by 0200 hours. The fight against the Red Army was soon to commence.

CHAPTER 2

The XXXXVIII Panzer Corps Thrusts to the Stalin Line

The first day of battle – crossing the Western Bug (22 June 1941)

The starlit night sky gradually faded at dawn. In the east, on the other side of the Western Bug, the first reddish rays of light appeared on the horizon.

The infantry advanced at 0315 hours with the support of the tremendous firepower of the artillery, smoke-shell mortars, rocket launchers, and anti-aircraft guns. The enemy was completely taken by surprise. He barely put up any resistance to begin with. The important bridge in Sokal fell into our hands intact. The crossing of the Western Bug ran smoothly. The infantry ascended the heights to the east of the river and reached the bunker positions, which were still under construction, without encountering any noteworthy resistance. It seemed that the enemy forces in those bunkers had also been caught unawares. Russian artillery, in a state of complete disorder and confusion, opened fire here and there. Our aerial reconnaissance reported that several columns of enemy troops were in retreat.

At 0500 hours, the 57th Infantry Division broke through the line of fortifications and seized the Sokal Hills. The 75th Infantry Division also penetrated the line and took Hill 222. Many of the bunkers were fiercely defended, so the fighting was tough. By 1000 hours, the infantry divisions had made further good progress. The leading elements of the 57th Infantry Division were in action on Hill 234, to the north of Perespa. The bulk of this division had marched through the woods south of Horbkov and was at that moment to the south of Tartakov. The 75th

Infantry Division had reached Kopytov and was advancing on Tartakov. While the enemy fell back to the east, the military bridges of the 57th and 75th Infantry Divisions were completed.

The bridge over the Western Bug in Krystynopol remained undamaged and was captured by the XXXXIV Army Corps.

The commander of the XXXXVIII Panzer Corps decided that the time was right to exploit our initial success by committing the 11th Panzer Division to a deep thrust. At noon, having obtained the approval of the panzer group, he ordered the panzer division to drive towards and seize the bridges over the Styr in Szczurowjce and Beresteczko.

The infantry divisions reached their first objective, the Perespa–Tartakov–Kopytov line, at 1500 hours, and the panzer division commenced its advance through Sokal with its reconnaissance battalion leading the way. Part of the road of advance of the panzer division lay within firing range of enemy forces that still occupied the bunker line near Rawszczynia. The fortifications were very modern. It was difficult to shoot directly at their deep firing ports, and the three-storey construction allowed the garrison to go deeper under the ground during a bombardment and to ascend and open fire again afterwards.

By the evening, the infantry, whose efforts that warm day had been nothing short of extraordinary, stood before a determined enemy along the Perespa–Tartakov–Bobiatyn–Royatyn line. The reconnaissance battalion of the 57th Infantry Division pushed as far as Torki, while the 11th Panzer Division reached the area to the west of Stoyanov, which was held by motorised enemy forces, at 2300 hours.

The first day of the offensive had been a great success. The strong and fully developed Russian defensive line along the Western Bug had been overcome. The panzer corps had advanced more than 20 kilometres into enemy territory.

The first tank battle near Radekhov (23 June 1941)

It was generally quiet overnight. The infantry divisions resumed their eastward advance at 0330 hours. Corps pioneer troops were at that time committed to the mopping up of the enemy forces that remained in the frontier fortifications. This task proved to be unexpectedly difficult.

After a short fight, the 11th Panzer Division took Stoyanov in the early hours of the morning. The first Russian tanks were encountered and destroyed. At 0530 hours, the spearhead of the panzer division clashed with strong motorised Russian forces, including tanks, to the north of Radekhov. Our aerial reconnaissance had reported earlier that these forces had been on their way from the area near and to the south-east of Kholoyov.

The situation that developed in the combat zone of the XXXXVIII Panzer Corps was what became the first tank battle of the campaign in the East. The 15th Panzer Regiment moved into position and then commenced an envelopment manoeuvre on the western side of Radekhov.[1] The enemy defended tenaciously and counter-attacked ruthlessly and repeatedly. But he suffered heavy casualties and was thrown back to the south towards noon. More than 30 destroyed tanks stood on the battlefield. Our own losses were by no means insignificant, but the victorious outcome of this first tank battle inspired the confidence of the troops.

The 110th Rifle Regiment of the 11th Panzer Division overcame resistance in Khmilno and then reached Lopatyn towards 1700 hours. The 61st Motorcycle Battalion carried out a rapid thrust and took the bridges over the Styr in Merva and Beresteczko intact.

Despite the poor condition of the roads in its sector, the 57th Infantry Division put in the utmost effort and pushed beyond the Stoyanov–Volitsa–Drutskopol line.

The 75th Infantry Division marched beyond the Drutskopol–Pieczychowsty line and sent advance companies to the Kholonov and Staro Stavy crossings. The enemy counter-attacked ferociously, but the crossings fell into our hands by the evening. Horokhov and the high ground to its north-east remained under the control of Russian heavy artillery.

On the deep northern flank of the panzer corps, enemy forces started to push forward from the forests to the south and south-west of Poryck. The strength of the enemy in those forests was unknown. The 175th

---

[1] The 15th Panzer Regiment was commanded by Lieutenant-Colonel Gustav-Adolf Riebel, who would later fall during the advance on Stalingrad in 1942.

Reconnaissance Battalion was therefore committed to the protection of the flank.

Fighting was still taking place in the vicinity of the fortifications near Rawszczynia. The enemy forces there severely disrupted the advance of the rear formations and the flow of supplies.

Towards 1830 hours, the 110th Rifle Regiment reached Szczurowjce and established a bridgehead there. The bridge in the village had been destroyed by the enemy.

The advance detachment of the 297th Infantry Division relieved the panzer reconnaissance battalion of the 11th Panzer Division in Radekhov, while the XXXXIV Army Corps relieved the forces protecting the endangered southern flank of the XXXXVIII Panzer Corps shortly afterwards.

By 2100 hours, the 57th Reconnaissance Battalion had executed a brilliant lunge and had crossed the Styr at Plaszowa. In the meantime, the headquarters of the panzer corps had been shifted to Perespa.

Over the Styr towards Dubno (24 June 1941)

Aerial reconnaissance reported towards 0700 hours the concentration of strong Russian tank forces to the south of the route of advance of the 11th Panzer Division. A panzer company of the panzer division was sent to defend the area on the southern outskirts of Lopatyn.

The 57th Infantry Division had been advancing without any difficulty towards the Styr since the early hours of the morning. It encountered no enemy resistance. The 75th Infantry Division, which had left some of its forces behind in the region to the north of Tartakov, was also making good progress to the east. From noon, this division was to come under the command of the LV Army Corps.

The 61st Motorcycle Battalion seized Ostrov at 0800 hours, but the 11th Panzer Division experienced difficulties due to enemy air raids on the road of advance and on the bridge in Szczurowjce.

The 16th Panzer Division, under the command of Major-General Hans-Valentin Hube, was assigned to the XXXXVIII Panzer Corps. This panzer division had advanced via Krystynopol and reached Radekhov at 1700 hours. However, it could proceed no further due to traffic congestion caused by the rear elements of the 11th Panzer Division.

By the evening, the 11th Panzer Division had pushed beyond Ostrov as far as Kozyn and Ptycza (12 kilometres south of Dubno). In the meantime, the infantry divisions reached the area near and to the north of Beresteczko.

We received more reports from our aerial reconnaissance that confirmed the Russians were assembling strong armoured and motorised forces in the area to the south of Radekhov and Leshnev. Additionally, there were several motorised columns heading north through Brody. This was a clear indication that the enemy intended to strike the southern flank of the panzer corps, which was at that time already 80 kilometres in length. The 57th Infantry Division therefore pivoted to the south in order to protect the flank.

The seizure of Dubno (25 June 1941)

The road of advance between Horbkov and Tartakov was disrupted by enemy machine-gun and artillery fire. The enemy forces to the south of Poryck were attempting to press forward against our weak security units in the direction of Tartakov and Sokal, so the rifle battalion of Infantry Regiment Großdeutschland was committed there in order to strengthen our defence.

While the 57th Infantry Division sent ahead elements of its motorised units to secure Lopatyn and Leshnev, there was a revival of the fighting around the fortifications near Sokal. About 20 bunkers had come to life again. The enemy was obviously putting up stiff resistance and was refusing to give up. Only his complete annihilation would resolve the situation. It was therefore decided that the 51st Pioneer Battalion would be employed to knock out the bunkers one by one.

After the 110th Rifle Regiment of the 11th Panzer Division had smashed through weak enemy forces overnight, its spearhead arrived in the area to the south of Dubno at 0730 hours. The reconnaissance battalion of the panzer division approached Dubno by going around the northern side of the woodlands through Mlynov. At 1100 hours, we attacked Dubno from the north and south. Russian tank formations struck our flanks, but we repelled them. By 1410 hours, Dubno had been taken.

The leading battalions of the 57th Infantry Division reached Lopatyn and Leshnev at 1500 hours. To the south of these villages, the enemy appeared to be making preparations for an attack.

The bulk of the 16th Panzer Division rolled forward out of the forest east of Radekhov once the rear elements of the 11th Panzer Division had left the area.

In the evening, the rumour that Russian tanks had appeared near Ostrov and the area to the north of Beresteczko spread like wildfire. This 'tank terror' spread along the northern march road as far as Stoyanov. Many of our columns turned back, causing utter confusion and terrible traffic congestion. The headquarters of the panzer corps, which had by that time moved to Beresteczko, managed to put a stop to any retreat along the southern march road. Some of our troops were about to set fire to the timber bridge over the Styr in Merva, but this was prevented just in time.

The enemy seizes the initiative (26 June 1941)

The 16th Panzer Division reached the Styr near Plaszowa towards 0600 hours. By 1430 hours, its reconnaissance battalion, motorcycle battalion, and panzer regiment had pushed as far as the area to the west of Kremenets.

The 11th Panzer Division captured Mlodava at 0630 hours. The attack carried out by its panzer regiment only gradually gained ground. From 1400 hours, near Warkowicze, our tanks were engaged in combat with enemy tanks that had approached from the north-east. The rifle brigade of the panzer division made better progress. Its leading elements advanced through Wielka Moszczanica and reached Buszcza by the evening.

At 0900 hours, the 57th Infantry Division reported that the anticipated Russian tank attack from the south towards Leshnev had begun. The situation there became critical by noon. The reinforced I Battalion of the 179th Infantry Regiment, despite its courageous resistance, suffered heavy casualties. The large formation of Russian tanks, supported by powerful artillery fire, advanced over the stream and surged northwards past Leshnev. There had been no chance to blow up the bridge to the south of the village the day before. Enemy fire had become too overwhelming to be able to carry out such a task safely. Some of the Russian tanks

THE XXXXVIII PANZER CORPS THRUSTS TO THE STALIN LINE • 11

reached Mytnitsa and even penetrated as far as the Styr to the west of Beresteczko. So great was the pressure applied by the enemy that German infantry and artillery units to the north of Leshnev were pushed back. Yet the aimlessness of the Russian attack and the personal intervention of the commander of the 57th Infantry Division prevented the enemy from being able to fully exploit his success. Elements of the reinforced 199th Infantry Regiment, which had been on its way to provide flank protection in Sitno, wheeled to the south with the intention of hurling back the enemy forces that had broken through.

The panzer corps utilised all the anti-tank weaponry it could muster. At its request, waves of Luftwaffe aircraft bombed the enemy forces that were concentrated on either side of the Brody–Leshnev road.

It was not yet possible at noon to fully assess the situation in the combat zone of the panzer corps. There was much that remained unclear. However, there could be no doubt that the panzer corps was in great danger. Enemy tanks had approached Radekhov and were attempting to achieve a breakthrough.

In the afternoon, the spearhead of the 16th Panzer Division was fighting near Kremenets. The bulk of the panzer division, though, was still to the west of the Styr and had been cut off by the enemy attack on Leshnev.

To the south and south-east of Beresteczko, the enemy carried out multiple armoured strikes through Redkov against Ostrov. This meant that the road of advance of the panzer corps was disrupted on several occasions. As a precaution, preparations were made to detonate the bridges over the Styr. However, by concentrating all available anti-tank weapons under the leadership of the commander of Motorised Regiment Hermann Göring, Colonel Paul Conrath, it was possible to destroy a large number of Russian tanks and to push the enemy away from Ostrov.

The situation urgently demanded the presence of General Kempf at the headquarters of the panzer corps. Constantly under fire from the enemy, he made the dangerous journey from Dubno and eventually arrived safe and sound in Beresteczko.

The enemy carried out several air raids against the command post of the panzer corps, and his tanks managed to reach a position that was only 6 kilometres away from it. The command post was therefore relocated to an estate 2 kilometres north-west of Beresteczko.

The elements of the 199th Infantry Regiment that had wheeled to the south succeeded, along with the 179th Infantry Regiment, in establishing a stable defensive front to the south of the road of advance.

The enemy had not recognised the importance of the need to exploit his success against the severely wounded flank of the panzer corps. His tank attacks were conducted sporadically and without a point of main effort. They also received little infantry support. As a result, our numerically inferior forces were able to carry out an effective defence and ensure the security of the road of advance. The enemy's attempt to achieve a breakthrough had failed.

The number of destroyed Russian tanks was considerable. In the area to the north of Leshnev alone lay the wrecks of 30 or 40 tanks. With the seizure of Dubno, large quantities of food, fuel, and ammunition had fallen into our hands, not to mention several light and medium batteries as well as 42 Russian 21-centimetre howitzers.

The situation that evening could be regarded as having been brought under control. A day filled with fierce fighting had come to an end.

The advance continues – Ostrog is taken (27 June 1941)

The 16th Panzer Division came across well-built enemy emplacements outside Kremenets and was therefore unable to enter the city. It struggled to create a small bridgehead across the Ikva and soon found that the enemy had gone around it to strike from behind. The route of advance of the panzer division was disrupted in the vicinity of Sitno due to an attack by enemy tanks from the south. In the early hours of the morning, the enemy sent more forces across the Ikva to the north of our bridgehead and executed a number of powerful attacks. The rifle brigade of the panzer division tried to reach and provide assistance to the advance detachment, but it experienced its own difficulties due to the multiple assaults launched by enemy tanks from the forests on the southern side of the road of advance. Ever more Russian tanks continued to be spotted in the region to the south of the Sitno–Kremenets line. Yet the precise

THE XXXXVIII PANZER CORPS THRUSTS TO THE STALIN LINE • 13

location of the bulk of those forces could not be ascertained. Our troops could not see them from the ground, nor could the Luftwaffe from the air.

The rifle brigade of the 11th Panzer Division reached Ostrog towards 0500 hours. The panzer regiment was at that time engaged in combat to the west of Mizocz.

The 57th Infantry Division retook Leshnev against barely any enemy resistance. It was thereafter detached from the XXXXVIII Panzer Corps and assigned to the XXXXIV Army Corps. The army corps was at that moment positioned on the south-western side of the panzer corps.

Nevertheless, the panzer corps still urgently required flank protection. The panzer group therefore promised that the 16th Motorised Infantry Division (Lieutenant-General Sigfrid Heinrici) would be made available to the panzer corps. The leading elements of the division had at that point arrived in Beresteczko. The 670th Anti-Tank Battalion and a flak battery were also allocated to the panzer corps.

An immediate pursuit of the large numbers of enemy forces falling back to the east was impossible in the prevailing situation. The units of the panzer divisions were spread over a large area and would be unable to assemble for the next leap until the threat to the flanks had been resolved.

In the meantime, the 11th Panzer Division entered Ostrog and seized the crossing over the Horyn. The bridgehead that was established there soon came under constant attack. Near Mizocz, the panzer regiment had hurled back the enemy forces that had barred its way and was advancing towards Ostrog. The panzer division was ordered to bring its supply troops forward to Dubno and to keep them closer to its combat troops so that the traffic congestion on the supply road could be cleared up.

The command post of the panzer corps remained where it was for the time being. The road that led to Dubno via Demidovka was often under attack by the enemy. The 108th Corps Artillery Command drove on ahead with an advance party to assume command of German forces near and to the east of Dubno.

The situation of the 16th Panzer Division in the vicinity of Verba had worsened by nightfall. A large enemy tank unit appeared to be making an attempt to break through from Brody to Dubno. Our aerial reconnaissance confirmed the presence of a motorised column of tanks and other vehicles advancing along the road between the two cities. The advance detachment that was in combat near Kremenets was thereby cut off from the rest of the panzer division. The rifle brigade was at that time fighting enemy forces near Honoratka. For the third time since the commencement of the campaign in the East, the main road of advance of the panzer corps had been disrupted. The spearhead of the enemy tank forces struck as far as Dubno, overcoming the elements of the corps signal battalion and the units of the supply troops that had been sent to Tarakanov. Yet the mass of the enemy's forces still remained to the south of the road of advance. The first heavy tanks (50–60 tonnes) were spotted there. Major-General Hube (16th Panzer Division) and some of the staff officers of his headquarters were encircled near Verba. If the enemy were to succeed in taking the weakly secured Dubno, there would be no guarantee that the 11th Panzer Division would receive the supplies it needed. If the enemy were to pivot to the south-east, the 16th Panzer Division would be put in an extremely difficult position. It was of the utmost importance that the rifle brigade of the panzer division reach the advance detachment near Kremenets, even if this meant that German tanks would have to be assigned to the protection of the rifle brigade. Only then would the German forces in the vicinity of Kremenets be capable of resisting any Russian tanks that came their way. The 11th Panzer Division would in the meantime have to stay in and hold on to the Ostrog bridgehead.

The 16th Motorised Infantry Division was placed under the command of the panzer corps that night. It was ordered to concentrate all its forces in Beresteczko in preparation for further operations.

Another difficult day of fighting was over. The performance of the troops had been outstanding, the result of which was that the road of advance remained in the hands of the panzer corps despite the challenging situations that had arisen, the constant threats that had been posed to the flanks, and the multiple breakthroughs that had been achieved by the enemy. The defence against the waves of innumerable Russian tanks had placed the greatest demands on our men, for they were usually lacking in sufficient and effective anti-tank weaponry.

A total of 120 enemy tanks had been put out of action on 26 and 27 June.

THE XXXXVIII PANZER CORPS THRUSTS TO THE STALIN LINE • 15

Danger on the southern flank (28 June 1941)

The concentration of the forces of the 11th Panzer Division in the vicinity of Ostrog took place throughout the day of 28 June. The bridgehead there was subjected to constant attack by the enemy, and his efforts were supported by aircraft and artillery. The panzer division consequently suffered heavy losses.

In the combat zone of the 16th Panzer Division, the advance detachment and the rifle brigade were still separated from one another as a result of the thrust that had been carried out by the enemy motorised and armoured column from Brody towards the north-east the previous evening. The rifle brigade had been fighting in the woods near Honoratka throughout the night. Russian tanks that had in the meantime approached Dubno were repelled.

Aerial reconnaissance in the early hours of the morning spotted the well-camouflaged enemy column in fields to the south and west of the road of advance of the panzer corps. Our aircraft also identified another enemy motorised column with tanks advancing along the road from Brody to Dubno. Even if the approach of the 111th Infantry Division of the LV Army Corps from Mlynov towards the area east of Dubno were to alleviate the immediate danger to the city, it was nonetheless decided that the road of advance would be sealed off just to its south.

The forces of the 16th Panzer Division were finally reunited towards noon. The divisional commander and those accompanying him had been encircled for a long time, but they had by this time broken out successfully. Enemy resistance before Kremenets had been reinforced with heavy artillery. The tremendous firepower of this resistance compelled the motorcycle battalion to withdraw from the bridgehead over the Ikva. In the area near and to the south of Kozyn, the rifle brigade annihilated several Russian infantry units and disabled a large number of Russian tanks. It would have been too difficult and time-consuming at that moment to launch an attack over the Ikva towards the high ground (Hills 369 and 354) near Kremenets. Enemy tank and motorised forces in the woods to the west of the Verba–Dubno road presented too great a threat.

General Kempf decided that the attack towards Kremenets had to be abandoned so that the bulk of the 16th Panzer Division could be employed to resolve the situation south of Kozyn and to attack the enemy forces south-west of Dubno once they emerged from the woods. This plan, whose execution would mean a slight delay before the 16th Panzer Division caught up with the 11th Panzer Division, was approved by the headquarters of the panzer group. There was no chance of employing the 16th Motorised Infantry Division instead to carry out this task. Its forces were still approaching and were too greatly spread out. They would have struggled against the overwhelming numerical superiority of the enemy tanks.

The 111th Infantry Division had in the meantime gone through Dubno with the intention of advancing further to the south on the eastern side of the Ikva. However, due to the fact that the enemy had increased the strength of his forces near Dubno in the course of the late afternoon, the LV Army Corps, on the request of the XXXXVIII Panzer Corps, left behind a reinforced battalion in the city.

The situation in Dubno had become critical as evening approached. The enemy attacked the city from the west with tanks and infantry. It was no longer possible that night for the panzer corps to fulfil the demands of the commandant of the city, Major-General Hans-Joachim von Stumpfeld, for more support. The 16th Panzer Division was nevertheless given the task of sealing off the Brody–Dubno road and of making ready a strong combined-arms battle group for an attack against the enemy forces south-west of Dubno. The panzer division would leave behind only a few security forces in the vicinity of Kremenets.

The 11th Panzer Division continued to concentrate its units near Ostrog. The number of casualties it suffered climbed ever higher, for the bridgehead over the Horyn remained under attack from Russian aircraft and artillery.

The struggle for Dubno (29 June 1941)

Dubno was repeatedly struck by enemy forces on the night of 28/29 June. Only by making use of all available forces, including the men of the signal troops, was it possible for the panzer corps to repel these attacks on the outskirts of the city. The intended relief of the forces there by a reinforced battle group of the 16th Panzer Division could not take place, for the motorcycle battalion, which had been assigned the task of manning the security line near Kremenets, was attacked by heavy tanks and cavalry not only from the south-east but also from the west. The motorcycle battalion was withdrawn to the north-west, as it would have been unable to resist the immense pressure applied by the enemy. The panzer division was compelled to keep its panzer regiment ready in the Verba–Kamienna–Stobyets area so that, depending on the development of the situation, it could be sent into action either towards the south-east (in the direction of Kremenets) or the north-east (in the direction of Dubno).

The situation near Dubno was approaching its climax. Since 0400 hours, the enemy had been storming our defences with rifle and tank units. He possessed several 15-centimetre assault tanks. It was reassuring when the panzer group informed the panzer corps that elements of the 44th Infantry Division were on their way to help resolve the situation. These elements had already reached a point 15 kilometres to the north of the city. Less reassuring was the fact that the enemy had penetrated the defensive line of the 111th Infantry Division on the south-east side of Dubno towards noon and was continuing his advance towards the eastern outskirts of the city.

The bulk of the 16th Motorised Infantry Division still stood on the west bank of the Styr. Traffic was slow, and the roads were in poor condition. Only the reconnaissance battalion of the division had managed to drive on ahead. It had secured Bokiyma so that the northern road to Dubno via Mlynov could at least be kept open. It was hoped that the heavy armour-piercing weapons of the division would be able to reach the garrison in Dubno along this road. The division then received the order to prepare a regimental group in Beresteczko as soon as possible for use against the enemy forces that were striking northwards from the vicinity of Verba.

Verba changed hands a couple of times that day. It had been taken by the enemy forces that were on the western side of the road of advance and was retaken by the 16th Panzer Division at 1400 hours.

The reports from Dubno followed in quick succession. More Russian forces had been attempting to infiltrate the city since 1300 hours.

General Kempf made his way to the combat zone of the 16th Panzer Division so that he could intervene personally in the resolution of the situation to the south-west of Dubno. There could not be any thought of sending the panzer division further to the east in accordance with the orders of the panzer group until such a resolution had occurred.

Finally, at 1700 hours, the commandant of Dubno reported that all the attacks carried out by the enemy had been repelled and that several enemy tanks had been destroyed. Fortunately, the feared loss of Dubno to the Russians had not come to pass. The 44th Infantry Division and the reconnaissance battalion of the 16th Motorised Infantry Division had not even arrived in the city at that point.

Far ahead, in the Ostrog–Wielbowno bridgehead, the 11th Panzer Division was on its own. It was not yet in contact with its northern neighbour, the III Panzer Corps, and was still being hit hard by enemy tanks and artillery. The enemy enjoyed aerial supremacy in this sector of the front and inflicted heavy casualties through bombing and strafing. There had been some concern at the headquarters of the XXXXVIII Panzer Corps that the strong enemy tank forces to the north of Ostrog might begin to make inroads into the bridgehead, and this was what now took place. Nevertheless, the panzer group ordered that the task of the panzer corps for the following day would be to thrust further to the east. Szepetowka, which lay 45 kilometres east of Ostrog, would be the first objective; Polonne, another 30 kilometres beyond Szepetowka, would be the next objective after that.

The immediate objective assigned to the 11th Panzer Division was the high ground to the north-east of Krupets (18 kilometres east of Ostrog). However, given that the panzer corps received no news that evening as to the situation in the combat zone of the panzer division, the possibilities of carrying out such a thrust could not be assessed.

Once the situation to the south-west of Dubno had been resolved, the 16th Panzer Division was to advance through the city towards Zaslav, which was 30 kilometres to the south-east of Ostrog. Meanwhile, the 16th Motorised Infantry Division would assume responsibility for the obstacle line across the Brody–Dubno road so as to prevent the southward escape of the enemy forces that were at that time situated immediately to the south and west of Dubno.

The 57th Infantry Division had been marching southwards from Leshnev throughout the day and had reached Brody at 1530 hours, while the 75th Infantry Division had advanced through Sitno and had thereby hurled the enemy forces in the vicinity of the village back towards the south-east. This helped to reduce the threat to the 16th Panzer Division from the area of Kremenets.

The reports received overnight boded ill for the plans for the next day. While it remained quiet in the vicinity of Dubno, the battle group of the 16th Panzer Division that had advanced through Verba encountered strong enemy tank forces near Ptycza and had to disengage. Struck again in the middle of the night by large numbers of Russian infantry, all of whom roared wildly as they wielded their flamethrowers, the battle group had to retreat further to the area south of Verba. The violent night fighting exacted a considerable toll on the troops. The movement of the panzer division to Dubno, which was intended to take place on 30 June, had to be postponed. Thorough reconnaissance and artillery preparation would be required beforehand.

The enemy tank forces that we were threatening to encircle resisted tenaciously by carrying out multiple heavy counter-attacks. It was quite likely that these forces would soon be reinforced with or relieved by enemy troops from the forested region south-east of Dubno.

The threat to the Ostrog bridgehead – the advance comes to a temporary halt (30 June 1941)

The difficulties faced by the 11th Panzer Division in the Ostrog–Wielbowno bridgehead had become greater overnight. The fierce assaults that had been launched by enemy tanks and infantry against Wielbowno the previous day had compelled the panzer division to withdraw its garrison from the village at nightfall. In spite of the heavy casualties he suffered, the enemy continued to attack the bridgehead from the north-east and the south-west. He always seemed to have new forces at his disposal. Yet the panzer division held out with its last reserves against the heavy artillery fire and constant air raids. The crossings over the Viliya remained in its hands.

The attempt to resupply the panzer division with fresh ammunition overnight had failed. The unbelievably terrible condition of the roads in Russia had not been too serious thus far, as it had often been possible for German forces to advance through the fields on either side of those so-called roads. But there had been a sudden downpour of rain during the night, transforming the fields into impenetrable bog. It became more difficult to supply the panzer division, whose defensive power decreased as a result. The delivery of supplies by air would have helped slightly, but not enough.

The enemy maintained his pressure against the Ostrog bridgehead on the morning of 30 June. It was our estimate that his forces there were of about divisional strength, but he continued to send in ever more reinforcements. His constant attacks, especially from the air, convinced the headquarters of the panzer division that the earliest point at which it could continue its advance to the east would be on 1 July, and that was only if the panzer division managed to regroup to the north of Ostrog.

In addition to the enemy tanks attacking from the north-east (from Hoszcza), it was reported that more enemy tanks were approaching throughout the day from the south-east (from Zaslav).

On the morning of 30 June, in the combat zone of the 16th Panzer Division, our aerial reconnaissance spotted large groups of enemy tanks assembling in the fields to the north and south of the road in the vicinity of Ptycza. More than 100 tanks were identified. Amongst them were heavy tanks with two turrets. The panzer corps, whose headquarters would shortly be moved forward to the northern road that led to Dubno, therefore requested that ground-attack aircraft be employed most urgently against these forces. Unfortunately, the Luftwaffe was unable to fulfil this request. Not only would the panzer division have to further postpone its advance; it would also have to resist to the best of its ability the tank assaults the enemy was bound to conduct against Verba.

The panzer division did not make any better progress in the afternoon. Its panzer regiment had been engaged in heavy fighting overnight and was not yet entirely ready for further action. Only on 1 July, after systematic preparatory fire by our artillery, would the panzer regiment be able to attack. It would be fully occupied for the next few days with the task of annihilating the enemy tanks south-west of Dubno. In the meantime, the 16th Motorised Infantry Division would be brought forward to the area south-east of Wierchow after nightfall.

The order that had been issued by the panzer group to the effect that the 11th Panzer Division was to cross the Horyn and thrust towards Szepetowka was one that had not been able to be carried out on 30 June. An attempt to follow this order had to be made on 1 July instead.

Relief attempts by the enemy from the north (1 July 1941)

Thundery showers turned all roads in the combat sector of the 11th Panzer Division into mud. The crossing of the Horyn was thus further delayed. Only to the south-west of Ostrog, near Kuniow and Kamionka, did the motorcycle battalion manage to establish a small bridgehead over the Viliya. But the enemy counter-attacked there throughout the day, making bridge construction difficult. The motorcycle troops near Kamionka had to move back to the west bank of the river due to the overwhelming numerical superiority of the enemy.

The 16th Motorised Infantry Division, which had set off from Warkowicze towards the east at 0500 hours, pivoted to the south-east. Its leading elements reached Kuniow in the afternoon, but the bulk of the division was still struggling along the incredibly bad roads.

To the north of Ostrog and on the west bank of the Horyn, the 11th Panzer Division clashed with Russian tanks and infantry that were pushing southwards. Our aerial reconnaissance identified several Russian trains steaming westwards over the railway bridge in Brodov and unloading in Ozhenin, which lay 12 kilometres to the north of Ostrog. A battle group was hastily organised from elements of the panzer regiment of the 11th Panzer Division as well as from the motorcycle battalion of the 16th Motorised Infantry Division to deal with this threat. The battle group rolled forward at noon and struck the advancing enemy. It was the desire of the commander of the panzer corps that the enemy tank forces to the west of the Horyn be annihilated that day and that the railway bridge in Brodov be taken as well, but the small battle group could not quite carry this out. Khorov was seized at 2200 hours, but no further progress was made after that.

Ever more enemy forces were arriving and assembling in the Ozhenin–Khorov–Rovats–Brodov area as well as near Badovka. The panzer corps requested that the employment of the Luftwaffe against these forces be made a priority.

An attack was executed by the 11th Panzer Division from the southern sector of the Ostrog bridgehead, but it ground to a halt when it ran into thick forest and heavy artillery fire a few kilometres to the south-east. In contrast, Battle Group Bohlmann conducted a bold and skilful thrust in the late afternoon and retook Wielbowno in the evening. The significance of this achievement cannot be overstated. The thrust could only be carried out along a narrow 2-kilometre stretch of road that was bordered on either side by marshy terrain, but its success created the conditions for the further advance of the panzer division to the east. All that was required now was the elimination of the enemy forces to the north.

The victorious tank battle near Verba (1 July 1941)

The encircled enemy tank forces in the combat zone of the 16th Panzer Division began their desperate attempts to break out. With artillery support, the enemy had tried to push in the direction of Verba overnight. The panzer division had prevented this, but by morning it was short of ammunition. The attack that had been planned for 0900 hours had to be postponed. Our aerial reconnaissance reported that the enemy tank forces were splitting up into smaller groups. After the failure of his united push, it now seemed that the enemy was going to try a multipronged breakout. Some groups sought to escape eastwards towards Nosovitsa; our howitzers shot them to pieces. Other groups were spotted pressing to the west and north-west. But most of the enemy tanks seemed to be in the vicinity of Ptycza. This meant that they stood in the path of the 44th Infantry Division, which was at that moment approaching from the north.

The 16th Panzer Division therefore abandoned the planned thrust to the north-east and attacked on the western side of Verba directly towards Ptycza. While a battle group remained in the vicinity of Verba to provide security to the north-east, the attack itself was a tremendous success. Numerous Russian tanks were put out of action. In the afternoon, the area to the east of Ptycza was reached at the very moment the main group of enemy tanks commenced their northward advance against the 44th Infantry Division. Both the panzer division and the infantry division coordinated their efforts and saw to the destruction of almost all the enemy tanks.

The battle group near Verba pushed to the north-east at noon and eliminated whatever was left of the enemy forces in the vicinity of Ptycza. Towards 1700 hours, the battle group ran into a desperate attack launched by Russian forces that were attempting to escape to the south-west after being hurled back over the Ikva by the 111th Infantry Division. This enemy attack shattered into bloody pieces against the hastily established defensive front of the battle group.

At 1715 hours, the commander of the 16th Panzer Division reported: 'The tank battle near Verba has come to a victorious conclusion, and contact has been made with the 44th Infantry Division.'

The tank battle had lasted four days. The performance of the troops had been most impressive. They had overcome the many severe crises that had arisen as a result of the numerical and often materiel superiority of the Russian tank arm. Moreover, they had triumphed over the will to fight of the Russian soldier, who was defending his native soil with the utmost fanaticism.

An indication of the severity of this battle is best demonstrated by the number of Russian tanks that had been destroyed. In the combat zone of the 16th Panzer Division, 261 combat vehicles had been destroyed, of which 10 were Kliment Voroshilov (KV) tanks. Meanwhile, the 11th Panzer Division had destroyed 150 combat vehicles.

The grand total of enemy tanks that had been captured or destroyed by the panzer corps since the beginning of the campaign in the East amounted to more than 600.

An examination of the dreaded KV tank revealed its mass to be only 60–70 tonnes rather than the 90 tonnes we had believed. Its armour possessed an average thickness of 90 millimetres. The tank came in two types: one had a high turret with vertical surfaces and was armed with a 15-centimetre gun as well as two machine guns, while the other had two gun turrets of medium calibre and three machine guns. The only way we could combat these tanks was with 8.8-centimetre anti-aircraft artillery at a range of less than 1,000 metres or with artillery fire of heavy calibre.

The threat that had been posed to the extended southern flank of the panzer corps by the enemy tanks had been removed. It was now hoped that the continuation of the advance to the east could proceed smoothly.

The 16th Panzer Division was unable to drive through Dubno towards Ostrog at that stage, for the few roads in the area that could be used were in bad condition and were occupied by the 16th Motorised Infantry Division. It was therefore decided that the 16th Panzer Division, on 2 July, would instead advance through Kremenets (to the south of which the 75th Infantry Division had recently arrived) towards Szumsk and in the direction of Zaslav so that both panzer divisions would finally be reunited for further operations. This plan was approved by the panzer group.

The new threat from the north (2 July 1941)

On the evening of 1 July, at approximately 2000 hours, the XXXXVIII Panzer Corps received alarming news from the XXIX Army Corps, the northern neighbour of the III Panzer Corps. Strong enemy tank forces had burst forth from the forests near Klevan, between Rovno and Lutsk, and had swiftly advanced southwards as far as the Moszkow–Borbin line. Facing this enemy was nothing more than a reinforced infantry regiment. The XXIX Army Corps had no further forces at its disposal, and the III Panzer Corps already stood to the east of Rovno, roughly as far forward as the 11th Panzer Division, with the 13th Panzer Division and the 25th Motorised Infantry Division.

Without delay, the XXXXVIII Panzer Corps sent the 670th Anti-Tank Battalion to the area east of Mlynov and elements of Motorised Regiment Hermann Göring to the area north-east of Dubno so as to ensure the protection of its road of advance. The 16th Panzer Division was given the order to keep its forces on standby for the time being. Perhaps its reinforced panzer regiment would need to be sent northwards via Dubno to deal with the new enemy tanks, or perhaps the panzer division would proceed with the plan of advancing through Krements and then eastwards towards Szumsk. There was even the possibility that the 16th Panzer Division might yet follow the 11th Panzer Division and the 16th Motorised Infantry Division through Ostrog.

Apart from this piece of news, the night of 1/2 July was quiet in the area of the panzer corps. It was the first time that this had been the case since the commencement of the campaign.

The 670th Anti-Tank Battalion headed north from Dubno early in the morning so that it could support the defensive efforts of the infantry regiment near Moszkow. It successfully hurled back the enemy forces there, destroying six Russian tanks in the process. The panzer group had also sent SS Motorised Division Leibstandarte Adolf Hitler through Lutsk to attack the western flank of this enemy. In the meantime, the Smoke Mortar Training Regiment and the 651st Pioneer Battalion were employed to set up a defensive front against some enemy forces that had been reported heading south towards the Dubno–Rovno road. The panzer regiment of the 16th Panzer Division was ordered to proceed through Dubno so that it would be ready to advance either to the north against the enemy forces near Moszkow or to the north-east in the direction of Rovno. Just in case, the reconnaissance battalion of the panzer division was also sent to Dubno.

The 11th Panzer Division was at that time continuing its attack to the east of Ostrog in the face of stiff enemy resistance. While the reconnaissance battalion took the high ground to the east of Wielbowno, the rifle brigade, to its north, was making progress in the direction of Lisicze. Importantly, the railway bridge in Brodov was taken intact by the panzer regiment of the 11th Panzer Division with the assistance of the reconnaissance battalion of the 16th Motorised Infantry Division. This bridge would be extremely valuable for subsequent operations. The enemy had vacated the area, so the panzer regiment drove over the bridge and advanced to the south-east in the direction of Badovka so as to join up with the rifle brigade.

After crossing the Viliya in the vicinity of Kuniow, the 16th Motorised Infantry Division pushed back the enemy troops in the forest to the south of the village and advanced throughout the afternoon in the direction of Zaslav. It reached Maydan by the evening, from where it carried out reconnaissance to the south-east and security measures to the south.

The Smoke Mortar Training Regiment, along with elements of the reconnaissance battalion of the 16th Panzer Division, routed the enemy forces that had been approaching the Dubno–Rovno road. At around the same time, Kremenets fell into the hands of the 111th Infantry Division.

During his visit to the front of the panzer corps later that day, the commander of the panzer group, Colonel-General von Kleist, decided that the 16th Panzer Division ought to advance through Kremenets and then drive to the east on the southern side of the 16th Motorised Infantry Division. This course of action would place the three divisions of the panzer corps (the 16th Panzer Division, the 16th Motorised Infantry Division, and the 11th Panzer Division) alongside one another. Each would thereby have its own attack sector and its own route of advance, yet they would still be close enough to each other in order to be able to coordinate their efforts.

The resistance of the enemy before the front of the panzer corps had become weaker throughout the course of the day. Nevertheless, there were still difficulties for the 11th Panzer Division. Its rifle brigade had been in constant combat with enemy tanks and had eventually, despite Russian heavy artillery fire, reached the high ground south-east of Ruska Moszonanica. The progress of the reconnaissance battalion was slower, for it was still struggling in the woods to the west of Krzywin before an enemy who was armed with anti-tank artillery and tanks.

The 16th Panzer Division set off for Kremenets that evening, with its panzer regiment departing from Dubno and its rifle brigade from Verba.

The whole front continues the advance (3 July 1941)

After a quiet night, the movements of all the divisions of the panzer corps continued according to plan.

By noon, the leading elements of the 11th Panzer Division had fought their way through to the fortified line that stood to the north-west of Krupets and to the south-west of Lisicze. The commander of the panzer corps, who was accompanying the panzer division, formed the opinion that the fortified line was only weakly defended. He ordered that the rifle brigade attack at once. But it had started to rain, so the attack was delayed until the middle of the afternoon. When that time came, the attack was successful. One battle group conducted a direct assault against the fortified line while another went around its northern end, via Annopol, in order to strike from behind. Towards 2100 hours, the fortified line was overcome without any significant resistance. The northern battle group took the village of Hubelce and seized the high ground to the north of Slavuta shortly thereafter. The view of the headquarters of the panzer corps that the area had been occupied by nothing more than a few rearguard units and that the bulk of the enemy forces were in retreat had been proven to be correct.

The 16th Motorised Infantry Division had been pushing the enemy back the whole day. However, the bad condition of the roads meant that only slow progress was made. There was not even one single good road that the division could use. On the northern wing, the division took Borysov and inflicted heavy casualties on the enemy. Reconnaissance units drove as far as Luterka and even approached Zaslav. On the southern wing, the motorcycle battalion rolled forward a little later and arrived in the vicinity of Yurkowce. The muddy roads made almost any movement impossible. Another battalion was committed to mopping-up operations in the forested region to the south of Ostrog. Once this task was completed, the battalion continued its advance and entered Stonicze in the evening.

Our reconnaissance indicated that the fighting in the combat zone of the 16th Motorised Infantry Division would probably be fierce the next day. The field emplacements defending Zaslav were heavily occupied.

In the sector of the 16th Panzer Division, one battle group had been committed against the enemy in the vicinity of Wielkie. His resistance was broken by noon, and the battle group thrust towards the Liski–Sivki line. More enemy forces were waiting there in entrenchments and behind old fortifications. Although it was possible to overcome these forces and to take the nearby hills before nightfall, the bad roads hindered further progress. Another battle group that had been diverted to repel an enemy counter-attack from Yampol got bogged down. A third battle group on the left wing of the panzer division also struggled to make progress. Once more, this was due to the terrible state of the roads. The bridge in Szumsk had been destroyed by Russian aircraft, so the bulk of this battle group was unable to cross the Viliya there. Reconnaissance therefore had to be conducted over a stretch of the river that lay north-west of the Russian-occupied Lachowce.

The headquarters of the panzer corps departed for its new command post in Ostrog at noon and arrived there at 1900 hours. For 4 July, the task of the panzer corps would remain the same, namely the relentless pursuit of the retreating enemy.

The 11th Panzer Division pursues the enemy – the remaining elements of the XXXXVIII Panzer Corps are stuck in mud (4 July 1941)

It was another quiet night. Non-stop rain made the muddy roads muddier. Neither the 16th Motorised Infantry Division nor the 16th Panzer Division could gain much ground.

Only the 11th Panzer Division managed to continue its drive into the depths of enemy territory. It captured Slavuta towards 0500 hours against little resistance and then thrust further to the south-east along the main road of advance, which was in surprisingly good condition. The road had probably built for use by Russian troops against Poland, for it led to the former Russo–Polish frontier in the vicinity of Ostrog. The spearhead of the panzer division thus made rapid progress. It smashed through the resistance put up by enemy rearguard tank units near Kamionka and then obliterated another line of resistance in order to take Szepetowka.[2]

The 110th Rifle Regiment had veered slightly to the north, had fought its way through Januszowka and Waczow, and was advancing on Romanov. Meanwhile, the spearhead of the panzer division continued along the main road. It had to battle against enemy tanks to the east of Szepetowka, after which it carried out a bold thrust to Polonne. After a brief period of combat, the city was taken in the evening. By 2300 hours, a vast quantity of materiel had been captured and a bridgehead had been established on the east bank of the river that ran through the city. The rifle regiment, which had soon given up its push towards Romanov due to the bad roads, had returned to Slavuta and was following the bulk of the panzer division in the direction of Szepetowka.

---

[2] Translator's note: this particular village of Kamionka lies to the east of Ostrog and should not be confused with the village of the same name which is situated to the south-west of Ostrog.

The other two divisions trailed behind. The 16th Motorised Infantry Division sent some of its forces to take the bridge over the Horyn in the vicinity of Mikhnov. There was little enemy resistance, and the bridge was soon seized intact. Other battle groups approached the river on a wide front. Zaslav and the stretch to its north was heavily occupied by the enemy. Along the stretch to the south-west, small bridgeheads were successfully created near Bielezynce and Myslatyn, although the resistance put up by enemy forces immediately to the north of the latter could not be broken. Throughout the afternoon, there was no success on either side of Zaslav. The enemy there was too strong, and it seemed as if he was being further reinforced by Russian units that had been pushed back to the south by the 11th Panzer Division. Elements of the motorised infantry division infiltrated Zaslav in the evening, but the strength of the enemy was so great that we suffered heavy losses and were compelled to evacuate the city shortly afterwards.

The rifle troops of the 16th Panzer Division entered Yampol in the early hours of the morning, following which they advanced over the Horyn and towards Pohorelce. The defensive efforts of several Russian cavalry and artillery units were thwarted, leading to the German seizure of Pohorelce that afternoon. The northern wing of the panzer division advanced on Lachowce, took the town after some heavy fighting, and established a bridgehead over the Horyn. However, the bulk of the panzer division was bogged down, and those that had pressed on ahead on foot had used up all their ammunition. Even though it had stopped raining, there was no way in which more ammunition could be supplied for as long as the roads remained muddy.

It would be the task of the panzer corps for 5 July to ensure the full exploitation of the success that had been achieved by the 11th Panzer Division on 4 July. Specifically, the panzer division would need to lunge towards the so-called Stalin Line in a surprise attack and take possession of Miropol. The 16th Motorised Infantry Division and the 16th Panzer Division were to advance towards Lubar. Both towns lay on the Slucz River.

CHAPTER 3

The XXXXVIII Panzer Corps Penetrates the Stalin Line

The 11th Panzer Division prises open the Stalin Line (5–6 July 1941)

The 11th Panzer Division set off from the Polonne bridgehead in the early hours of the morning and pushed into Miropol at 0600 hours despite determined resistance. The road bridge there had been destroyed, but the railway bridge to its south remained intact. A few elements of the panzer division managed to cross to the east bank of the Slucz, although the fortified position of the enemy soon brought them to a halt.

Our aerial reconnaissance that morning reported columns of enemy forces approaching along the Miropol–Chudnov road. An air raid by the Luftwaffe shortly afterwards caused them heavy casualties.

At 1630 hours, the panzer division launched a well-prepared attack against the fortified position near the railway bridge. The enemy forces in that position defended tenaciously, but they were crushed nonetheless. With that, the first penetration of the Stalin Line had been achieved. The attack wheeled to the north in the evening so that Miropol in its entirety would fall into German hands.

Several enemy tanks were put out of action, 23 guns were captured, and, in addition, 24 Russian aircraft were destroyed on the ground.

Now that a gap had come into being in the Stalin Line, a course of action that could possibly be pursued was to pour all available forces of the panzer corps, whose headquarters was now in Horodyszcze (slightly south of Szepetowka), into that gap. The panzer group was certainly in favour of sending the 16th Panzer Division through Miropol after the

11th Panzer Division, but the panzer corps rejected this idea. It would have required that the 16th Panzer Division cross the route of advance of the 16th Motorised Infantry Division, a process that could well have been chaotic enough without taking into account the bad roads. The panzer corps therefore ordered that the motorised infantry division continue with its advance, and this was to begin with the seizure of Zaslav. General Kempf suspected that the enemy had evacuated the city. This was indeed the case, and the city was taken by noon. It would then be the task of the division to advance on Lubar via Szepetowka and Polonne and to seize the crossing over the Slucz in a single stroke. But the roads were still in poor condition. Tractors were needed to pull our vehicles out of the mud one by one. By the evening, our troops were utterly exhausted and were only able to march as far as the area to the west of Polonne.

In the meantime, the 16th Panzer Division had clashed with large numbers of Russian tanks and artillery to the south and east of Lachowce, as well as along the Polkva. The stubborn resistance of the enemy meant that only the hills to the west of Czelhuzow, and eventually the village itself, could be taken. The panzer division hastily established a bridgehead there whilst under heavy counter-attack from enemy tanks. Little ground could be gained after that, and it was looking unlikely that much progress would be made the next day. So strong was the enemy and so terrible were the roads that the headquarters of the panzer corps was beginning to think that it might perhaps be best after all to withdraw the 16th Panzer Division and to send it through Zaslav so that it could follow the 11th Panzer Division through the gap in the Stalin Line and then possibly provide additional impetus to the continued thrust of the 11th Panzer Division in the direction of Chudnov. As it turned out, this would not take place.

During the night, supported by artillery fire, the enemy launched multiple counter-attacks against the 11th Panzer Division. The panzer division repelled these counter-attacks, and, by the morning of 6 July, it was in possession of the whole of Miropol. The enemy recognised the danger that was developing for him near Miropol as well as in the area of the road that led south from Zvyahel, which had already been crossed by the 13th Panzer Division (of the III Panzer Corps). He therefore sought to stop the 11th Panzer Division in its tracks by sending aircraft to bomb the road of advance and by hurling motorised forces and artillery towards Miropol.

Aerial reconnaissance revealed that large numbers of enemy troops were retreating before the front of the XXXXVIII Panzer Corps. They were also retreating in the sector of the III Panzer Corps, along the Zvyahel–Zhitomir road. It appeared as if the counter-attacks that the enemy had conducted against Miropol had been designed to cover this large-scale withdrawal, and they had indeed been effective enough to ensure that the 11th Panzer Division managed only to push slightly further beyond the eastern outskirts of the town before coming to a halt. If the enemy were to continue his counter-attacks, the panzer division would have to hold on to the Miropol bridgehead at all costs. It was likely that the arrival of more German forces would need to be awaited before the further advance to the east could proceed.

The 16th Motorised Infantry Division had advanced through Szepetowka and had reached Labun, 25 kilometres south-west of Miropol, by noon. The 156th Infantry Regiment, as the spearhead formation, pushed another 10 kilometres to the south-east in the direction of Lubar and unexpectedly came across a well-built fortified position. The presence of these three-storey modern bunkers, camouflaged as straw stacks, in a position 15 kilometres to the west of the Slucz came as a complete surprise to the XXXXVIII Panzer Corps. Our available intelligence had indicated that the enemy ought to have had nothing more than a few weak field positions on either side of Lubar. Breaking through the Stalin Line in this sector of the front was going to be more difficult than expected.

Due to the enemy withdrawal movements that had been reported by our aerial reconnaissance, we could anticipate that the 16th Panzer Division would be able to make better progress in its attack sector than it had done the previous day. The ease with which it crossed the Horyn near Lachowce was a clear indication that the enemy had indeed fallen back to the east. Encouraged by this new situation, the commander of the panzer corps ordered that the panzer division be divided into two groups. The southern group was to advance through Okopy and Starokonstantinov, while the northern group would go through Bialogrodka and Werbowce. Only towards 1900 hours did these groups catch up with the retreating enemy. The southern group fought the enemy in the vicinity of Zielona, and the northern group did so near Dracze. The fighting lasted well into the night and resulted in the annihilation of many of the Russian forces and the capture of 21 guns.

Our aerial reconnaissance had reported in the afternoon and again in the evening that enemy motorised columns were approaching from the south and were going through Starokonstantinov towards and to the east of Lubar. These columns were retreating from the front of the XXXXIV Army Corps, the formation to the right of the XXXXVIII Panzer Corps. Although they did not appear to have any intention of attacking the southern wing of the panzer corps, it could be expected that they would try to defend their route of withdrawal against any attempt by the 16th Panzer Division to push further in the direction of Starokonstantinov. It was therefore important that the panzer division advance on a wide front as quickly as possible so as to break through the Stalin Line to the south of Miropol and then continue with the pursuit of the enemy to the east.

The drive of the 11th Panzer Division towards Berdichev – the fighting for the security of the southern flank (7–8 July 1941)

At the crack of dawn on 7 July, the 11th Panzer Division punched into the depths of Russian territory beyond the Stalin Line. It took Szulayki at 0900 hours and Chudnov at 1000 hours, reached the gates of Berdichev at 1400 hours, and seized the city at 1900 hours. Troyanov was taken at about the same time by the left wing of the panzer division. It was clear that the enemy had fled, for there was little that stood in the way of our rapid advance.

The long southern flank of the 11th Panzer Division had to be taken care of. It had been intended that the 16th Motorised Infantry Division advance through Lubar so as to see to the protection of the right flank of the panzer division. However, the motorised infantry division remained in the vicinity of the fortified line on either side of Lubar. The panzer corps therefore detached the reinforced 60th Infantry Regiment from the motorised infantry division and sent it through Polonne and Miropol towards Chudnov. The regiment was placed under the command of the panzer division and was given the task of covering the south-western flank against the enemy forces near Lubar. Furthermore, the point of penetration in Miropol, which was only a few hundred metres in width, needed to be shielded, so the panzer corps assigned the 670th Anti-Tank Battalion the role of sealing off the roads that led to Miropol from the north and north-east, and SS Motorised Division Leibstandarte Adolf Hitler, which had gone through Ostrog, the responsibility for the defence of the flanks and for keeping open the point of penetration.

Significant traffic problems arose from all these movements. The railway bridge in Miropol remained the only site where the Slucz could be crossed, and the area around it had become very muddy. It was necessary for the panzer corps to set up a forward command post to look after traffic control.

Although the 16th Motorised Infantry Division had been able to overcome many of the bunkers to the south-east of Labun the previous evening, it only made slow progress after that. The division had become much weaker after the detachment of the 60th Infantry Regiment, and the resistance put up by the enemy was particularly fierce. Multiple counter-attacks by Russian tanks had to be repelled. The division was soon brought to a halt and was compelled to place the 165th Motorcycle Battalion on its flank to the south-west in order to provide security against the enemy forces in the vicinity of Starokonstantinov.

The 16th Panzer Division had been driving forward near the woods to the north-west of Starokonstantinov in the early hours of the morning when it clashed with large numbers of enemy forces. Our reconnaissance units confirmed that more enemy troops were assembling in and approaching from the city. Amongst them were tank and artillery units, and they sought desperately to strike to the north. This made for a lot of work for the panzer division, and constant support from the Luftwaffe was required. Additional enemy forces appeared from the forested region near Werbowce and attacked the reconnaissance battalion and even the divisional command post. The road of advance was thereby interrupted, and the combat troops were cut off from the supply troops. The situation had become critical. Nevertheless, the panzer division managed to destroy the enemy forces near Werbowce by nightfall, and all the attacks that had been launched from Starokonstantinov had been repelled. Following the elimination of so many enemy forces, the panzer division was able to draw closer to the city. It reached the Hrebeninka–Popowce line that night.

The day had brought success for the panzer corps. The 75-kilometre drive to the east by the 11th Panzer Division was a bold manoeuvre that sliced through the road and rail routes leading to the south from Zhitomir. Also noteworthy was the performance of the 16th Panzer Division. It had eradicated a vast quantity of enemy forces and had prevented the retreat of what was left to the north-east.

Colonel-General von Kleist visited the command post of the panzer corps in the afternoon. He agreed with the plan presented to him by General Kempf regarding the continuation of operations. The 16th Motorised Infantry Division was to follow in the wake of the 11th Panzer Division, while the 16th Panzer Division was to cover its flank facing Starokonstantinov, which the 111th Infantry Division was approaching, whilst pushing further to the east via Lubar and thereby widening the attack front. However, the intended continuation of the thrust of the 11th Panzer Division beyond Berdichev had to be postponed for the time being. The XIV Panzer Corps was still a long way behind, and the formation immediately to the north of the 11th Panzer Division, the 13th Panzer Division (of the III Panzer Corps), had yet to break through the Stalin Line.

The enemy launched some small attacks against Berdichev overnight and again on the morning of 8 July. These were all driven off by the 11th Panzer Division. The Russians probed the city from all sides, but this did not prevent the expansion of the German bridgehead. In the early afternoon, faced only by weak enemy resistance, the panzer division took the high ground to the east of the city (Hill 285) as well as the area to its south.

It was at that point the desire of the headquarters of the panzer group that a battle group of the 11th Panzer Division carry out an immediate attack to the north so that it could seize Zhitomir in conjunction with the 13th Panzer Division. But the bulk of the 11th Panzer Division was still in the process of arriving in the vicinity of Berdichev and the 13th Panzer Division was still too far behind. A thrust to the north would have split up the forces of the 11th Panzer Division and would have been too weak on its own to guarantee the capture of Zhitomir.

The reconnaissance battalion of SS Motorised Division Leibstandarte Adolf Hitler had in the meantime reached Romanov and, since 1100 hours, had been in combat with enemy troops to the east of the village. The bulk of the SS division, navigating bad roads and subjected to attack from Russian aircraft, had been further behind for quite some time and had only gradually caught up. By the evening, the SS division still stood to the east of Romanov, for the enemy resisted tenaciously and was supported by heavy artillery. Even so, the SS division persisted in its push to the east and eventually succeeded in widening the Miropol gap to the north and south.

The panzer corps had shifted its command post to Polonne at 0930 hours. Towards noon, the corps reconnaissance squadron suffered heavy casualties when waves of Russian bombers and fighters struck the roads and airfields in the combat zone of the panzer corps.

In the immediate vicinity of Chudnov, the 60th Infantry Regiment had attacked a small group of enemy forces and had taken Krasnovolka. Most of the troops of the 16th Motorised Infantry Division were by then ready to move forward from Luban through the region south of Chudnov in the direction of Krasnopol and Januszpol. The remaining elements of the motorised infantry division were further to the rear and were therefore subordinated to the 16th Panzer Division. These elements pushed in the direction of Lubar in cooperation with the reconnaissance battalion and the motorcycle battalion of the panzer division. This push gained little ground, even though it seemed as if the enemy had withdrawn eastwards from the fortified area near Lubar.

The rest of the 16th Panzer Division sought to advance further to the east by bypassing Lubar to its south. Signal communications were lacking between the panzer division and the panzer corps that day, the result of which was that it was not until the evening that the headquarters of the panzer corps could gain a clear picture of the situation in the sector of the panzer division. It could not be expected that the panzer division would have an easy time in crossing the Slucz to the south-west of Lubar. The decision was therefore taken that the 60th Infantry Regiment would approach Lubar from the north-east the next morning in order to help the panzer division cross the river and thrust towards Makhnovka, which lay 18 kilometres to the south of Berdichev.

SS Motorised Division Leibstandarte Adolf Hitler had been veering to the north and was for that reason placed under the command of the III Panzer Corps. However, it had yet to make much progress in the direction of Zhitomir, so the panzer group came to the conclusion that it might not be a good idea after all for a battle group of the 11th Panzer Division to be sent northwards from Berdichev. The panzer division would instead prepare for the renewal of its eastward advance.

The fighting in the Miropol–Lubar–Berdichev area (9 July 1941)

The 11th Panzer Division was eager to strike from the Berdichev bridgehead and continue with the thrust to the east. There was no enemy presence to the north of the city, and reconnaissance units had already advanced eastwards through Bialopol and had damaged the railway line that lay beyond. Since the III Panzer Corps had in the meantime taken the strongly fortified Zvyahel and had already launched its 13th Panzer Division towards Zhitomir, the panzer group granted the request of the XXXXVIII Panzer Corps for the continuation of the advance by the 11th Panzer Division. However, it was first necessary to repel a couple of attacks carried out by the enemy against the high ground south of Berdichev. In addition, our aerial reconnaissance had spotted long columns of Russian vehicles, including tanks, approaching Berdichev from the south via Makhnovka. The planned advance in the direction of Bialacerkiew would have to wait until the approaching columns had been destroyed. They had already reached Khazhyn, and a large part of the panzer division, as well as the Luftwaffe, had to be committed against them.

The 16th Motorised Infantry Division had repelled an attack by armoured reconnaissance vehicles to the south-east of Chudnov during the night and had encountered enemy tanks and entrenchments in the area between Babuszki and Volosovka. The 60th Infantry Regiment set off from Krasnovolka in the direction of Lubar in order to facilitate the crossing of the Slucz by the 16th Panzer Division.

The 16th Panzer Division had still been advancing towards the Slucz on the evening of 8 July. The panzer corps was now aware of this thanks to the fact that communications had been restored between it and the panzer division. A group on the southern wing of the panzer division had been sent to establish a bridgehead near Przewalowka, for the bridge in Lubar had been blown up by the enemy. This bridgehead soon had to be given up when the enemy conducted a powerful attack against it. The northern group of the panzer division had made little progress. The roads were in poor condition, and enemy resistance remained strong. On the morning of 9 July, this northern group parried a strong attack from Lubar before lunging towards the town. Only once some of our tanks crossed the Slucz on a small bridge to the north of Lubar was there success, towards noon, in breaking the stubborn resistance of the enemy and in taking the town itself. An advance detachment of German tanks immediately started to push towards Krasnopol. This success by the panzer division meant that the task that had been assigned to the 60th Infantry Regiment had been fulfilled. The regiment stayed where it was to the north-east of Lubar so that it could soon follow in the wake of the advance of the 16th Panzer Division.

Elements of SS Motorised Division Leibstandarte Adolf Hitler were still in fierce combat with enemy forces to the east of Romanov, but the bulk of the formation was at that stage proceeding through Miropol.

The 60th Motorised Infantry Division was on this day assigned to the panzer corps. Its first task would be to reach Polonne as soon as possible.

In the afternoon, the 16th Motorised Infantry Division was repeatedly attacked by enemy forces from the area near Babuszki. The enemy suffered heavy casualties and was kept at bay, but, that evening, he carried out two attacks simultaneously: one from the south-east and another, comprising countless tanks, from the east along our road of advance. Our aerial reconnaissance indicated that there were at least 50 tanks near and to the south of Tiuturniki. The defensive fighting to the south-east of Chudnov lasted until the evening. The road of advance remained under enemy control, so the division was at that stage unable to move forward in the direction of Berdichev. Furthermore, the planned shift of the command post of the panzer corps to Chudnov could not take place just yet.

In the afternoon, after some heavy fighting on the high ground near Khazhyn, the 11th Panzer Division managed to hurl back the enemy forces that had attacked from the south. At the same time, a handful of enemy tanks rolled forward from the area west of Makhnovka and caused trouble immediately to the west of Berdichev.

Could the 11th Panzer Division resume its eastward advance? Russian motorised forces were approaching from the south, but our aerial reconnaissance reported that these forces were pivoting to the east through Makhnovka. In the assumption that the 16th Panzer Division, after its successful breakthrough at Lubar, would probably soon arrive in the vicinity to the west of Makhnovka, the panzer corps decided to order the 11th Panzer Division to drive towards Bialacerkiew at once and to cut off the eastward movement of the Russian motorised forces.

Yet it came to light that evening that the 16th Panzer Division had been held up by the enemy to the west of Troszcza and that it was therefore still making its way through the hills near Krasnopol. On top of that, the enemy forces that stood to the south-east and east of Chudnov before the front of the 16th Motorised Infantry Division were particularly strong and needed to be dealt with right away. The motorised infantry division did not possess sufficient striking power to be able to do this on its own. The constant threat to Berdichev from the south meant that the bulk of the 11th Panzer Division would have to stay where it was. An advance in the direction of Bialacerkiew at that moment would have been too difficult. A new decision was made to the effect that a battle group of the 11th Panzer Division would head back towards Chudnov in order to partake in the destruction of the enemy forces in the vicinity of the city.

The 60th Motorised Infantry Division reported that it had reached Polonne. Once it reached Miropol, it would be able to relieve the elements of SS Motorised Division Leibstandarte Adolf Hitler that were still securing the point of penetration.

There were thundery showers during the night. The roads became muddier than ever.

The crisis in the sector of the XXXXVIII Panzer Corps – the 11th Panzer Division is cut off (10 July 1941)

On the morning of 10 July, the three-sided envelopment of the enemy forces south-east of Chudnov went according to plan.

Battle Group Angern of the 11th Panzer Division drove through Pyatki in the early hours of the morning. It then wheeled to the south and struck some enemy tank units that were deployed near Datski.

At about the same time, the 16th Motorised Infantry Division attacked the entrenched enemy forces between Babuszki and Volosovka. Large numbers of enemy tanks were also to be found there. The 156th Infantry Regiment, upon breaking through the Babuszki–Volosovka line, reported that it had identified approximately 30 tanks withdrawing to the south towards Januszpol. Battle Group Angern was therefore given the order to lunge to the south beyond Datski so as to prevent the enemy tanks from escaping into the large forest region that lay not too far away.

The 16th Panzer Division was to conduct a simultaneous attack from the west in the direction of Januszpol. Unfortunately, it had been in combat with strong enemy tank forces to the east of Krasnopol since 0500 hours and had only been able to push forward gradually. It was 1100 hours by the time it reached the area to the south of Januszpol. The enemy's resistance there had in the meantime been strengthened by the tanks that had withdrawn from the north.

So as to assist the 16th Panzer Division in its advance, the 11th Panzer Division was ordered to send another battle group from Berdichev to the south-west. This battle group was to go through Rajgrodek and then approach Januszpol.

The commander of the panzer group emphasised the importance of seeing to the destruction of the enemy forces near Januszpol, and also made it clear that there were to be no further overextended thrusts by the panzer divisions to the east of the kind that had been conducted thus far if there were no motorised divisions available to provide flank protection. Even Kiev was not to be taken until the infantry divisions had caught up.

The 11th Panzer Division had in the meantime been successful in repelling all attacks carried out by the enemy near Khazhyn. However, our aerial reconnaissance revealed that more enemy forces were on the way. Several tanks and other motor vehicles were being concentrated in the area to the north of Makhnovka, and multiple trains were delivering troops to the north and south of Koziatyn. Because of this situation, it was decided that the planned dispatch of a battle group towards Rajgrodek would be cancelled.

Towards noon, the command post of the 11th Panzer Division in Holodki, which was situated to the north-west of Berdichev, was attacked from two sides, and its situation became ever more precarious throughout the course of the afternoon. An advance detachment of the 60th Motorised Infantry Division charged towards Holodki via Pyatki in order to free the command post of the panzer division from the enemy pincer movement. The rest of the motorised infantry division was to follow as soon as possible.

The relocation of the headquarters of the panzer corps to Chudnov was delayed until the evening. Traffic congestion had become a problem. The four divisions of the panzer corps had just one major road at their disposal. This road went through Miropol, where only the railway bridge could be used to cross the Slucz.

The 16th Motorised Infantry Division had been pursuing the enemy forces that had fallen back to Januszpol, but it had now come to a standstill. In addition, the tanks of Battle Group Angern were bogged down in mud. This necessitated a reorganisation of forces, but there was no chance that they would catch up with the retreating enemy that day. Only the 156th Infantry Regiment could be committed in the direction of Januszpol. Its leading battalion arrived at the northern outskirts of the town by nightfall, and was soon in combat with enemy tanks and infantry.

Even the 16th Panzer Division barely gained ground in its push towards Januszpol from the south. It launched one assault after another all afternoon, but the tremendous firepower of the enemy's artillery, the tough resistance of his tanks, and the defensive strength of his anti-tank weaponry proved to be too overwhelming. The envelopment from the south that the panzer division was supposed to carry out would not be able to be completed just yet. But the situation for the 11th Panzer Division that night was even more critical. Its command post was threatened by enemy tanks and infantry from the north, south, and west. Our main road of advance was increasingly populated by enemy troops, and they edged ever closer to Holodki and Pyatki. The enemy encirclement was almost complete. Moreover, offensive preparations were underway to the south and south-east of Berdichev. A new Russian tank brigade had arrived by rail, in addition to the several tanks and six to eight batteries that had already reached the area by road. The 11th Panzer Division requested that reinforcements be sent to Berdichev with the utmost urgency. General Kempf therefore ordered that Battle Group Angern turn around and go back to Berdichev via Pyatki. The loss of either location could not be allowed to occur under any circumstances. The advance detachment of the 60th Motorised Infantry Division was also ordered to move forward as quickly as possible. A difficult night was in store for the 11th Panzer Division.

More setbacks (11–12 July 1941)

The 60th Motorised Infantry Division drove forward throughout the night and attacked the enemy forces that lay slightly beyond Pyatki at 0330 hours. The enemy was compelled to withdraw, thereby relinquishing control of the road of advance to us once more. Elements of the motorised infantry division pursued the southward retreat of the enemy, and contact was re-established with the 11th Panzer Division.

An intercepted radio message revealed that a Russian assault on Berdichev would take place at 1100 hours. Our aerial reconnaissance confirmed that preparations were being made by the enemy to the south-west of the city. The panzer corps, whose headquarters had by then arrived in Chudnov, ordered the 11th Panzer Division to go over to the defensive. The divisional command post was shifted to Berdichev at the same time.

The 16th Panzer Division had been in combat with enemy artillery to the south of Januszpol since the early hours of the morning. It eventually linked up with the 16th Motorised Infantry Division, which had been approaching from the north. A battle group of the panzer division had in the meantime been sent in the direction of Berdichev so as to envelop the enemy forces from the south. It took Smiala shortly before noon and was then attacked by a large formation of tanks to the west of Buraki in the early afternoon. There was also heavy fighting in the vicinity of Podorozna, and additional cavalry, artillery, and tank forces were confirmed to be assembling around Ulanov. Parts of this enemy group plunged into the deep flank of the panzer division, reaching the area to the north of Stefskowce in the course of the afternoon. The 60th Infantry Regiment, which still stood to the east of Lubar, pushed back these enemy troops, but it had to defend itself against a new infantry attack in the evening.

The advance of the 16th Motorised Infantry Division from Januszpol to the south-east was held in check by fierce enemy resistance. Several heavy tanks hit the division hard. Although it managed to repel them, its progress was slow.

The anticipated enemy assault on Berdichev failed to materialise. Aside from an increase in artillery activity and scouting raids, enemy action in the combat zone of the 11th Panzer Division had died down. It seemed as if the enemy felt compelled to turn to the south-west so as to avoid the growing pressure being applied by the 60th Motorised Infantry Division. Our aerial reconnaissance reported that enemy troops were heading south away from Makhnovka and that trains were departing Kalinovka for the south-east. Nevertheless, the enemy had established a strong defensive flank to the south-east of Januszpol and was resisting with the greatest tenacity both the 16th Motorised Infantry Division and the 16th Panzer Division. As a result, the latter was still experiencing difficulties in carrying out its southern envelopment manoeuvre. The enemy also seemed to be pulling back his motorised forces. Overall, it had become clear that he was conducting a large-scale withdrawal. Because of this, the panzer group ordered the renewal of the advance. The panzer corps decided that the 60th Motorised Infantry Division would assume responsibility for the defence of Berdichev and that the 11th Panzer Division would thrust from the city to the east. Even though the situation remained a challenging one, there would be no danger to this eastward thrust from the north. The III Panzer Corps had taken Zhitomir on 10 July, and its 13th Panzer Division had already reached a position east of Korostyshev.

Despite the best efforts of our fighter defence, the enemy successfully conducted air raids against the forces of the XXXXVIII Panzer Corps the entire day. The 16th Panzer Division in particular suffered heavy casualties. It had taken Podorozna, but then had to give it up again in the evening. Its progress the next day was negligible, as the defensive strength of the Russian tank and artillery units proved to be too great. On the northern wing of the panzer division was the panzer regiment, and it tried in vain to seize Buraki. The southern wing of the panzer division attempted to infiltrate Podorozna, but it soon found that its whole flank from there to Severynovka was under attack from strong Russian forces. These forces achieved a breakthrough and pushed almost as far as the southern outskirts of Krasnopol. A relief attack by the 60th Infantry Regiment via Nosovki was brought to a halt by a powerful enemy counter-attack. The northern wing of the panzer division managed to reach the western outskirts of Buraki in the afternoon, although the effort was costly for the panzer regiment. It was attacked by several heavy enemy tanks and lost five of its own tanks. The southern wing captured Podorozna at about the same time, but the flank attack from the south and the tank threat from the north-east meant that it could go no further. The enemy forces that had reached the area south of Krasnopol sought to push further to the north, and the hills to the south-east of the village changed hands many times. The infantry regiment eventually forced its way through Nosovki at 1700 hours and could render valuable assistance to the flank of the panzer division. Although the 57th Infantry Division was at that moment approaching from the west and the 75th Infantry Division from the north, they were too far away to be able to release the infantry regiment, which the 16th Motorised Infantry Division needed if it were to drive towards Berdichev.

The 16th Motorised Infantry Division fought its way through impenetrable woods throughout the morning, took the fiercely defended village of Rajgrodek, and established a bridgehead over the stream that ran through the village. Eleven enemy tanks were destroyed. The right wing of the division encountered tough resistance to the west of Rajgrodek. This enemy still held on to Buraki. The fighting there did not reach a conclusion before the end of the day. The division saw to the protection of its north-east flank by setting up a security line between Martsinovka and Slobodka Lesna, for there remained strong enemy forces, including tanks, in the Berdichev–Holodki–Rajgrodek area.

Since the morning, the 60th Motorised Infantry Division had been driving off one enemy attack after another along the line that ran from the area south of Holodki to that just to the west of Berdichev. Towards noon, the enemy succeeded in breaking through this line. He occupied Kuscin and pushed as far as our main road of advance. By rapidly committing its reserves to this front, the division inflicted heavy casualties on the enemy. Kuscin was retaken in a counter-attack that afternoon, and the 120th Infantry Regiment, which belonged to the division, even managed to wrest control of the firmly held Ozadovka before nightfall. The fighting there continued into the night.

Although the 92nd Infantry Regiment (of the 60th Motorised Infantry Division) was able to relieve elements of the 11th Panzer Division in Berdichev, the panzer division could not set off just yet. The enemy, with strong artillery support, had launched a surprise attack in the early hours of the morning towards the high ground to the south-east of the city, and he conducted repeated attacks in this direction right up until noon. The entire panzer division had to go over to the defensive, creating a main line of resistance that ran around the eastern, southern, and south-western outskirts of Berdichev so that any attempt by the enemy to infiltrate the city could be opposed. While the positions facing east were secure, those to the south, south-west, and west were not. The divisional commander therefore recommended that all available forces of the panzer corps be employed to annihilate the enemy formations that faced those positions. This would enable the defensive front of the panzer corps, which was 85 kilometres in width, to be shortened somewhat. There were a number of discussions with the headquarters of the panzer group at that time. The difficult situation that confronted the panzer corps, not to mention the impossibility of an advance to the east by the panzer division under the prevailing circumstances, needed to be made clear to the panzer group. Consideration was given to the idea of sending the 9th Panzer Division (of the III Panzer Corps) from the north to the area east of Berdichev, but this did not end up taking place. Another idea was to release the 16th Panzer Division so that it could move to the area to the north of the city, but the danger to the flank of the panzer division and the poor condition of the roads in its sector meant that this idea could not realistically be pursued. The third solution – for the 11th Panzer Division to hand over the defence of Berdichev to the 60th Motorised Infantry Division once the latter had been relieved by the 111th Infantry Division so that the panzer division would be free to focus its attention towards the south-east – was rejected by the commander of the panzer division, Major-General Ludwig Crüwell, for he regarded it as one that could not be carried out without suffering heavy casualties. He also thought it out of the question that a motorised infantry division would be capable of holding on to the city on its own.

The situation became critical for the 11th Panzer Division towards the evening. The enemy carried out multiple powerful assaults against Berdichev from the east and south-east. He had a large number of tanks at his disposal, and his artillery fire caused such destruction that our own artillery formations were torn to shreds. Only by making use of all the forces at its disposal and by conducting a counter-attack with its panzer regiment was the panzer division able to keep the city in its grasp. It was obvious that the enemy's reinforcements consisted of much artillery, and our aerial reconnaissance confirmed the presence of innumerable tanks in the vicinity of Makhnovka. Some of them were heading north, others east. Late in the evening, enemy tanks probed Berdichev from the north and north-east for the first time. It could be expected that the enemy would continue to assault the city on 13 July.

Resolution of the situation – the first supply difficulties (13 July 1941)

The enemy defensive front before the 16th Panzer Division showed no signs of diminishing in strength. It was therefore the plan of the XXXXVIII Panzer Corps for 13 July that the panzer division exploit the advance of the 16th Motorised Infantry Division near Rajgrodek by circumventing the enemy to the north and regaining freedom of movement to the east. The protection of the deep southern flank of the panzer division, against which the enemy would foreseeably conduct further attacks, would be assigned to the infantry. It was possible that the 60th Infantry Regiment would become available for this task. The 11th Panzer Division was to hold on to Berdichev and was also to participate in the elimination of the enemy forces to its west in conjunction with the other three divisions of the panzer corps.

Thunder and rain during the night, in addition to cloudbursts on the morning of 13 July, once more caused the condition of the roads to deteriorate. A strong battle group created from the panzer regiment of the 11th Panzer Division and from elements of the 60th Motorised Infantry Division was sent towards the south-west. It encountered little resistance, reached Piatyhorka, and thrust further in the direction of Rajgrodek. The bulk of the 60th Motorised Infantry Division captured Hardyszowka and Zydowce before reaching the eastern edge of the large forest that lay to the west of Piatyhorka. The difficulties presented by the roads meant that the 16th Motorised Infantry Division could only roll forward from the Rajgrodek bridgehead at noon, but it was nonetheless able to establish contact with the 11th Panzer Division shortly thereafter. This compelled the enemy to fall back to the south-east.

The attempt by the panzer regiment of the 16th Panzer Division to wheel around the northern flank of the enemy forces failed due to the terrible condition of the roads. For this reason, the panzer division, following the seizure of Buraki at noon, sought to conduct a frontal assault against the enemy. It gained some ground before coming to a halt that afternoon near Andrejaszowka. As ever, the roads were in a bad state, but it was also the case that the enemy refused to give in. However, considering that the region to the west of Berdichev had in the meantime been cleared of enemy forces, that the battle group of the 11th Panzer Division could now return to the city, and that elements of the 16th Motorised Infantry Division and 60th Motorised Infantry Division were providing security to the south, it was best at that point that the 16th Panzer Division abandon its useless frontal assault and instead head towards Berdichev. Furthermore, the 60th Motorised Infantry Division could be released for action elsewhere thanks to the rapid arrival, on trucks, of the troops of the 50th Infantry Regiment (of the 111th Infantry Division). It had originally been envisioned that the 60th Motorised Infantry Division would advance to the south via Berdichev, but now it was the 16th Panzer Division that would be heading towards the city. It was therefore decided that the latter would proceed through the city, thrust to the south as far as Makhnovka, and then pivot towards the east.

Enemy artillery fire continued to inundate the 11th Panzer Division. Our Stuka dive bombers were utilised to good effect against the tank and artillery formations that stood to the south of Berdichev, near Iwankowce. Towards noon, waves of Russian forces surged forward from the woods that lay to the east of Berdichev. These forces were blown to pieces by the seven batteries and heavy rocket projectors that we had positioned on the eastern outskirts of the city. The enemy suffered heavy losses. Our reconnaissance units attempted to patrol the area to the south of the city, but they were pushed back by the enemy troops there. When

Russian tanks rolled forward from the south that evening, our men had to fight hard to repel them.

A major source of concern on this day was the flow of our supplies. The unpaved roads became so muddy when it rained that they could barely be used, yet none of the divisions were prepared to take the risk of ordering their rear units to travel off-road. As a result, all the supply vehicles of all the divisions had just the one route at their disposal. Even without the unfavourable weather, the long queue of vehicles would have led to traffic congestion. For the troops at the front, the most pressing concern was the shortage of ammunition, the expenditure of which had been considerable during the heavy defensive fighting. Such expenditure of ammunition was always at its highest whenever our units were spread out and forced to defend in multiple directions (e.g. at Berdichev and Werbowce).

All measures were taken by the panzer corps to guarantee the delivery of what was most urgently needed. It was made clear to the men and their commanders that the movement of supply traffic took priority.

The renewal of the attack meets with little success (14 July 1941)

The headquarters of Panzer Group 1 ordered that the XXXXVIII Panzer Corps should roll forward once more and that it should advance to the area south of Skvira. The XIV Panzer Corps had in the meantime been shifted from its position south-east of Tarnopol to a new position, much further north, on the left wing of the XXXXVIII Panzer Corps. This was because a wide gap had developed between the XXXXVIII Panzer Corps and the III Panzer Corps. The latter was tied down in combat before Kiev, so the XIV Panzer Corps would be given the task of driving directly towards Skvira, which lay 80 kilometres to the south-east of Berdichev.

The 11th Panzer Division was preparing for the renewal of the advance on the morning of 14 July when it was yet again struck by heavy artillery fire. Given that its ammunition supply column was stuck in mud in the vicinity of the Miropol bridge, the only way in which the panzer division could return fire with its field howitzers was to obtain shells from the 60th Motorised Infantry Division. This process took time and resulted in the delay of the renewed advance, although the panzer division could hardly set off without being properly resupplied first. With the assistance of our aerial reconnaissance, the panzer division specifically targeted the enemy artillery units when it returned fire towards noon. The 92nd Infantry Regiment, which had been transferred from the motorised infantry division to the panzer division, attacked southwards shortly afterwards and took the high ground near Khazhyn, thereby creating the preconditions for the planned route of advance for the 16th Panzer Division.

The 16th Panzer Division had in the meantime been released by elements of the 111th Infantry Division and had started its journey towards Berdichev via Rajgrodek. Its progress was slow. The roads were in a bad state, the bridge to the south of Rajgrodek had been destroyed, and enemy aerial activity and artillery fire caused a great deal of trouble. At noon, only 26 tanks of the panzer regiment and a few other weak units of the panzer division reached Berdichev. They were ordered to exploit the success of the 92nd Infantry Regiment by pushing southwards towards Makhnovka. The bulk of the panzer division remained a long way behind and could not be properly employed in combat. Nevertheless, the leading elements fought hard and captured Lezhelov in the late afternoon.

The 60th Motorised Infantry Division, now without the 92nd Infantry Regiment, secured the Obukhovka–Markusze line. Parts of the division then proceeded to mop up the enemy forces in the large forest region to the west of Piatyhorka, a task that lasted until the evening.

Providing security to the south was the 16th Motorised Infantry Division. It stood along the muddy road between Rajgrodek and Berdichev and suffered heavy losses throughout the day thanks to the bombs of enemy aircraft and the harassing fire of enemy artillery.

A Stuka raid that afternoon inflicted significant damage on the battery positions in the enemy-held villages of Iwankowce and Nizgorce. This made up to some degree for the shortage of ammunition of the artillery units of the 11th Panzer Division. At 1600 hours, Battle Group Angern was able to commence the attack. Its tanks infiltrated Nizgorce, but they soon had to withdraw when confronted with the enemy's artillery fire and tank defence. Clearly, the Russian artillery formations had not yet been destroyed. The German artillery still lacked the ammunition needed to take them out, and the onset of thunderstorms meant that another Stuka raid could not happen that day. There was no other option than for the panzer division to abandon the attack. The 92nd Infantry Regiment also faced heavy artillery fire, and only in the evening did it manage to enter Iwankowce.

It seemed that the enemy had given up any idea of trying to retake Berdichev. He sought simply to amass as much artillery firepower as possible to check the eastward advance of the XXXXVIII Panzer Corps.

The 11th Panzer Division had been in non-stop combat for 23 days. Enemy artillery fire had been raining down on it for the last four days. Although the panzer corps had dispatched the last of its artillery units to Berdichev, and although the bulk of the artillery of the 60th Motorised Infantry Division had supported the attack of the panzer division, a decisive success against the overwhelming numerical superiority of the enemy artillery had not been achieved. The headquarters of the panzer corps knew that a remedy somehow had to be found to help overcome the enemy forces near Berdichev and that something needed to be done to alleviate the supply difficulties arising from the use by four divisions of just one relatively good road.

Breaking out of Berdichev (15 July 1941)

The advance of the 9th Panzer Division (of the XIV Panzer Corps) through Zhitomir to the south-east led to the capture of Skvira on the evening of 14 July. Threatened with an envelopment to his east, the enemy withdrew many of his motorised formations from the area east of Berdichev towards the south-east via Bialopol and Rozyn.

These were favourable circumstances for the 11th Panzer Division. On the morning of 15 July, the panzer division smashed through the limited artillery resistance that remained to the east of Berdichev and re-entered Nizgorce. Slightly to the south, the 92nd Infantry Regiment fought enemy troops near Sadki. It paused there briefly and was once more placed under the command of the 60th Motorised Infantry Division. The panzer division continued to overcome what little resistance the enemy could muster and reached Bialopol towards noon. The bridge there had been blown up, so the panzer division had to wait until an emergency bridge had been constructed. It was completed by 1900 hours, at which time an advance detachment of the panzer division immediately set off in the direction of Rozyn.

In the meantime, the 16th Panzer Division had departed Lezhelov in the early hours of the morning and had taken Makhnovka a short time later. The German forces had therefore managed to break out of the partial ring of encirclement that the enemy had established around Berdichev. Both panzer divisions of the XXXXVIII Panzer Corps finally had the chance to gain more territory to the east. However, our aerial reconnaissance at that moment reported that an enemy motorised column was approaching Makhnovka from the south. It was 30 kilometres in length and included a number of tanks. The motorcycle battalion of the 16th Panzer Division sealed off the crossings that permitted access to Makhnovka and managed to hold off this enemy for the time being. Yet it could be expected that the pressure applied by the enemy would increase. For that reason, a battle group that had already begun to advance on Koziatyn was ordered to stop temporarily, just in case it was needed. A Stuka raid against the motorised column in the afternoon rendered the enemy incapable of executing a systematic attack. Although the threat from the south remained, the panzer division could now continue the advance to the east more easily. It succeeded in taking the railway junction in Koziatyn that evening. Russian aircraft carried out one strike after another against the forces of the panzer division, causing heavy losses in men and materiel.

The 16th Motorised Infantry Division had advanced from the area of Rajgrodek towards Frydov in order to support the attack of the 111th Infantry Division. It then assembled near Januszpol towards noon and was placed in panzer group reserve.

The 60th Motorised Infantry Division brought the 92nd Infantry Regiment back to Berdichev, after which it reorganised and assembled its units immediately to the north-west of the city.

At 1800 hours, the command post of the panzer corps was relocated to Berdichev.

Pursuing the enemy and pivoting to the south-east (16–17 July 1941)

On the occasion of his visit to the headquarters of the panzer corps on the morning of 16 July, Colonel-General von Kleist outlined his plans for the further conduct of operations. It could immediately be seen from the divisional boundaries set in his new order that the formations under the command of the panzer group were to wheel towards the south-east.

The withdrawal of strong enemy forces from the Lvov region towards the Dnieper had led to the decision to abandon the rectilinear thrust to the east. We were to give up the creation of a large pocket in favour of a small one, which we anticipated would still result in the envelopment of approximately 40 divisions. For this plan to succeed, the III Panzer Corps and the XIV Panzer Corps would need to be free to turn to the south-east as soon as possible so as to cut off the route of retreat of the Russian forces. But the former would be tied down in the vicinity of Kiev until relieved by the infantry divisions, while the latter had encountered strong resistance near Bialacerkiew.

The XXXXVIII Panzer Corps ordered all its forces to continue with the advance. Slowed down by the bad roads, the 11th Panzer Division pushed forward throughout the night and reached Czerniawka in the morning. It overcame the weak resistance there and continued onwards, although the multitude of blown-up bridges hindered its progress. The reports of our aerial reconnaissance indicated that more enemy resistance could be expected along the stream to the east of Rozyn.

The 16th Panzer Division left Koziatyn early in the day and seized Bialolowka shortly afterwards. In so doing, it wiped out whatever few enemy forces stood in its way.

It had been the special request of the panzer corps that the 16th Motorised Infantry Division rather than the 60th Motorised Infantry Division remain under its command. While the latter went into panzer group reserve, the former was given the task of protecting the southern flank of the 16th Panzer Division. It would therefore proceed through Berdichev and establish a security line between Makhnovka and Koziatyn.

In the afternoon, the enemy resistance that the 11th Panzer Division had anticipated in the vicinity of Rozyn was nowhere to be seen. Battle

Group Angern took Rozyn with the bridge there intact. There were a few enemy units that tried to attack the bridgehead created by the battle group, but they were thrown back easily. By late evening, the battle group was on the move again. It reached Skvira at 2200 hours and established contact with the leading elements of SS Division Wiking, which had arrived in the city at approximately the same time. Due to the bad state of the Czerniawka–Rozyn road, the rest of the panzer division advanced through Wczerajsze towards Pawolocz, where it met the rear elements of the SS division.

The 16th Panzer Division advanced beyond Bialolowka and clashed with strong enemy tank forces near Zaradynce towards noon. More enemy tanks were reported to be approaching from the north. These additional forces had probably fled from the area of Rozyn in order to avoid combat with the 11th Panzer Division. This enemy was driven away to the east in the course of the afternoon, and the 16th Panzer Division set off in pursuit. It conducted a rapid thrust through Ozerna towards the south-east and reached Borszczahowka by midnight. There was no noteworthy enemy resistance.

The day was a tremendous success, especially when considering the extended period during which the panzer corps had been tied up in and around Berdichev. Despite the bad roads and the presence of some enemy units, both panzer divisions had covered approximately 50 kilometres that day. According to our aerial reconnaissance, the enemy was in full retreat. It was necessary for the panzer corps to continue the advance and keep the enemy at sword-point.

On the morning of 17 July, the reconnaissance battalion of the 11th Panzer Division drove southwards as far as Kosovka. There was no encounter with the enemy. The motorcycle battalion had in the meantime taken Volodarka. Bridgeheads were established in both locations over the Roska. A third bridgehead over the river was created by the 16th Panzer Division at roughly the same time near Tetiev. The spearheads of both panzer divisions had thereby achieved the objectives that had been set that day, although it is worth bearing in mind that their rear elements were still catching up.

An enemy tank assault had plunged into the road of advance of the 16th Panzer Division that morning at a point slightly to the south-east of Bialolowka. A battle group had to be put together in the rear area of the panzer division in order to deal with this threat.

The 16th Motorised Infantry Division had also been attacked that morning to the south of Koziatyn. The fighting lasted until the evening, although elements of the division managed to push the enemy back to the south-east in the afternoon and take Zurbince. To the north of Koziatyn, enemy tanks appeared from the woods and blocked the road of advance. Nevertheless, by the evening, the situation was once more under control.

It had been the plan of the panzer group that the 16th Motorised Infantry Division be relieved by the XXXXIV Army Corps so that the division could continue with the advance on the right wing of the XXXXVIII Panzer Corps. But this was delayed, for the exhausted infantry of the XXXXIV Army Corps desperately needed a day's rest before pushing onwards.

The enemy enjoyed aerial superiority over the rear areas of the 16th Panzer and 16th Motorised Infantry Divisions on 17 July. Even the headquarters staff of the panzer corps were frequently held up and dispersed by the multitude of air raids as they tried to make the 100-kilometre journey to their new command post in Skvira. The traffic congestion and poor roads would have sufficed to slow their progress, and it was only at midnight that some of them started to arrive at their destination.

For 18 July, the task of the panzer corps would be to conduct a deep thrust to the south-east in the direction of Uman so as to deny the enemy forces earmarked for encirclement the ability to escape to the east. This thrust would have to be executed with the utmost rapidity if there was to be any chance of success. It was important that the pivot to the south-east come as a surprise to the enemy. He would be expecting the advance of the panzer group to continue directly towards Kiev. It was also important that the 16th Motorised Infantry Division be relieved by the infantry of the XXXXIV Army Corps as soon as possible. The motorised infantry division would then be available for the protection of the long southern flank of the panzer corps. Unfortunately, this plan would not be fully realised in the course of the day of 18 July.

Slow progress in bad weather (17–18 July 1941)

The bridge in Volodarka was unable to bear the weight of our tanks and heavy artillery, so the 11th Panzer Division could only send an advance detachment over it. This detachment arrived in Stawiszcze, which lay 18 kilometres to the east of Volodarka, and eliminated the weak enemy resistance to be found there. It pressed a little further through the woods to the south-west of Stawiszcze and reached the southern end of those woods. Its reconnaissance units identified strong concentrations of enemy troops in and around the city of Zaszkow, which was situated 15 kilometres to the south of Stawiszcze. Stukas were dispatched in the afternoon to strike this enemy. In the meantime, a new bridge had been constructed in Volodarka and the bulk of the 11th Panzer Division was able to roll forward. However, its progress for rest of the day was slow. Heavy downpours of rain transformed all roads into mud yet again.

The roads were in a particularly poor state in the combat zone of the 16th Panzer Division, but an advance detachment nonetheless set forth from Tetiev towards noon and, without encountering the enemy, entered Oratov in the evening. The bulk of the panzer division had assembled in Borszczahowka that morning, but it could barely move forward through the mud after that. A security unit that stood to the east of Pohrebyszcze for the protection of a major fuel depot had to be withdrawn when the enemy launched a powerful assault against it in the afternoon. Furthermore, the movement of the rear elements of the panzer division was considerably delayed between Bialolowka and Ozerna. The road along that stretch was difficult enough without the occasional appearance of enemy tanks.

Yet to be relieved by the XXXXIV Army Corps, the 16th Motorised Infantry Division instructed the 60th Infantry Regiment to go on ahead and assume responsibility for the protection of the flank of the XXXXVIII Panzer Corps between Horodok and Borszczahowka. However, the regiment was unable to move quickly. Once again, the road conditions were abysmal, and there was also traffic congestion caused by the rear elements of the 16th Panzer Division. Only the reconnaissance battalion managed to reach Horodok by the evening, while the motorcycle battalion secured the area around Zaradynce. The 156th Infantry Regiment, which remained in the area to the south-east of Koziatyn, had to repel several attacks carried out by the enemy near Pruszynka in the afternoon. Regrettably, the infantry of the XXXXIV Army Corps could not be expected to arrive before 20 July.

The XXXXVIII Panzer Corps now possessed a western flank that was 100 kilometres in depth and was by no means safe from enemy attack. The situation was a difficult one, but there was a good chance that it would improve as a result of the creation on 18 July of Group Schwedler, which unified the XXXXIV Army Corps and the LV Army Corps. Subordinated to Panzer Group 1, it could be expected that the infantry of Group Schwedler would move forward at an energetic pace.

Temporary cessation of the advance to the south (18–19 July 1941)

By the evening of 18 July, the XIV Panzer Corps had made good progress to the south-east and was engaged in fierce fighting on its front and its eastern flank. Strong elements of the Russian 26th Army (seven divisions) had been spotted in the region to the north, east, and south-east of Bialacerkiew. The possibility existed that these forces would attack the panzer group, so it was decided that the advance to the south would be ceased temporarily until their precise intentions were clear. The XXXXVIII Panzer Corps was given the order to concentrate its forces, with the 16th Panzer Division to repel any attempts by the western enemy to break out and the 11th Panzer Division to be prepared to help the XIV Panzer Corps if need be.

It rained non-stop on the night of 18/19 July. The state of the roads deteriorated further.

The 11th Panzer Division kept a battle group ready in Stawiszcze. The rest of the panzer division gathered in the vicinity of Volodarka, a task fraught with difficulty and requiring the use of all available tractors. No contact was made with the enemy. Not even the reconnaissance units sent to the south and south-west saw anything.

Neither was there any encounter with the enemy in the combat zone of the 16th Panzer Division. The panzer division established a westward-facing security line, 50 kilometres in width, that ran from Oratov to Novofastov. Its movements were slow along the impossibly muddy roads.

The 60th Infantry Regiment (of the 16th Motorised Infantry Division) reached Starostynce during the night, but it could go no further following the rainfall. Only the reconnaissance battalion was able to make it as far as Hopczycia, where it hurled back an enemy tank attack from the south-west the next morning. The enemy also conducted multiple assaults from the south towards Bialolowka. Protecting the village was the 156th Infantry Regiment, which, despite heavy losses, kept the enemy at bay. The relief of elements of the 16th Motorised Infantry Division by the 57th Infantry Division had been delayed due to the fact that the latter had been under constant attack from enemy forces, and it was only towards the evening that the relief of the former could finally be carried out. However, it can hardly be claimed that this helped to reduce the length of the front of the motorised infantry division.

There was an increase in the number of Russian deserters at that time. The enemy forces that were being squeezed in between the envelopment wing to the east and the approaching mountain divisions to the west were beginning to suffer from a shortage of supplies.[3] They would desperately try to break through the front of the XXXXVIII Panzer Corps to the east. Given the overextended lines of the panzer corps, the terrible state of the roads, and the gap that had yet to be closed between the 16th Panzer Division and the 16th Motorised Infantry Division, any such breakout attempts by the enemy would undoubtedly present a great danger.

---

[3] See Hans Steets, *Gebirgsjäger bei Uman: Die Korpsschlacht des XXXXIX. Gebirgs-Armeekorps bei Podwyssokoje 1941* (Heidelberg: Vowinckel, 1955) (Die Wehrmacht im Kampf, vol. 4).

CHAPTER 4

The XXXXVIII Panzer Corps in the Battle of Uman

The advance is resumed despite all difficulties (20 July 1941)

On the evening of 19 July, the panzer group informed the panzer corps that it appeared as if the Russian 26th Army intended not to launch an attack but rather to maintain a bridgehead to the south of Kiev. Based on this assessment of the situation, it was decided that the advance towards the south-east would resume. This advance, the objective of which was Uman, would have to be carried out as quickly as possible if the enemy were to be taken by surprise.

The panzer corps emphasised to the panzer group how important it was that the infantry formations catch up so that the mobile units would be free to charge ahead. It also urged the divisions under its command to keep the rear elements as close as possible to the leading units. This would minimise the degree to which supply traffic was blocked.

In the early hours of the morning of 20 July, a battle group of the 11th Panzer Division drove southwards and took Zaszkow. The enemy troops that had previously been spotted there were gone. Due to the condition of the roads, the rifle troops rode on tanks, the motorcycle riflemen proceeded on foot, and the motorcycles were loaded onto horse-drawn wooden wagons. After the light enemy resistance near and to the south of Buzovka had been broken, Sokolovka was taken at 1500 hours. Russian aircraft constantly bombed and strafed our troops, so progress was slow. Our aerial reconnaissance indicated that Uman was firmly held by the enemy and that several trains were moving eastwards around the northern side of the city. The Luftwaffe was unable to conduct a bombing raid against the railway line at that moment, but an armoured reconnaissance car section of the 11th Panzer Division managed to reach and damage the line. There was also a continuous flow of Russian road traffic withdrawing to the east via Bratslav, Gaysin, and Uman. The city of Uman was obviously an important traffic junction that needed to be seized at once. A battle group of the panzer division therefore set off that evening from Sokolovka towards the south.

The 16th Panzer Division had been compelled the day before to relinquish its hold on Oratov. The enemy tanks in the area had been too great a threat. The reconnaissance battalion departed Zywotow in the morning in order to retake the town. The bad roads prevented the bulk of the panzer division, still in Tetiev, from rolling forward until the afternoon. Once it was on the move, it advanced via Piatyhory and then headed towards the south. It soon had to halt once more when a bridge along its route of advance collapsed. Until the evening, the multiple road junction to the west of Zaszkow was the furthest the panzer division could go. A reconnaissance patrol unit was sent on ahead and was able to ascertain that Monastyryshche, although free of enemy forces, was heavily mined. In the meantime, the reconnaissance battalion had pushed through Oratov to Honoratka, with an armoured reconnaissance car section proceeding further, as far as the railway station in Frantovka, and bringing eight fully loaded trains to a standstill. The tanks on those trains immediately went into action, but their hasty attack towards Honoratka failed spectacularly.

German aerial reconnaissance spotted large enemy formations near Spiczynce and Lipovets as well as long columns moving to the east and north-east. In addition, trains continued to travel in a south-easterly direction from Pohrebyszcze to Uman. The western flank of the panzer corps, now 120 kilometres in depth, was in danger.

The objective of the 16th Panzer Division that day had been the railway junction to the north-west of Uman. However, the extent to which the panzer division had been delayed meant that it could not yet reach that objective. The panzer corps therefore ordered the panzer division to edge just a little more to the south so that it could set up a defensive line that ran from Monastyryshche to Zywotow via Oratov, and thereby prevent any attempt by the enemy to force his way through to the east.

It had been the desire of the panzer group that the 11th Panzer Division drive through Uman and take possession of the traffic centre to the south of the city, but it was doubtful that the panzer division would be able to carry out such a task at that moment. Neither the threat to the overextended flank of the panzer corps nor the gap in the defensive front between the 11th and 16th Panzer Divisions could be ignored.

With the arrival of the 57th Infantry Division, the relief of the whole of the 16th Motorised Infantry Division could finally get underway. The enemy probed the flank of the motorised infantry division throughout the day, after which he conducted a powerful northward attack in the evening on either side of the road and railway line from Pohrebyszcze. This attack was pushed back. A smaller attack near Hopczycia managed to penetrate the flank, but it was eliminated in close combat before nightfall. It could be expected that the enemy would continue to try to break through to the east, so it was of great importance that the motorised infantry division push to the south in order to free some of the forces of the 16th Panzer Division for closing up the gap to the 11th Panzer Division.

Establishment of a fragmentary westward-facing front (21 July 1941)

It rained heavily on the night of 20/21 July and continued to do so in the morning. Any kind of movement was dreadfully difficult.

Against fierce enemy resistance, the 11th Panzer Division advanced beyond the railway line and took Hill 251, a location of vital importance for the final push to the south on Uman. No reinforcements reached the panzer division, as the roads were too muddy. Neither rifle and artillery units nor fuel and ammunition supplies could make it to the front. The panzer regiment, the mounted rifle troops, and the elements of the motorcycle battalion on the hill therefore had to establish a hedgehog defensive position. The assault on Uman had to be postponed until the next day. In recognition of the dangerous situation that was developing for him, the enemy launched a tank attack from Uman against the front and western flank of the leading battle group of the panzer division. The battle group destroyed 30 Russian tanks, and our artillery routed additional columns of troops that were approaching Uman from the west. Yet a shortage of ammunition meant that the battle group would be unable to hold out for long. The bulk of the panzer division was still spread out between Volodarka and Sokolovka.

German warplanes were in the air in the combat zone of the panzer corps that day. They repeatedly struck the enemy forces in Uman and along the road to the west of the city.

The 16th Panzer Division rolled forward from Zaszkow towards the south-west in the early hours of the morning, and its leading elements entered Monastyryshche at 0800 hours. By the evening, the city had been cleared of enemy forces. Seven Russian tanks had been destroyed and 500 prisoners taken. The right wing of the panzer division advanced only gradually, reaching the line between Kniaza Krynycia and Hill 261 (north-west of Lukaszowka) in the evening. The reconnaissance battalion had reported that morning that trains were being unloaded on the stretch of railway line to the south of Oratov. Reconnaissance patrol troops approached the line and blew it up in several locations. The detrained forces behaved only defensively to begin with, but their tanks and heavy artillery began to attack Oratov in the afternoon. Some of the troops of the panzer division remained in the vicinity of Zywotow in order to maintain the continuity of the security line.

The enemy conducted an assault that morning near Dziunkow, but the 16th Motorised Infantry Division hurled him back to the south. The division then set up a security line, 40 kilometres in width, that ran from Starostynce to Zywotow via Dziunkow. Before long, the 57th Infantry Division pushed as far as the high ground in the vicinity of Pohrebyszcze, thereby releasing elements of the 60th Infantry Regiment for an advance further to the south.

In the afternoon, the headquarters staff of the panzer corps went to Stawiszcze via Bialacerkiew.

There were no major attempts by the enemy during the day to achieve a breakthrough. The fighting to the north of Uman and to the south-west of Oratov was a result of the efforts of the enemy to ensure the safety of the railway line and to secure his retreat to the east and south-east. However, when he renewed his attack on Oratov in the evening, it was clear that he was aiming to penetrate the flank of the panzer corps and escape to the north-east. This western flank, thanks to the southward push of the 11th Panzer Division, was now well over 120 kilometres in length and was extremely vulnerable. The concern at the headquarters of the panzer corps was all the greater given that the eastern flank was by then 75 kilometres in length. This situation had arisen due to the failure that day of the XIV Panzer Corps, hindered by enemy attacks and atrocious roads, to advance further to the south.

Heavy defensive fighting – a large gap comes into being (22–23 July 1941)

On the night of 21/22 July, the motorcycle and reconnaissance battalions of the 16th Panzer Division found themselves in a particularly difficult position. Heavy artillery and mortar fire thundered like lightning in the darkness, and under torrential rain, as the enemy struck Oratov from three sides. Holding on to the town was impossible, but so was the withdrawal of our vehicles through knee-deep mud. Almost all combat and supply vehicles had to be left behind as the troops of both battalions fell back to the north-east. There were barely any losses in personnel as they reached the Osiczna–Rozyczna line. The enemy, who was much stronger than we had thought, pressed the attack without delay so as to exploit his initial success. Our early-morning reconnaissance discovered that at least two Russian regiments, consisting of several tank and artillery units, had arrived at a position beyond Osiczna. A little to the north, the II Battalion of the 65th Rifle Regiment had to retreat from Zywotow to the north-east on the morning of 22 July, for the enemy pressure there was too great to resist. The battalion was still in combat with the enemy when it reached the edge of the forest that lay 3 kilometres to the north-east of Zywotow. It was struggling hard and unable to push to the south-east for the purpose of closing the 18-kilometre gap that the enemy had prised open.

The 16th Motorised Infantry Division was given the order to thrust southwards through Tetiev with all available forces right away. But this thrust was delayed. The roads were in a bad state and there were traffic jams caused by the leading elements of the 57th Infantry Division.

In the afternoon, the 16th Panzer Division ordered a group of 30 recently serviced tanks to advance through Wysokie and resolve the situation to the north of Osiczna. At the same time, a battalion of the panzer regiment was to strike from Ivakhny in the direction of Oratov. Enemy forces attacked Monastyryshche and Kniaza Krynycia that afternoon, although they did so in an unsystematic fashion and were swiftly repelled. In contrast, the efforts of the enemy on either side of Oratov were very much systematic. His strength there was roughly equivalent to that of a division. The panzer battalion reached Balabanovka, routed the enemy forces that had been assembling there, and returned to Ivakhny in the evening. The whereabouts at that moment of the 30 tanks that had gone through Wysokie remained unknown.

The elements of the 16th Motorised Infantry Division that arrived near Zywotow in the afternoon were placed alongside the II Battalion of the 64th Rifle Regiment. Together, just to the south of Buhayovka, they repelled a series of assaults conducted by the enemy that lasted until the evening. Yet they were far too weak to be able to carry out their own attack and take Zywotow. Further German forces arrived that evening in the area to the south of Tetiev, where they set up a defensive front against the Russian forces that were breaking through. Some of the units of the 57th Infantry Division reached the area to the west of the town, but the ongoing combat made it impossible for them to relieve the 16th Motorised Infantry Division.

The 11th Panzer Division experienced a no less difficult day of fierce fighting. Neither reinforcements nor fuel nor ammunition had reached its spearhead during the night, so the push towards Uman had come to a temporary halt. In the morning, more Russian troops were brought by train to a position that lay south-west of where the panzer division controlled the railway line. These troops sought to reach Uman on foot. Only by employing all the tractors at its disposal could the panzer division bring its most essential elements to the front by noon. The now reinforced spearhead surged forward in the afternoon and entered the northern outskirts of the city despite the tremendous firepower of the enemy's artillery pieces, anti-tank guns, and infantry troops. It even managed to withstand a counter-attack against its flanks. Five of the enemy tanks that had approached from Palanka and Voytovka were put out of action. Waves of Russian aircraft struck our spearhead, and, in the evening, an attack by Russian tanks and infantry along the railway line from the west penetrated as far as the level crossing, thereby interrupting the march route of the panzer division. A battle group of the panzer division that had just reached the area to the south of the railway line found itself in heavy defensive fighting against overwhelming numbers of enemy troops and had to be withdrawn to a position near Zibermanovka during the night. The enemy's assault against the western flank of the 11th Panzer Division was all the more serious given that the gap to the 16th Panzer Division in Monastyryshche was still open. The panzer corps had no forces available with which to close this gap, for it had already committed everything possible to the defence of the western flank of the 16th Panzer Division against the enemy breakthrough there.

Less endangered was the eastern flank of the XXXXVIII Panzer Corps. The 9th Panzer Division had already reached the area to the south-east of Stawiszcze, and it was in any case the tendency of the enemy to retreat to the east.

So as to help with the annihilation of the enemy forces that had infiltrated its western flank, the panzer corps made a special request for the 57th Infantry Division to be placed under its command. There could be no mistake that the enemy would continue to try to smash through the front of the panzer corps and strive with all the means at his disposal to regain full control of the railway line to the north of Uman for the purposes of his eastward withdrawal.

The situation became critical for the 11th Panzer Division on the morning of 23 July. It had been possible overnight for the panzer division to concentrate its forces and hurl back the enemy forces to the north of Zibermanovka. This reopened the march route and removed the threat of encirclement. The spearhead of the panzer division had by then withdrawn, so the German forces now stood along the Podobna–Zibermanovka line. The enemy assaulted this position throughout the morning from the south and south-east, and he also carried out a tank thrust from the west. The panzer division managed to hold out, but it was clear that the strength of the enemy was increasing by the hour. Large numbers of Russian tanks and artillery continued to approach from all sides. The enemy had obviously noticed the gap between the 11th and 16th Panzer Divisions. His forces poured into this gap in the afternoon and took Konela. Although the 11th Panzer Division had sufficient forces with which to defend Sokolovka, its counter-attack towards Konela had to be abandoned that evening after heavy fighting. The only extra unit that the panzer corps could send to this area was a reinforced company of the motorcycle battalion of Motorised Regiment Hermann Göring, which arrived in Buzovka and defended the village against the enemy breakthrough. The spearhead to the south of the railway line was attacked by enemy tanks well into the night, and it was also subjected to the fire of six to eight enemy batteries. The divisional commander, Major-General Crüwell, regarded it as inevitable that the current position of the spearhead would be lost. For that reason, he recommended a withdrawal to a new position south of Nesterovka. General Kempf could not ignore the seriousness of the situation, so he gave the panzer division the authority to destroy and relinquish the railway line and to establish a defensive position further to the north, from where that railway line could at least remain within range of German artillery. The most pressing task after that would be to close the gap to the 16th Panzer Division.

In the combat zone of the 16th Panzer Division, the enemy breakthrough to the north-east of Oratov failed to gain further ground. The 30 tanks whose whereabouts had been unknown were reported that morning to be in Sitkowce. They had encountered no enemy forces whatsoever. It had been the original plan of the panzer division to regroup near Monastyryshche and to advance to the south-east, especially due to the fact that 15 trains had been observed bringing vast quantities of enemy forces to the railway station in Khristinovka. But the enemy launched a tank assault against Monastyryshche that very morning, and the pressure he applied against the western flank of the panzer division increased dramatically throughout the afternoon. He repeatedly attacked the entire defensive front from Monastyryshche through Kniaza Krynycia to Lukaszowka, and his artillery fire in particular caused tremendous destruction. Our tanks had to conduct one counter-thrust after another in order to deny the enemy entry into Monastyryshche. Yet the panzer division soon came to the conclusion that the only way in which it could master the situation on its southern wing was to give up Monastyryshche and withdraw slightly to the north. The panzer corps approved this measure, even though it meant that the gap to the 11th Panzer Division would become larger. The II Battalion of the 64th Rifle Regiment, which was still fighting in the vicinity of Zywotow, had to be relieved at the earliest possible moment so that it could be sent into action on the southern wing of the 16th Panzer Division and thus help to close the gap to the 11th Panzer Division.

The 16th Motorised Infantry Division had made good progress on the morning of 23 July in its attack against the enemy forces that had broken through to the north-east of Oratov. The 179th Infantry Regiment had been placed under its command and had pushed forward to the line that ran from the northern side of Zywotow past the northern outskirts of Kalinovka to Stadnitsa. But the attack had come to a standstill against the stubborn resistance of the enemy, who then launched a number of strong armoured counter-attacks, especially against the right flank near Zywotow. The fighting was of the utmost ferocity, but it subsided in the evening due to the heavy casualties suffered by the enemy, although his artillery fire continued to wreak havoc. It seemed that the enemy was of at least divisional strength in this sector, and he was doing everything possible to force his way to the north or north-east. So as to prevent the enemy from evading our defensive line with a manoeuvre to the east, the motorcycle battalion was deployed in the vicinity of Kluki, where it set up an obstacle line. The annihilation of the enemy forces that had pushed into the western flank of the panzer corps would no longer take place that day. The losses of the 16th Motorised Infantry Division had been considerable, and the overextension of its front meant that it could not move effectively. It was highly likely that the division would only be capable of defensive action the next day.

One of the regiments of the 57th Infantry Division pushed energetically in the direction of Zywotow, but it neither took the village nor improved the situation for the 16th Motorised Infantry Division. By the evening, the 57th Infantry Division was back under the command of Group Schwedler.

Reflecting on the difficult situation in which the panzer corps found itself as a result of the systematic efforts of the enemy to break through to the east, the panzer group promised it would allocate to the panzer corps not only SS Motorised Division Leibstandarte Adolf Hitler but also additional infantry forces on 24 July. The SS division would initially remain on standby between Skvira and Bialacerkiew and would intervene further to the south if need be.

Deterioration of the situation – employment of last reserves (24 July 1941)

The 11th Panzer Division had managed to hold its position near Zibermanovka. Masses of Russian infantry had applied an enormous amount of pressure against the panzer division on the night of 23/24 July, but our tanks eliminated them after dawn. Another enemy attack to the north of the railway line was repelled. A rifle battalion of Motorised Regiment Hermann Göring seized Konela following the success of a Stuka raid against the enemy forces there, reopening the road of advance and establishing contact with the panzer division by noon. The situation became increasingly bad for the southern group of the panzer division throughout the morning. All its available strength had to be summoned in order to resist the powerful strikes of the enemy from the south-east and south-west. For the first time, the enemy coordinated the use of his artillery to systematically target our batteries. He scored multiple direct hits against our guns, putting them out of action.

During his visit to the command post of the panzer corps, Colonel-General von Kleist said that he would see to it that as many Stukas as possible were employed against the Russian formations and artillery groups. SS Motorised Division Leibstandarte Adolf Hitler, which had already received the order to march to the area to the north of Stawiszcze, was now placed under the command of the panzer corps. It was the intention of the panzer corps to insert this SS division in between the 11th and 16th Panzer Divisions.

The situation worsened ever more in the afternoon, as the enemy pushed forward against both the eastern and western wings of the 11th Panzer Division. This compelled the panzer corps to send its last reserves to Sokolovka. Those reserves were the motorcycle battalion of Motorised Regiment Hermann Göring as well as the 670th Anti-Tank Battalion. The latter was still in action in the combat zone of the 16th Motorised Infantry Division. Fortunately, our Stukas appeared at that moment and were employed most effectively, making it possible for the panzer division to restore the situation on its right wing. Nevertheless, it still turned out to be necessary for the panzer division to conduct a withdrawal. Its eastern flank remained in danger, and the enemy received non-stop reinforcements of tanks and artillery. The divisional commander wanted to bring his forces outside the range of the enemy artillery. It was therefore his plan to disengage during the night, ideally unbeknownst to the enemy, and to withdraw to the line that connected Sokolovka and the northern outskirts of Kiszczynce. This would give the panzer division a brief respite, as the enemy would need time, first, to become aware of the German withdrawal and, second, to reposition his artillery. Both the panzer group and the panzer corps understood the necessity of this measure, but they stipulated that a strong battle group be left behind so that the German forces could still exert their influence on the railway line and thereby ensure the continued disruption of the eastward retreat of the enemy.

It was a quieter day for the 16th Panzer Division. Although a shortage of forces meant that Monastyryshche had to be evacuated overnight and a new defensive position had to be taken up to the north of the city, the eventual arrival of the II Battalion of the 64th Rifle Regiment on the eastern flank permitted a part of the gap to the 11th Panzer Division to be closed with a thrust along the Monastyryshche–Sokolovka road. Fortunately, it turned out to be the case that the enemy forces that had poured into the gap were not particularly strong. The small number of guns and tanks to be found there were either destroyed or driven away. Meanwhile, the weak attacks conducted by the enemy against the western flank of the 16th Panzer Division throughout the day were easily dealt with. Yet the enemy artillery fire remained quite strong along the entire front.

In the combat zone of the 16th Motorised Infantry Division, the enemy executed a powerful thrust in the morning against the 179th Infantry Regiment. He suffered heavy casualties and had to withdraw. He continued to attack the central and southern sectors of the division for the rest of the day, with his preparatory artillery fire becoming ever stronger and more systematic. In the evening, he managed to infiltrate the southern part of Stadnitsa. The division estimated that the enemy forces it was facing possessed the strength of approximately two divisions. The arrival by then of some of the forces of the 57th Infantry Division in the northern part of Stadnitsa enabled the relief of elements of the 156th Infantry Regiment and in turn the commencement of the relief of the northern wing of the 16th Panzer Division.

By the end of 24 July, the enemy forces on the western flank of the panzer corps were yet to be eliminated. It would be important on the following day to prevent all attempts by these forces to break through to the east and, above all, to make use of SS Motorised Division Leibstandarte Adolf Hitler to fully seal the gap between the two panzer divisions.

Withdrawal of the 11th Panzer Division – closing the gap (25 July 1941)

The 11th Panzer Division successfully disengaged from the enemy on the night of 24/25 July and established itself in its new position further back. This small retreat was carried out according to plan and without being noticed by the enemy, who edged forward only gradually. A reinforced panzer reconnaissance battalion had been left behind, but by morning it too had to be withdrawn to the high ground of Nesterovka, for it was unable to resist the overwhelming strength of the Russian tank and artillery formations. More Russian reinforcements arrived in the afternoon. The reconnaissance battalion soon had to be committed to the protection of the left flank in the vicinity of Khizhnya. This was because the reconnaissance battalion of the 9th Panzer Division, which had been standing near Antonovka in readiness to assist the 11th Panzer Division, had by then been shifted further to the east. Many more attacks by the enemy could be expected before long. In the area to the south of Sokolovka, he was moving his large formations and relocating his artillery units. As soon as he had completed his preparations, he conducted a number of deep strikes and air raids against the 11th Panzer Division.

A battalion of SS Motorised Division Leibstandarte Adolf Hitler approached the gap between the panzer divisions in the morning, hurled back some enemy forces that stood in its way, and reached the line for which it had been aiming by noon. The gap was finally sealed. An assault against the right wing of the SS division took place towards the evening, but it was able to be repelled.

The new boundary between the 16th Panzer Division and the 16th Motorised Infantry Division ran along a line that started in the area north of Balabanovka and extended beyond the northern outskirts of

Ivakhny. On the left wing of the panzer division, the panzer regiment was employed to eliminate enemy forces that had advanced into the woods to the south-east of Tsybulov. Nothing happened on the right wing.

Supported by artillery, the enemy attacked the 16th Motorised Infantry Division in the vicinity of Sitkowce and Stadnitsa, but he was pushed back. Additional enemy forces, also supported by artillery, managed to enter Lukaszowka, but they too were pushed back. Our Stukas bombed a large formation that was assembling in the woods to the south-west of Stadnitsa that afternoon. The enemy was hit so hard that he carried out no further attacks for several hours. His batteries also fell silent. It was the plan of Panzer Group 1 that the 16th Motorised Infantry Division release the entire 16th Panzer Division for a thrust around the eastern flank of the 11th Panzer Division and beyond Uman to the south-east, yet this plan could not be pursued due to the fact that all the divisions of the XXXXVIII Panzer Corps were fully occupied with the task of thwarting the attempts of the Russian forces to punch through to the east. The most that was possible was the relief of the northern wing of the 16th Motorised Infantry Division thanks to the arrival that day of the 68th Infantry Division.

The situation improves – a successful panzer thrust (26 July 1941)

It was quiet on the night of 25/26 July, and it remained so in the morning aside from some artillery fire and a weak attack near Lukaszowka, which lay in the combat zone of the 16th Motorised Infantry Division. The infantry of Group Schwedler had by that time made their way slowly to the east and had reached a position on the high ground on either side of Ilince. Further south, the 100th Light Infantry Division already stood along the Gaysin–Ladyzhyn line and would soon be on its way to Granov. Even further south were Hungarian troops who had just advanced through Troscianice. The enemy had therefore begun to evacuate the northern part of the pocket that was forming around him. We spotted large numbers of Russian troops boarding trains on the railway line that led to Uman from the north-west. By noon, 17 trains had already departed the stations in Frantovka and Monastyryshche for the south-east. Marching parallel to the railway line were long columns of Russian forces. A rapid advance by Group Schwedler was of the greatest necessity at that moment, especially because the 16th Motorised Infantry Division was parrying one enemy attack after another whilst still partway through the process of being relieved on its northern wing.

The 16th Panzer Division held a position that projected somewhat into the pocket and was therefore exposed to much of the pressure being applied by the enemy in his attempts to escape. Russian artillery bombarded the front of the panzer division relentlessly. Nevertheless, the panzer division was given the order to launch its panzer regiment towards the railway station in Monastyryshche so as to disrupt the flow of eastbound Russian traffic. The thrust that was conducted turned out to be a success. An ammunition train was blown sky-high, and the surrounding railway infrastructure was destroyed. Enemy artillery fire intensified against the southern wing of the panzer division in the afternoon, and Russian aircraft attacked in multiple waves.

There was little combat in the sector of SS Motorised Division Leibstandarte Adolf Hitler. The enemy had withdrawn, leaving behind just a few units in the marshy terrain to the south of the stream near Konela.

In the afternoon, the 11th Panzer Division repelled an attack that the enemy executed from the south in the direction of Sokolovka. The enemy carried out more attacks against the left wing of the panzer division right up until the evening, but they were lacking in strength and achieved nothing whatsoever. There had been reports of motorised Russian forces advancing through the Buki–Kiszczynce–Mankovka area against the eastern flank of the panzer division, yet there was no sign of those forces by nightfall. A battle group that was sent to the area to meet them made slow progress due to the bad roads. No encounter with the enemy took place.

The impression of the situation at the headquarters of the panzer corps was that the enemy sought to evade the encirclement by withdrawing the bulk of his forces to the south-east. He was covering this withdrawal by leaving behind some artillery units and conducting local assaults with limited objectives. It was therefore decided that the retreating enemy be pursued ruthlessly and that the area to the south-east of Uman be occupied swiftly. To carry out this plan, the 16th Motorised Infantry Division would need to be pulled out from its current sector and placed to the left of the 11th Panzer Division. Even if it meant the inability to relieve the 16th Panzer Division for the time being, this measure would allow the 11th Panzer Division to push forward in conjunction with SS Motorised Division Leibstandarte Adolf Hitler so as to take Uman and thrust further to the south-east.

But then there were downpours of rain, and the roads became muddy again. It was doubtful whether the combat elements of the 16th Motorised Infantry Division would make it to their new position the next day.

The Uman pocket (27–28 July 1941)

It continued to rain! The roads became muddier and hindered the movements of the 16th Motorised Infantry Division. Only by the evening of 27 July did its leading elements reach the area to the north-east of the 11th Panzer Division, where they occupied the high ground near Khizhnya and Kislin. The enemy forces facing them had dug in.

The left wing of SS Motorised Division Leibstandarte Adolf Hitler advanced beyond the stream near Konela, and its leading elements took Zibermanovka in the morning. On the right wing, in the vicinity of Panskij List, there was heavy fighting throughout the day. Enemy forces constantly flowed into the area that lay opposite the front of the SS division. Amongst those forces were 10 batteries whose tremendous firepower proved difficult to withstand.

The right wing of the 11th Panzer Division was likewise subjected to heavy artillery fire. Nevertheless, the enemy withdrew to Krasznosdowka and shifted many of his forces towards the east. The motorised forces that had been reported on the eastern flank of the panzer division the previous evening were now seeking to push towards the north-west.

Group Schwedler made good progress on 27 July. Its left wing was well on the way to Kniaza Krynycia. The enemy forces fleeing from this group conducted a few feeble attacks to the north of Monastyryshche against the 16th Panzer Division, but they were repulsed with little effort.

It was by then quite clear that the enemy was indeed falling back to the south-east. This led to the decision, taken by the panzer group, not to seize Uman as originally planned but rather to bypass the city to its east so that the escape of large enemy formations could be prevented before it was too late. The line of attack of the panzer corps, whose spearhead would comprise the 11th Panzer Division and SS Motorised Division Leibstandarte Adolf Hitler, would be towards the south-east in the direction of Kirovograd.

On the morning of 28 July, the leading elements of the left wing of the SS division were increasingly under attack in the vicinity of Zibermanovka. The bridge in the village had been destroyed by a direct hit from enemy artillery, so the rear elements of the left wing had to advance via Sokolovka. By the evening, they had managed to seize Dobra. The right wing of the SS division remained where it was in the marshy terrain near Panskij List. Enemy resistance there was particularly fierce. In the meantime, the enemy continued to assault the position in Zibermanovka well into the night, but the German forces there were able to hold on.

The repositioning of the 16th Motorised Infantry Division had been delayed due to the poor condition of the roads, and it was only at 1500 hours that both it and the 11th Panzer Division rolled forward. The resistance of Russian infantry was weak; that of Russian artillery strong. But the German formations gradually gained ground and reached the line that ran from Nesterovka through Mankovka and Ivanki to Chernaya Kamenka.

The 16th Panzer Division maintained its defensive position against the heavy weaponry and artillery of the enemy. Our own artillery prevented him from being able to restart railway operations from the station in Monastyryshche. It was planned that the panzer division be withdrawn from its current combat zone upon the arrival of Group Schwedler, that it be placed in panzer group reserve, and that it assemble in the area to the south of Zaszkow. This battle-tried panzer division had been under the command of the panzer corps since the commencement of the campaign in Russia. It was hard for the headquarters of the panzer corps to have to hand it over.

Pivoting to the south (29 July 1941)

The escape of many of the Russian forces from the pocket that was being created and the arrival by rail of more Russian forces in the area to the north of Shpola (90 kilometres north-east of Uman), which threatened the eastern flank of the panzer group, led on 29 July to the abandonment of the current direction of advance. The panzer corps was ordered to pivot to the south immediately. A large operational envelopment was to be given up in favour of a small encirclement. According to our assessment of the situation, this course of action would still amount to the encirclement of large portions of the Russian 6th and 12th Armies. The new line of advance ran roughly through Novo Arkhangelsk (40 kilometres south-east of Uman) and then in the direction of Pervomaisk (70 kilometres south of Novo Arkhangelsk). The leading elements of the Seventeenth Army, which were to seal the southern side of the pocket, were already standing to the south of Uman and advancing slowly against a stubborn enemy towards Golovanevsk.

It had mostly been a quiet night for the divisions of the panzer corps, and, in the morning, they were informed by telephone of the new line of advance.

In the early hours of the morning, the 11th Panzer Division annihilated a small group of enemy forces between Sokolovka and Nesterovka that had thus far prevented the divisional artillery from being able to be brought forward closer to the front. The right wing of the panzer division pushed forward against the bitter resistance of the enemy and took Podobna and Pomoynik. Given that enemy units were still present on the right flank of the panzer division, it was necessary for some security forces to be left behind to defend that flank. The left wing of the panzer division destroyed the Russian forces that sought in vain to hold on to Mankovka, but it had less success after that in trying, against a determined enemy, to push further through the dense forest in the direction of Rogi. Several enemy tanks were disabled. The fighting power of the enemy began to subside in the evening, making it easier for the panzer division to enter Rogi.

Opposed by barely any enemy forces, the 16th Motorised Infantry Division advanced through Popuzhintsy and, with its reconnaissance battalion, took Talnoye in the evening. The division had to devote many of its units to the security of its eastern flank, as the formation on its left, the XIV Panzer Corps, had remained behind in order to stop enemy troops that were reported to be approaching from the east.

By noon, SS Motorised Division Leibstandarte Adolf Hitler had overcome stubborn enemy resistance and powerful artillery fire and had reached the line that ran from Leshchinovka to the area south of Dobra. Progress through the cornfields to the south of that line was slow, and it was only in the evening that the stretch of railway line to the north of Zibermanovka was seized. With a strong position soon established along the Krasnopolka–Zibermanovka line, the enemy fell back to the south through Uman.

The defence against further attempts by the enemy to break out (30–31 July 1941)

In the early hours of 30 July, the 16th Motorised Infantry Division concentrated most its forces in the vicinity of Talnoye while its reconnaissance battalion took Zelenkov. The battalion lunged further through Kamyaneche and reached Novo Arkhangelsk towards noon. Enemy resistance was almost non-existent.

In contrast, both SS Motorised Division Leibstandarte Adolf Hitler and the 11th Panzer Division, standing along the Leshchinovka–Zibermanovka–Pomoynik–Molodetskoye line, were assaulted by enemy forces throughout the morning. All these attacks had been repelled by noon. However, a battle group of the 11th Panzer Division that had forced its way through the tough resistance of the enemy to the northern outskirts of Legezino had to be withdrawn shortly afterwards to the high ground south of Rogi due to the overwhelming superiority of the Russian counter-attacks. The situation remained challenging in the afternoon, with the enemy launching multiple armoured counter-thrusts. He possessed vast quantities of heavy tanks, and our ability to counteract the destructive firepower of his artillery was severely limited because of our shortage of ammunition at that time.

The western flank of the panzer corps was by then almost 60 kilometres in length. So that this flank could be protected against the immense and increasing pressure of the enemy forces trying to escape encirclement, the panzer corps requested that the 16th Panzer Division be returned and placed alongside the 16th Motorised Infantry Division. Yet the only unit that the panzer group could place at the disposal of the panzer corps was the reinforced SS Regiment Westland of SS Division Wiking. The SS regiment initially stood in the vicinity of Tarashcha, but it reached Talnoye in the evening and was subordinated to the motorised infantry division.

The panzer corps did not think it possible for the motorised infantry division to push further to the south beyond Novo Arkhangelsk before the end of the day. It requested that Group Schwedler continue its advance with the utmost urgency so that SS Motorised Division Leibstandarte Adolf Hitler could be relieved at the earliest possible moment and shifted to the left wing of the panzer corps, thereby providing the necessary strength for the thrust to the south. The development of the situation in the afternoon demonstrated that such a course of action was correct. The pressure being applied by the enemy against the rather fragmentary front of the motorised infantry division to the west of the road connecting Talnoye and Novo Arkhangelsk became ever greater. It required the absolute commitment of all the forces at the disposal of the motorised infantry division to be able to hurl back the enemy that evening.

The forces of the panzer corps had barely been sufficient to prevent the enemy from breaking through the German front. If the front were to be further extended with a renewed advance to the south, it might have become so weak that it may have been unlikely to survive another attack by the enemy.

On the evening of 30 July, the 11th Panzer Division pushed back a strong tank assault on the high ground south of Rogi. A total of 15 enemy tanks were put out of action. The enemy renewed his assault on the morning of 31 July, but he suffered heavy casualties and was compelled to withdraw.

Group Schwedler had made good progress in the meantime. Its 297th Infantry Division relieved SS Motorised Division Leibstandarte Adolf Hitler, enabling the latter to proceed through Ivanki towards Talnoye. The spearhead of the SS division had reached Lashchova towards the evening when it was struck by an enemy thrust that had punched through the front on the boundary between the 16th Motorised Infantry Division and the 11th Panzer Division. The SS division brought the enemy thrust to a halt and forced it to retreat, whereupon a new defensive front was set up in the evening along the Ivanki–Lashchova line. Unfortunately, it was not possible that day to seize the stretch of railway line on either side of the station near Potash, which stood at that time in the gap between the panzer division and the motorised infantry division.

Such was the progress of the 297th Infantry Division that even the battalion on the right wing of the 11th Panzer Division could be released for action elsewhere. This battalion was able to advance on Legezino and Talyanki in the afternoon, although both locations were heavily defended and could only be taken after nightfall. On the left wing of the panzer division was the reconnaissance battalion, and it secured Potash against the enemy forces that had pushed through the gap between it and the motorised infantry division in the direction of Mashurov.

The 16th Motorised Infantry Division defended itself the entire day against multiple enemy attacks on Novo Arkhangelsk, on either side of Kamyaneche, and to the north of Maidanetske towards Talnoye.

Meanwhile, the panzer corps had been informed by the panzer group that the 9th Panzer Division had wheeled in the direction of Tishkovka. The panzer division reached Lipnyazhka in the evening and drove further towards Dobryanka and Olshanka. Because the mountain divisions of the Seventeenth Army and the units of the Hungarian Mobile Corps had at that time arrived at the Golovanevsk–Ladyzhinka–Uman line from the west, the envelopment manoeuvre was almost complete. There remained only a gap of approximately 40 kilometres to the south. Our aerial reconnaissance reported that several Russian motorised columns were desperately rushing towards this gap, trying to reach Olshanka before the German forces did so.

The Uman pocket would soon be sealed!

A smaller pocket had already been created with elements of the 11th Panzer Division, the 16th Motorised Infantry Division, and SS Motorised Division Leibstandarte Adolf Hitler. It was planned that the rifle battalion of Motorised Regiment Hermann Göring as well as a battalion of the SS division would eliminate this pocket the next day by sweeping towards the Potash–Mashurov line and, if possible, also towards the Talyanki–Talnoye road.

Unfortunately, the panzer corps would be incapable on the following day of advancing through Novo Arkhangelsk in the direction of Ternovka. The enemy pressure against the western flank of the 16th Motorised Infantry Division remained too great, so this flank would first need to be reinforced by the entire SS division. The panzer corps therefore recommended to the panzer group that forces of the XIV Panzer Corps be employed to close the gap to the south of Novo Arkhangelsk.

The fall of Uman (1–2 August 1941)

The 11th Panzer Division, standing in the vicinity of Legezino and Talyanki, had been assaulted by enemy forces from the south, east, and west since the early hours of the morning of 1 August. Casualties were heavy on both sides. The panzer division generally managed to hold its position, although the connection between Legezino and Talyanki was interrupted. By the afternoon, the offensive activity of the enemy abated somewhat. The 297th Infantry Division approached from the north and assumed responsibility for the Legezino–Talyanki sector in the evening, permitting the bulk of the panzer division to assemble in the vicinity of Rogi. A battle group was made ready to execute an attack on 2 August against the enemy units that still held Mashurov.

Those enemy units were supposed to have been destroyed by the rifle battalion of Motorised Regiment Hermann Göring, but it had been unable to overcome the defensive strength of the enemy. By the end of the day, the battalion stood along the Potash–Gordashevka line.

The 16th Motorised Infantry Division, under attack throughout the day by the enemy, drew on its final reserves in order to beat him back and cause him heavy losses. Although the reconnaissance battalion defended Novo Arkhangelsk with fierce determination, it had to withdraw by noon as a result of the overwhelming numerical superiority of the enemy forces that were attacking from the west and south-east. There was a serious shortage of artillery ammunition, and the long supply route from Bialacerkiew was far from secure. SS Motorised Division Leibstandarte Adolf Hitler, which could only make slow progress over a number of damaged bridges, was ordered to advance on Ternovka via Novo Arkhangelsk as quickly as it possibly could so as to close the gap to the 4th Mountain Division and thereby deprive the enemy of his last chance to flee from the pocket. The commander of the XXXXVIII Panzer Corps himself emphasised to the spearhead battalion the importance of the immediate recapture of Novo Arkhangelsk. While the reconnaissance battalion of the motorised infantry division reached a point on the western outskirts of Novo Arkhangelsk in the afternoon, the SS division struggled to infiltrate the town. Two battalions of the SS division were still engaged in house-to-house fighting with a tenacious enemy well into the evening.

Elements of the 9th Panzer Division held the high ground to the south-east of Novo Arkhangelsk, but the panzer group could not make them available for an attack on the town. Nevertheless, the desperate attempts by the enemy to break out of the Uman pocket on 1 August failed thanks to the firm defence that had been established by the divisions of the panzer corps. Aerial reconnaissance in the evening reported that the enemy forces in the pocket were heading in all directions. It seemed that they were trying to find the weakest point against which they could renew their efforts to break out the next day.

The western part of Uman was in our hands by the evening. The area in which the encircled enemy could move was ever more constricted. According to the information gleaned from deserters, the enemy forces in the pocket comprised not only the combat elements but also the staff headquarters of each of the Russian 6th and 12th Armies. The enemy troops had been made aware by their superiors that they were encircled and that the only way in which they could escape total annihilation was to courageously break through the German defensive line. It was clear that the panzer corps had to prevent any attempt by the enemy to escape the pocket. Most important at that moment was that SS Motorised Division Leibstandarte Adolf Hitler somehow push through Novo Arkhangelsk as far as Ternovka so that the enemy would be unable to flee over the stretch of the Sinyukha River that flowed between the two towns.

On 2 August, the point of main effort of the attempts by the enemy to break out of the pocket lay in the vicinity of Kamyaneche and Sverdlinovo. Both villages were in the combat zone of the 16th Motorised Infantry Division. Enemy troops had slipped through the thinly defended line of the I Battalion of the 156th Infantry Regiment overnight and had then attacked the battalion from all sides in the morning. The battalion lost some ground despite the brave defensive fighting of its men, but it managed to regain that ground with the help of the 670th Anti-Tank Battalion as well as of the I Battalion of SS Regiment Westland. The Russians fought bitterly. Despite the multitude of Stuka raids and the accuracy of our artillery fire, waves of Russian forces attacked again and again from the woods south-east of Kamyaneche. Further attacks were carried out by the enemy near and to the north of Kamyaneche as well as in the vicinity of Sverdlinovo. Although he suffered bloody losses, the enemy persisted with his mass assaults. He managed to infiltrate the village of Sverdlinovo and strike the rear of the III Battalion of the 60th Infantry Regiment, yet the German forces were able to hold on to the village. By noon, the motorised infantry division was once more the master of the situation. Every single metre of ground that had been seized by the enemy was retaken. The attacks conducted by the enemy in the afternoon became progressively weaker. It was apparent that he was reaching a state of utter exhaustion. The heroic efforts of the units of the motorised infantry division had seen to it that the enemy forces that they had faced, whose strength had been roughly that of two divisions, had been repelled. The enemy had sought, and had failed, to escape the German formations approaching from the west and to avoid the fate of being completely destroyed. Near Sverdlinovo alone lay roughly 1,200 dead Russians! Our losses were also quite considerable.

After hours of bitter house-to-house fighting, SS Motorised Division Leibstandarte Adolf Hitler had recaptured Novo Arkhangelsk late in the evening on 1 August and had subsequently repulsed a powerful counter-attack that had been launched by the enemy, putting five of his tanks out of action in the process. The SS division held the town throughout the day on 2 August despite being subjected to an endless series of assaults from the west, south, and south-east. It was unable to carry out the planned thrust towards Ternovka that day, for the resistance of the enemy was still too strong and the condition of the roads still quite atrocious.

The 11th Panzer Division mopped up the Rogi–Talnoye–Legezino area and then started to move to a position to the east of Talnoye. It was the intention of the panzer corps to send the panzer division to the area east of Novo Arkhangelsk so that it would then be available for action on the southern front of the pocket. But the movement of the panzer division was delayed. The muddy roads were packed with columns of troops from three different divisions. Only in the evening did the reconnaissance battalion reach Yampol, but the bulk of the panzer division was still in the vicinity west of Talnoye.

The command post of the panzer corps was placed in Talnoye in the afternoon. Our aerial reconnaissance spotted many of the enemy forces marching to the south, so there existed the very real possibility that they would try to escape the pocket by proceeding over the aforementioned stretch of the Sinyukha. All the means at the disposal of the panzer corps had to be used in order to occupy this stretch and establish contact with the XIV Panzer Corps. As SS Motorised Division Leibstandarte Adolf Hitler lacked the strength to be able to undertake this task on its own, the XXXXVIII Panzer Corps decided that a battle group of the 11th Panzer Division would work in conjunction with the SS division for the purpose of pushing as energetically as possible in the direction of Ternovka.

The final phase of the battle of encirclement (3–8 August 1941)

Combat and movement on 3 August were severely hindered by hours of rain. Once again, the roads were transformed into mud.

At dawn, SS Motorised Division Leibstandarte Adolf Hitler had to push back multiple enemy attacks on Novo Arkhangelsk from the west. Only after that could the SS division finally roll forward from the line between Novo Arkhangelsk and Novo Grigoryevka in the direction of the Sinyukha. It encountered little resistance to begin with and crossed the road leading from Novo Arkhangelsk to Tishkovka. It met with strong resistance shortly thereafter, and the enemy seemed to become stronger in this sector as the afternoon wore on. So slowly did the advance proceed that, by nightfall, the SS division remained only just to the west of the road that it had crossed. It did not help that the roads were in such bad shape and that it was therefore impossible to bring forward our heavy weaponry.

Although it had been planned that the 11th Panzer Division would partake in the push towards Ternovka, this did not end up taking place. The roads remained in a terrible state, so the combat elements of the panzer division had not managed to reach and assemble in Novo Grigoryevka in time. With great difficulty, a few units made it as far as Novo Arkhangelsk by nightfall, where they then made attack preparations for the following day.

The 16th Motorised Infantry Division finally enjoyed a relatively quiet day at the front. There was little combat activity aside from an easily repulsed attack from Sverdlinovo and some harassing fire from enemy artillery. Contact was established that day with the 297th Infantry Division, which had approached the area to the north of Kamyaneche from the north-east. The relief of some of the units of the motorised infantry division could therefore commence.

The battle of Uman had entered its final decisive stage. Our reconnaissance that afternoon revealed that strong elements of the enemy forces, amongst them motorised columns, were proceeding towards Ternovka via Podvysokoye. It could thus be expected that the point of main effort of the breakout attempts by the enemy would be in the vicinity of Ternovka and that these attempts would be made overnight and on the following day. The occupation of the Sinyukha line was without question the top priority. The ring of encirclement had already been drawn tighter that day on its western and south-western sides.

Group Schwedler already stood to the east of Uman along the Babanka–Zelenkov line, while the 4th Mountain Division was located to the south-west of Novo Arkhangelsk along the Rassokhovatets–Kopenkovata–Rogovo–Dubovo line. Meanwhile, the 9th Panzer Division (of the XIV Panzer Corps) had advanced to a position to the west of the Tishkovka–Pervomaisk road. Pervomaisk itself was taken by the 16th Panzer Division. Further to the west, but drawing closer, were the 1st Mountain Division, the 101st Light Infantry Division, and the Hungarian Mobile Corps.

Squeezed between the German fronts to the east and west, many of the Russian motorised columns fell back to the south on the western side of Pervomaisk. The XIV Panzer Corps therefore set up a defensive front that circled from the east to the south, with the 14th Panzer Division positioned between Bolshaya Viska and Pletenyi Tashlyk and the 25th Motorised Infantry Division along the line connecting Novo Ukrainka, Peschanyi Brod, and Lysaya Gora.

On the night of 3/4 August, Russian aircraft dropped supplies into the pocket before the front of the 16th Motorised Infantry Division and that of SS Motorised Division Leibstandarte Adolf Hitler. Some of these supplies landed on our side of the lines. These efforts by the enemy to supply the pocket were an indication that there were still large quantities of forces in that pocket and that they would try to resist for as long as possible.

Towards 0600 hours, the SS division and the 11th Panzer Division renewed their advance towards the Sinyukha. Despite the ferocity of the fighting, the SS division reached the river in the early afternoon. In the combat zone of the panzer division, the panzer regiment took the high ground to the north of Konstantinovka (east of Ternovka) while a combat group to its north seized Losovatka. The long columns of enemy forces that fled from Ternovka towards the south-east were intercepted and annihilated in cooperation with the 9th Panzer Division. Many prisoners were taken, and a considerable number of guns also fell into our hands.

In the afternoon, once our artillery had moved into position, the southern wing of the 11th Panzer Division attacked the strongly defended Ternovka while the 9th Panzer Division launched a simultaneous strike from the south. German forces eventually entered the village in the evening, although there were multiple skirmishes that continued into the night. The right wing of the 11th Panzer Division fought hard to the west of Losovatka. The enemy there had dug in and was putting up tremendous resistance. But this resistance was broken before nightfall, enabling the XXXXVIII Panzer Corps to fully occupy the length of the Sinyukha between Novo Arkhangelsk and Ternovka.

There existed enemy batteries to the south-east of Torgovitsy as well as strong concentrations of enemy troops in Torgovitsy itself and in the forest to the south-east of Kamyaneche. The 16th Motorised Infantry Division fought against these forces with apparent success, for the enemy's artillery fire and offensive activity soon became weak and isolated.

After an uneventful night, the 11th Panzer Division approached Maslobrod, which lay slightly to the north of Ternovka, on the morning of 5 August. The bridge there was still held by the enemy, but the panzer division captured it in a single stroke. In the meantime, the house-to-house fighting in Ternovka had come to an end. The village had fallen into the hands of the panzer division, as had several thousand prisoners and large numbers of guns and other weapons.

No further assaults were launched by the enemy against the front of the panzer corps. The infantry divisions pressed firmly against the southern, western, and north-western sides of the pocket. Chaos reigned within that pocket, with the enemy finding himself in an increasingly cramped position. It was not long before the 1st Mountain Division and the 297th Infantry Division took up positions along the line of encirclement, thereby releasing most of the forces of the 11th Panzer Division and the 16th Motorised Infantry Division. SS Motorised Division Leibstandarte Adolf Hitler remained where it was. The possibility existed that the enemy might try to attack its front in the vicinity of Podvysokoye and Torgovitsy.

It was on this day that the III Panzer Corps occupied Kirovograd. This created the conditions favourable for a thrust by Panzer Group 1 towards the Dnieper. How precisely the XXXXVIII Panzer Corps would be utilised in carrying out this thrust was yet to be decided.

On 6 August, for the first time since the commencement of the campaign in the East, the XXXXVIII Panzer Corps partook in no combat whatsoever. It looked likely that the Uman pocket would finally be eliminated on that day or the next.

Some of the encircled forces broke through the front of the 4th Mountain Division and headed in the direction of Golovanevsk. As the XIV Panzer Corps had already advanced further to the east, with the 16th Panzer Division standing at that time to the south of Konstantinovka (on the Southern Bug), the XXXXVIII Panzer Corps, on the orders of Panzer Group 1, prepared the 11th Panzer Division for action in the vicinity of the breakthrough point. Yet this action did not end up taking place.

It was on 7 August that the remaining enemy forces in the Uman pocket were wiped out. The enemy had made a feeble attempt during the night to break out to the south of Novo Arkhangelsk, but he had been knocked back by SS Motorised Division Leibstandarte Adolf Hitler and had suffered heavy casualties.

According to the initial assessment of the situation at the headquarters of the XXXXIV Army Corps before dawn, there were strong enemy forces that had succeeded in breaking through the ring of encirclement in the combat zone of the 24th Infantry Division. The departure of the 16th Motorised Infantry Division to the south was therefore put on hold so that SS Regiment Westland could immediately reoccupy its old position in the vicinity of Sverdlinovo. The reconnaissance battalion of SS Motorised Division Leibstandarte Adolf Hitler placed itself on the western outskirts of Novo Arkhangelsk. However, it became clear towards 0700 hours that the forces that had broken through were small in number. The infantry alone could deal with them.

Additional Russian forces were at that moment advancing from Boguslav in the direction of the command post of the panzer group in Zvenigorodka. The XXXXVIII Panzer Corps therefore had to leave behind SS Regiment Westland and the bulk of Motorised Regiment Hermann Göring and head towards the east.

The command elements of the panzer corps set off for their new command post in Lipnyazhka. Thundery showers once more transformed all roads into mud, making movement difficult not only for the corps command elements but also for the 16th Motorised Infantry Division. The commander of the panzer corps and his chief of staff soon arrived in Lipnyazhka, but the first orderly officer and the radio detachment stood in Novo Arkhangelsk while most of the command elements were spread out along the road between there and Lipnyazhka. Meanwhile, the first general staff officer was still at the old command post in Talnoye. Only in the course of the day of 8 August did all the corps staff officers manage to reach the new command post.

The panzer corps was informed by the panzer group on 8 August that the Uman pocket had been eliminated. A total of approximately 103,000 enemy troops had been taken prisoner. Amongst them were the commanders of the Russian 6th and 12th Armies. With that, the battle of encirclement had come to an end. The panzer corps had contributed significantly to this victory, committed as it had been at the focal point of the battle. By driving boldly on Novo Arkhangelsk, the panzer corps had played a decisive role in sealing the pocket. And it had been against the firm defensive front of the panzer corps that the enemy, in vain, had sought most furiously to break out to the east. It was for their tremendous efforts that General Kempf, in an order of the day, expressed his thanks to the divisions under his command.

CHAPTER 5

The XXXXVIII Panzer Corps Thrusts to the Black Sea

The advance to the south (8–22 August 1941)

Even before the battle of Uman had drawn to a close, it had become clear what the new task of the XXXXVIII Panzer Corps would be. After assessing the situation on 6 August, Panzer Group 1 informed the panzer corps that it would be required, with the 16th Motorised Infantry Division and SS Motorised Division Leibstandarte Adolf Hitler under its command, to advance to the south through Voznesensk towards Nikolayev so that the enemy would be denied access to the remaining crossings over the Southern Bug. By the evening of 8 August, it was clarified that this task would encompass the seizure of Nikolayev itself so as to prevent the evacuation of enemy troops by sea. The panzer corps would have to carry out this operation with ammunition levels that would ordinarily last less than a day and a half, as the panzer group had no more to spare for the time being. A request made by the panzer corps to the effect that it be allocated the 16th Panzer Division for the new operation could not be fulfilled due to a shortage of fuel. It was also the plan of the panzer group that this panzer division be sent to the east. Even the 11th Panzer Division had been detached from the panzer corps on 8 August. It was placed in panzer group reserve and was to set off in the direction of Novo Mirgorod on 9 August. This meant that the panzer corps had lost an outstanding panzer division, a formation that had been under its command since the outset of the campaign in Russia and that had always fought at the front with brilliant success. Although the prospect of seeing the Black Sea generated enthusiasm, it was somewhat dampened by the knowledge that the panzer corps, for the first time, was supposed to advance without any panzer divisions assigned to it.

The reconnaissance battalion of the 16th Motorised Infantry Division departed Yampol for the south on 7 August at 1000 hours. Its leading elements reached Voznesensk on the evening of 8 August, relieving some of the units of the 16th Panzer Division that were already there. By the morning of 9 August, the entire panzer division had been relieved. There was barely any contact with the enemy, so it was without difficulty that the motorised infantry division reached the Arnautovka–Shcherbany line in the evening. Minefields briefly delayed the southward advance of the left wing, but, by noon on 10 August, Belousovka and Sukhoi Yelanets had been taken. Low-flying Russian aircraft struck at that moment and inflicted heavy losses, while Russian fighters neutralised our efforts to conduct aerial reconnaissance. As the fighter protection of the IV Air Corps was insufficient, the panzer corps requested that additional support be provided by the V Air Corps.

SS Motorised Division Leibstandarte Adolf Hitler had set off early on 8 August and had reached the area to the north of Konstantinovka (on the Southern Bug) later that day. Towards noon on 9 August, the SS division was ordered to occupy the area surrounded by Ivanovka, Bolshaya Serbulovka, Yelanets, and Medvedenki, after which it was to conduct reconnaissance further to the south. Due to the fact that the roads were in poor condition and that many of the bridges along the way had been destroyed by the enemy, only a few elements of the SS division were able to make it to the area to which they had been ordered before nightfall.

Russian forces had evacuated Bessarabia during the battle of Uman and were already in rapid retreat between the Southern Bug and the Dnieper. There probably remained only a few enemy forces to the west of the Southern Bug. It therefore seemed to the panzer corps that one division would be sufficient to carry out the Nikolayev operation. SS Motorised Division Leibstandarte Adolf Hitler was assigned the task, but it failed to follow the orders it had been given to begin with. Unbeknownst to the panzer corps, the SS division intended rather to attack the field positions to the north-east of Sukhoi Yelanets. The panzer corps, learning of this from the 16th Motorised Infantry Division, expressly forbade the SS division from executing this attack. The SS division ran off regardless and could only be reined in when ordered to turn back by the panzer group.

The command post of the panzer corps was shifted from Lipnyazhka to Konstantinovka on the morning of 9 August. It was at about that time that the area within and around the panzer corps became rather international in character. The Romanian Cavalry Corps and the Romanian Mountain Corps approached the high ground near Voznesensk from the northwest, while the Italian 9th Infantry Division Pasubio marched towards the city from the north. The Hungarian 1st Motorised Brigade stood along the Southern Bug between Pervomaisk and Konstantinovka on 9 August and was on that day subordinated to the panzer corps. This was a temporary measure to begin with, but it was decided on 10 August that the Hungarian brigade would remain under the command of the panzer corps for the duration of the Nikolayev operation. The Hungarian brigade relieved the 16th Motorised Infantry Division near Aleksandrovka and Voznesensk throughout the day of 9 August and drove towards the area to the south-west of Woszjatskoje on 10 August.

Chop and change of orders (10–11 August 1941)

On the evening of 10 August, a new order was received from the panzer group which completely changed the situation for the panzer corps. According to this order, the Hungarian Mobile Corps was to assume responsibility for the advance on Nikolayev on 11 August while the panzer corps, with the 16th Motorised Infantry Division and SS Motorised Division Leibstandarte Adolf Hitler, would remain at the disposal of the panzer group and would, as stated in a radio message on 11 August, depart for the north. This order was prompted by the growing danger to the rear lines of communication of the panzer group. A gap had developed between the Sixth Army and Panzer Group 1 near and to the north of Cherkassy, and enemy forces were pouring into that gap.

The Hungarian Mobile Corps arrived more quickly than expected, enabling the relief of the panzer corps to commence on 11 August. A shortage of fuel soon delayed the departure of the panzer corps, but preparations continued, with some regret, nonetheless. Any dreams of bathing in the Black Sea seemed to be at an end.

Yet the day of 11 August did not go by without further surprise. A new radio message from the panzer group reached the panzer corps at 1750 hours. The planned departure of the panzer corps was cancelled, as the Sixth Army and elements of the Seventeenth Army had counter-attacked in the meantime and had hurled the enemy back over the Dnieper.

At 1925 hours, the first general staff officer of the panzer group delivered a new order personally. It was the wish of the commander in chief of the German Army, Field-Marshal von Brauchitsch, that Nikolayev be taken as quickly as possible. Battle Group Kempf was to be formed for this purpose, and the units under its command would be the Hungarian Mobile Corps, the 16th Panzer Division, and SS Motorised Division Leibstandarte Adolf Hitler. The 16th Motorised Infantry Division, which had been subordinate to the panzer corps since the beginning of the campaign in the East and had always performed the role of flank protection with brilliance, was detached from the panzer corps and placed in panzer group reserve. Only gradually was the motorised infantry division relieved by the Hungarians, so it was not until 13 August that it could set off for its new assembly area to the north of Yelanets and Olgopol. The headquarters of the panzer corps regarded the detachment of this outstanding division to be most unfortunate and hoped that it was a measure that would only be temporary.

The command post of the panzer corps moved from Konstantinovka to Woszjatskoje on the morning of 12 August, and it was on that very day that the new thrust commenced.

The advance on Nikolayev (12–14 August 1941)

Between the Southern Bug and the Ingul, the Hungarian Mobile Corps advanced through the area of the German 16th Motorised Infantry Division towards the south. After that, the situation in the combat zone of the Hungarian formation remained unknown as a result of the poor signal communications. By the afternoon, it looked as if the mobile corps might not have made any progress. Thanks to the indecision on the part of the German military leadership on 11 August, the enemy had gained a full day to reinforce his defences in front of the mobile corps. According to Russian documents that were captured later, those reinforcements consisted of two divisions. The capacity of the enemy to resist was further enhanced by well-prepared field emplacements positioned behind extensive minefields. The Hungarian 1st Motorised Brigade had even been compelled to retreat 5 kilometres when attacked by a Russian battalion in the vicinity of Suvorovka. Multiple heavy attacks conducted by the enemy against Sukhoi Yelanets were repelled. The Hungarian 2nd Motorised Brigade took Troitskoye towards the evening, but otherwise gained little ground. It eventually succeeded in seizing Hill 91, which lay to the east of Kasnemovka, on 13 August, yet the 1st Motorised Brigade had by then evacuated Sukhoi Yelanets due to the enormity of the enemy pressure it faced. Strong concentrations of Russian tanks and artillery were spotted at that time by Hungarian reconnaissance units in the Petrovskoye–Pereszadew area.

On the morning of 14 August, both motorised brigades of the Hungarian Mobile Corps attacked. The enemy was pushed back. By the evening, the mobile corps stood along the Sebino–Petrovskoye line. The enemy quickly assembled his forces near the Ingul crossings. It was clearly his intention to withdraw over the river to the east.

The Romanian Cavalry Brigade also made good progress. It advanced along the east bank of the Gromokleya and reached the Peski–Khristoforovka line by the evening. That this advance placed considerable demands on the cavalry brigade is demonstrated by the fact that its cavalry regiments lost 50 horses from heatstroke.

The 16th Panzer Division had set off from the Olgopol area early on 12 August. A battle group of the panzer division crossed the Ingul near Kiryakovka and then turned to the south whilst leaving behind some security units to establish a defensive line against what appeared to be a strongly occupied Novyi Bug. The bulk of the panzer division advanced over the Ingul near Privolnoye and, by the evening, seized Novo Poltavka. It seemed that the new line of advance of the panzer corps on the east bank of the Ingul had taken the enemy by surprise. His forces there were generally few in number and poorly prepared. The panzer division resumed its advance early on 13 August. It thrust southwards along the railway line, drove through the station in Greiga, and arrived not only at the railway junction 5 kilometres to the south-east of Nikolayev but also at the nearby airfield. It was still morning. Barely any enemy resistance had been encountered. The spearhead of the panzer division swivelled to the west and approached Nikolayev itself in the afternoon.

Nikolayev and Kherson were strongly held by the enemy. Ships were sailing to and fro to the south of Nikolayev, and multiple columns and trains were making their way from Nikolayev to Kherson.

The 45-kilometre flank of the 16th Panzer Division was cause for some concern at the headquarters of the panzer corps. It was bound to be threatened by the enemy forces that had withdrawn to the east after being pushed back by the Hungarian Mobile Corps. Many of the troops of the panzer division were tied down near Novo Danzig and Greiga, for these were the locations where the enemy forces sought to cross the Ingul. This meant that a significant portion of the panzer division was unable to partake in the attack on Nikolayev for the time being. The entire 79th Rifle Regiment had to pivot to the east. Given that SS Motorised Division Leibstandarte Adolf Hitler was at that time tied down elsewhere and was therefore unavailable to provide flank protection, the panzer corps made several urgent requests for the 16th Motorised Infantry Division to be placed under its command. But the panzer group stated that it could not yet spare the motorised infantry division.

Fierce fighting on the Ingul – enemy forces escape (14–16 August 1941)

The situation along the Ingul deteriorated on the morning of 14 August. The strength of the enemy forces there increased constantly, especially in Novo Danzig, Greiga, and Kalinovka.[4] The 16th Panzer Division somehow needed to be reinforced, so it was decided that it would be given the IV Battalion of SS Motorised Division Leibstandarte Adolf Hitler. This battalion would relieve the 79th Rifle Regiment near Novo Danzig so that the latter could move further to the south. The enemy had been conducting a powerful push from Novo Danzig since noon. By the evening, the rifle regiment had lost contact with the southern

---

[4] Translator's note: the town of Kalinovka referred to here lies to the north-east of Nikolayev and should not be confused with the town of the same name that lies to the south of Berdichev.

group of the panzer division and was engaged in fierce defensive fighting between Novo Danzig and Greiga.

In the immediate vicinity of Nikolayev, the situation barely changed on the morning of 14 August. The panzer regiment and the 64th Rifle Regiment were weak and unable to enter the city. They stood opposite the entrenchments that had been prepared by the enemy and could do no more than fend off his multiple assaults. The left wing of the German spearhead was perhaps weakest of all, and this permitted large quantities of enemy troops a chance to withdraw to the south. Even so, it was still possible for our forces to defend themselves against a strong enemy group that had approached Nikolayev from Kherson. Part of this enemy group was destroyed; the rest was thrown back. In the afternoon, despite the fierce resistance of enemy artillery, anti-tank guns, and anti-aircraft guns, the II Battalion of the rifle regiment as well as some of the tanks of the panzer regiment managed to enter the eastern part of Nikolayev. They had to pause by nightfall. Enemy resistance remained strong.

The commencement of the advance of SS Motorised Division Leibstandarte Adolf Hitler on 12 August was delayed due to a misunderstanding of the order it had been given. The reconnaissance battalion of the SS division crossed the Ingul in the afternoon, but it soon came to a standstill in the vicinity of Novyi Bug. While the bulk of the SS division was engaged in combat near Novyi Bug and Novo Poltavka on 13 August, with the latter being taken towards the evening, the reconnaissance battalion proceeded further to the south, reaching Tavkino at noon and Saselye in the evening. Once the 16th Motorised Infantry Division arrived in the area of Novyi Bug and Novo Poltavka the following day, the bulk of the SS division was free to follow the reconnaissance battalion to the south.

Throughout the afternoon of 14 August, the reconnaissance battalion of the SS division had to repel one strong attack after another that the enemy launched towards Saselye from the east as well as from the south. The SS division therefore sent another battalion there as quickly as possible so as to reinforce the defensive measures of the reconnaissance battalion. The remaining elements of the SS division turned towards the west. This placed them beside the right wing of the 79th Rifle Regiment.

The enemy had been enjoying complete aerial superiority in the skies over the combat zone of Battle Group Kempf since noon on 14 August. Waves of Russian aircraft struck the road of advance between Novo Poltavka and Nikolayev. We suffered heavy losses. Not a single German fighter was to be seen! The panzer corps requested of the panzer group that the provision of fighter protection be given top priority.

On the evening of 14 August, despite the good progress that had been made by the Hungarian Mobile Corps, the overall situation had become quite unfavourable. There was no doubt that the enemy forces that had been pushed back by the Hungarian troops would do everything within their power to break out to the east. As the panzer corps lacked the forces needed to close the gaps on its western flank, it would be difficult to prevent the escape of many of the enemy's units. The eastern flank of the panzer corps was hardly covered at all. This meant that the strongly occupied Kherson presented a great danger, even though it might have been the general tendency of the enemy at that time to fall back to the east rather than to attack. In a situation such as this, it would not at all be possible to reinforce the spearhead of the 16th Panzer Division for its assault on Nikolayev.

It was on 15 August that the development expected by the panzer corps came to pass. The news reached the headquarters of the panzer corps at 0700 hours that the enemy had broken through in the vicinity of Novo Danzig. The defensive elements that the 16th Panzer Division had positioned near the town were heavily bombarded by enemy artillery throughout the morning. Large numbers of enemy troops flowed through the breakthrough point to the east and south-east. The panzer corps requested once more of the panzer group that it be allocated the 16th Motorised Infantry Division so that this division could be sent through Tavkino towards Novo Petrovka, where it would be able to cut off the route of retreat of the enemy forces that had escaped. However, the only unit that the panzer group could place at the disposal of the panzer corps was the reinforced 60th Motorised Infantry Regiment. This regiment immediately set off via Novo Poltavka. The panzer corps saw to it that the II and III Battalions of SS Motorised Division Leibstandarte Adolf Hitler were also committed to an attack towards the south. This would ensure that the enemy was not only intercepted but also destroyed.

The enemy forces that had broken out struck the I Battalion of the SS division later that morning in the vicinity of Saselye. The battalion counter-attacked, pushed the enemy back, and took several hundred prisoners.

The situation became ever more critical on the east bank of the Ingul throughout the course of the afternoon. The three SS battalions were advancing on Novo Danzig when they were subjected to heavy enemy artillery fire. Without any cover whatsoever on the increasingly high ground, the battalions were brought to a halt. On the southern wing of the panzer corps, the Hungarian 4th Cavalry Regiment was inserted into the gap that had been created when the II Battalion of the 79th Rifle Regiment had been pushed back by the overwhelmingly powerful enemy. The I Battalion and the reconnaissance battalion of the SS division established a south-ward-facing defensive front near Saselye. Further to the north, the bicycle battalion of the Hungarian Cavalry Brigade was stopped near Lalatskoye by enemy artillery. With his defensive positions firmly established, many of the enemy's troops were able to escape unhindered. Endless columns departed Mikhailovka for the south, and there were several more that departed the area south of the railway station in Greiga for the south-east. Our shortage of forces did not help. Only the immediate subordination of the 16th Motorised Infantry Division to the panzer corps would have enabled the encirclement and annihilation of these enemy forces.

Heavy fighting continued to take place on 16 August. In the combat zone of the 16th Panzer Division, the 79th Rifle Regiment took the railway station in Greiga and then, at 1400 hours, advanced along the railway line before turning to the south-east for the purpose of taking part in the destruction of the enemy forces that stood to the south-west of Saselye.

A battalion of the 60th Motorised Infantry Regiment had in the meantime thrust towards the south and was approaching Nikolayev. The remaining two battalions of the regiment fought to the south of Saselye and near Konstantinovka (east of Nikolayev).[5] The enemy, who sought

---

[5] Translator's note: this is the third Konstantinovka that has appeared in this narrative. The first was to the east of Ternovka, the second on the Southern Bug, and now this third one to the east of Nikolayev.

to move further to the east, had slipped between the two villages and was launching one strike after another against the two battalions. These battalions lost contact with the elements of SS Motorised Division Leibstandarte Adolf Hitler that stood near Saselye and that were defending themselves against enemy assaults from east and west. During the afternoon, the situation became critical for the II Battalion of the motorised infantry regiment. It had suffered heavy casualties and had been pushed back to the southern outskirts of Saselye. It was eventually relieved thanks to the arrival of the 76th Rifle Regiment (of the 16th Panzer Division). This regiment had advanced as far as the railway station in Saselye by the evening, and it then proceeded to veer towards Nikolayev.

The bulk of SS Motorised Division Leibstandarte Adolf Hitler took Novo Danzig on the morning of 17 August and started to push further to the south. The SS division was then given the order to send most of its forces to Saselye and to devote just one battalion to the task of combing through the villages along the Ingul as far as Nikolayev. By the evening, several elements of the SS division stood beside the II Battalion of the 60th Mobile Infantry Regiment along the defensive front near Saselye. A few other elements of the SS division had taken Greiga.

Enemy aerial activity was quite lively that day. Russian aircraft bombed the Konstantinovka–Saselye area and inflicted heavy losses on the German troops. The command post of the panzer corps, which had been situated in Novo Poltavka since 1430 hours on 14 August, was also subjected to enemy air raids. It suffered heavy casualties and lost many of its vehicles. By the evening, the command post had been moved to Novo Georgiyevka.

As expected, the Hungarian Motorised Corps made good progress in its advance towards the south on the morning of 15 August. The 2nd Motorised Brigade reached Peski towards noon, while the 1st Motorised Brigade fought slightly to its north and north-east. The enemy forces had been pushed back towards and were concentrated on the banks of the Ingul, so it was there that their resistance was greatest. An attack carried out there by units of the 1st Motorised Brigade and 1st Cavalry Brigade only gradually gained ground. The 1st Motorised Brigade slowly approached Ingulka and Peresadovka in the evening, but it was still striving to enter those towns on the morning of 16 August. Peresadovka was taken later that day.

By 17 August, the fighting along the Ingul had mostly come to an end. Any of the enemy forces that had not already escaped to the east had been destroyed instead.

Battle Group Nikolayev, as our group of forces near the city had been designated, found itself in a difficult situation on 15 August. Its front and right wing were bombarded by enemy artillery at dawn and were subjected to multiple assaults. The battle group suffered heavy losses and had to relinquish its control over the railway line. However, it conducted an armoured counter-attack in the afternoon, inflicted heavy casualties on the enemy, and retook the railway line. Elements of the panzer regiment proceeded to the south of the Nikolayev–Kherson railway line and eliminated enemy units that had been edging forward in that area. Our artillery fought with great success that day. Russian vehicles concentrated on the road leading south from the city were hit hard, and so too was enemy shipping on the Southern Bug.

Seizure of Nikolayev and Kherson (16–20 August 1941)

On the morning of 16 August, Battle Group Nikolayev renewed its attack. While the I Battalion of the 60th Motorised Infantry Regiment provided rear and flank protection, the battle group succeeded in infiltrating the city of Nikolayev despite the fierce resistance of the enemy. At noon, Major-General Hube, the commander of the 16th Panzer Division, hoisted the Reich War Flag on the water tower in the western part of the city. By the morning of 17 August, the fighting in the city had drawn to a conclusion.

The command post of the panzer corps was moved to Nikolayev on the afternoon of 17 August. It was the first time during the campaign that the headquarters staff of the panzer corps had seen a major Russian city. Even so, the sight of this city of 170,000 inhabitants was not particularly uplifting. Small, dirty stone houses lined the roads. Cheap, kitsch plaster statues stood in the sparse, neglected green spaces. The small number of large office buildings were almost all scorched. The people were cautious, but not unfriendly. It had been the hope of the panzer group that large quantities of provisions would be found in the city, but this was not to be the case. All shops and warehouses had been evacuated and plundered, and most the factories had been destroyed. At the shipyard, a 35,000-tonne battleship, as well as several submarines and ship frames, fell into our hands. The commander of the 108th Corps Artillery Command became the commandant of Nikolayev, while the 16th Panzer Division remained responsible for the security of the city for the time being.

Following the successful capture of Nikolayev, both the Hungarian Mobile Corps and the German 60th Infantry Regiment (of the 16th Motorised Infantry Division) were detached from Battle Group Kempf.

SS Motorised Division Leibstandarte Adolf Hitler thrust towards the east on 17 August and reached the road connecting Tavkino and Novo Petrovka. On the morning of 18 August, it took possession of Snigirevka (60 kilometres east of Nikolayev). The bridge in the city was ablaze, but still intact, so it was soon possible for a bridgehead to be established across the Ingulets. Enemy troops that advanced northwards from Kherson on the west bank of the river were either eliminated or taken prisoner. Furthermore, the enemy was compelled to abandon his bridgehead near Daryevka, although he had just enough time to blow up the bridge there.

Kherson was the objective of the SS division. The hills to the north of the city were strongly defended by the enemy. The attack against the port had already begun on the afternoon of 18 August, but it made such slow progress that it was still crawling forward on 19 August. The enemy fought fiercely and was supported by heavy artillery. Only in the afternoon did the SS division enter the northern part of Kherson, and it was already evening before the entire city was in our hands. Multiple troop transports, gunboats, and other small ships had been sunk in the fighting. Mopping-up operations were carried out and completed on the morning of 20 August. The enemy had evacuated the city and had destroyed anything that might have been of use to the German troops.

Aftermath

With the seizure of Nikolayev and Kherson, two of the small number of Russian ports on the Black Sea had fallen into German hands. Odessa was still held by the enemy. It was surrounded by the Romanian Fourth Army and would only fall on 16 October. But the XXXXVIII Panzer Corps had achieved a tremendous success. Its first rapid drive was at an end.

The thrust of Panzer Group 1 to the south-east had not quite managed to cut off all the enemy forces that had retreated before the front of the Eleventh Army and the Romanian armies. Substantial numbers of enemy troops escaped the Uman pocket and fled to the east over the Dnieper. The panzer group had been significantly delayed by multiple assaults that the enemy had launched from the Pripet Marshes. Nevertheless, it had still been possible to shatter considerable elements of the enemy forces to the west of the Dnieper. Within eight weeks, the entire west bank of the river from the Black Sea to Cherkassy had been occupied by German troops. It had also been possible to establish several bridgeheads across the river. This created a favourable position from which to cover the southern flank of the planned assault on Moscow.

CHAPTER 6

The III Panzer Corps Drives Towards Kiev

In Lublin, only a few weeks before the outbreak of hostilities, the III Army Corps had been upgraded from an infantry to a panzer formation and had correspondingly been redesignated the III Panzer Corps. Its commander was General of Cavalry Eberhard von Mackensen.[6]

Placed to the north of the XXXXVIII Panzer Corps, the III Panzer Corps commenced its drive to the east on 22 June 1941. Once the fiercely defended border fortifications had been overcome by the 44th and 298th Infantry Divisions, the two panzer formations of the panzer corps (the 13th and 14th Panzer Divisions) advanced deep into enemy territory. The first operational objective was the region surrounding Kiev.

The panzer divisions shortly gained freedom of movement in the area to the east and south-east of Wlodzimierz. Progress was rapid to begin with. The 13th Panzer Division was committed on the southern side of the sole road that led from Hrubieszow to Kiev via Wlodzimierz, Lutsk, Rovno, Zvyahel, and Zhitomir. It therefore had to force its way through difficult terrain. The 14th Panzer Division advanced along the road itself, although enemy resistance there was stronger.

While a great deal of combat occurred to the rear, the panzer divisions drove ahead and fought in their first tank battle near and to the south

---

[6] Translator's note: the operations of the III Panzer Corps in Russia in 1941 and 1942 are described in detail in the 42nd volume in the Wehrmacht im Kampf series – Eberhard von Mackensen, *Vom Bug zum Kaukasus: Das III. Panzerkorps im Feldzug gegen Sowjetrussland 1941/42* (Neckargemünd: Vowinckel, 1967) – which is yet to be translated into English.

of Aleksandrovka. A total of 267 enemy tanks were destroyed. As early as 25 June, German troops took Lutsk and crossed the Styr. The 14th Panzer Division had to go over to the defensive when the enemy assaulted Lutsk from the east and north-east, but the 13th Panzer Division, still off-road, bypassed the city to the south and swiftly conquered Rovno. The 298th Infantry Division soon reached Lutsk, enabling the 14th Panzer Division to follow in the wake of the 13th Panzer Division. The 25th Motorised Infantry Division was entrusted with the protection of Rovno, although it suffered heavy losses in the fighting there due to the relentlessness of the enemy.

Both panzer divisions quickly reached the Horyn. They crossed the river after some brief combat and continued towards the Slucz, along which the Stalin Line ran. If these obstacles could be overcome, it would pave the way for operations in the direction of Kiev. Yet the hitherto successful drive suddenly came to a halt. Torrential rain turned the roads in the black soil of Ukraine into mud and threatened to bring about the failure of the entire offensive in the East. The 14th Panzer Division had to make its way back to the main road of advance. Every single vehicle of the 13th Panzer Division struggled laboriously through the mud.

The 14th Panzer Division encountered enemy bunkers 20 kilometres to the west of Zvyahel and had to fight hard to knock them out. In the meantime, despite the difficulties presented by the terrain, the 13th Panzer Division managed to force the crossing of the Slucz near Hulsk. It established a bridgehead and, on 8 July, reached the main road of advance to the east of the enemy fortifications in Zvyahel. Yet taking the city itself was difficult. It was necessary for the 25th Motorised Infantry Division to be inserted between the two panzer divisions. Only after five days of intense fighting was the Stalin Line fully penetrated.

There were no delays after that. The 13th Panzer Division, once more the spearhead formation of the III Panzer Corps, reached Zhitomir in little more than 24 hours. By 10 July, the leading elements of the panzer division had already advanced as far as the Irpen. The panzer corps had therefore reached a point just before the inner circle of fortifications around Kiev. Its spearhead stood 120 kilometres ahead of its southern neighbour (the XXXXVIII Panzer Corps), which was still engaged in fierce combat in the vicinity of Berdichev, and 200 kilometres ahead of the infantry formations, which were at that time in the process of relieving the rear units of the III Panzer Corps.

The panzer corps had reached its first operational objective in a bold thrust. It had covered a distance of 450 kilometres in a period of only 18 days. But instead of exploiting the state of confusion of the enemy with an advance into Kiev and along the south bank of the Dnieper, the panzer corps, on the order of the High Command of the German Army (OKH), was to hold its position and await the arrival of the infantry. Standing before the gates of the city, it would be engaged in heavy defensive fighting in the meantime. This was especially the case for the northern flank, which was 70 kilometres in length and had to withstand the powerful assaults of the Russian 5th Army. These assaults frequently penetrated as far as the road along which the panzer corps had advanced. As a result, the panzer corps often had to be supplied by air. It was the view of the headquarters of the panzer corps as well as that of the panzer group that it ought to have been possible to take Kiev in a single stroke and even to hold on to it. The heavy casualties that the eventual capture of the city incurred could have been avoided.

The rapid drive of the panzer corps had demonstrated that the skilful leadership of armoured troops and the full exploitation of the weaknesses of the enemy can bring about significant results with relatively few losses. The first phase of the operation had been conducted swiftly and led to the destruction of 868 enemy tanks and 422 enemy guns. We suffered 806 fallen, 388 missing, and 2,426 wounded.

It was unfortunate from an operational perspective that the III Panzer Corps had to remain outside Kiev for so long. The XIV Panzer Corps had to be diverted to the north and placed between the III and XXXXVIII Panzer Corps. The immediate seizure of Kiev probably would have accelerated the subsequent encirclement of the Russian forces in the vicinity of the city. It had even been the original plan of the OKH to create a bridgehead on the east bank of the Dnieper without delay and to conduct operations to the north of the river. But the OKH had changed its mind on the grounds that there were insufficient German forces to carry out all the tasks that were necessary. It was the opinion of the OKH that the offensive operations of the panzer formations could not be exploited properly if the infantry divisions fell too far behind. The horse-drawn infantry troops were too slow, although they were doing their utmost to maintain contact with the panzer troops.

After being relieved by the Sixth Army, the III Panzer Corps was given the new task of covering the rear of Panzer Group 1 during the battle of Uman. For this purpose, the panzer corps advanced quickly to the south-east along the Dnieper in the direction of Cherkassy and Kremenchug. When the battle was over, the panzer corps pushed further to the south-east towards the large city of Dnepropetrovsk.[7] Amidst heavy fighting, the panzer corps entered the city on 25 August and established a bridgehead on the east bank of the Dnieper.[8] The major bridge across the river in Dnepropetrovsk had been blown up by the Russians. It was rebuilt and renamed Kleist Bridge, and would be of great importance for the conduct of operations in the direction of the Sea of Azov.

---

[7] Translator's note: the formations under the command of the III Panzer Corps in August 1941 were the 13th Panzer Division, the 60th Motorised Infantry Division, and the 14th Panzer Division. The northern flank along the Dnieper was defended by SS Division Wiking, which became overstretched as the panzer corps advanced. However, the arrival of the Italian Division Pasubio meant that the SS division could be relieved and could maintain its position on the left wing of the panzer corps. See Wilhelm Tieke, 'Das III. Armeekorps (mot.) im Brückenkopf Dnjepropetrowsk August/September 1941', *Allgemeine schweizerische Militärzeitschrift*, vol. 137, no. 11 (November 1971), 775–81, 775.

[8] Translator's note: the 13th Panzer Division entered the western part of Dnepropetrovsk on the morning of 25 August and fought hard to establish a bridgehead on the east bank of the Dnieper later that day. On 26 August, the forces of the 60th Motorised Infantry Division, having already secured the southern part of the city, started to enter the bridgehead and to relieve the forces of the 13th Panzer Division. The bridgehead was gradually expanded despite the ferocity of the enemy's constant counter-attacks and was, throughout late August and early September, reinforced with the 198th Infantry Division (which had meanwhile been placed under the command of the III Panzer Corps) and then SS Division Wiking. See Tieke, 'Das III. Armeekorps', 775–77.

CHAPTER 7

The XXIV and XXXXVIII Panzer Corps in the Battle of Kiev

The operational situation

The unexpected determination of the enemy's resistance, especially from the Pripet Marshes against the inner wings of Army Groups South and Centre, led to a decisive change in the overall operational plan. The situation on the northern wing of Army Group South had developed particularly unfavourably despite the rapid territorial gain of Panzer Group 1. As the fighting drew to a close along the southern bend of the Dnieper, the Sixth Army still stood before the strongly defended Russian bridgehead at Kiev. At the same time, the southern wing of Army Group Centre, which consisted of the Second Army and Colonel-General Heinz Guderian's Panzer Group 2, had driven far to the east and was increasingly threatened on its flank by hostile forces. A multitude of numerically superior, albeit battered, enemy units had separated the inner wings of the army groups from one another and had demonstrated no intention whatsoever of falling back to the east. Two different opinions arose as to how best to deal with this difficult situation. One group, whose leading proponent was Colonel-General Guderian, believed that the swift advance towards Moscow had to continue no matter what and that the city had to be taken before the onset of bad weather. The other group was of the view that the danger from the Pripet area needed to be eliminated first. Hitler was primarily concerned with political and economic matters. He attached great importance to the seizure of the industrial area in southern Russia and to the security of the oilfields in

Romania. The momentous decision was therefore taken to encircle and annihilate the Red masses in the vicinity of Kiev.

On 22 August 1941, in accordance with this decision, the southern wing of Army Group Centre was given the order to advance southwards from the Gomel–Starodub line towards the Desna. Whilst carrying out this advance, Panzer Group 2 was to execute an envelopment manoeuvre as far to the east as possible. A simultaneous northward advance would be conducted by the northern wing of Army Group South, with Panzer Group 1 also sweeping far to the east. The enemy forces near Kiev would thereby be cut off from their route of retreat and would subsequently be destroyed.

The operation commenced on the northern arm with the Second Army and Panzer Group 2 advancing over the Desna and approaching the city of Romny. In the meantime, on the southern arm, Panzer Group 1 assembled its forces in the Kremenchug bridgehead, which had been created by the Seventeenth Army. It would be the task of Panzer Group 1 to advance to the north and establish an obstacle line along the Sula between Romny and Lubny so that the withdrawal of the enemy to the east could be prevented.

To be examined now will be the offensive operations conducted by the spearhead formations of the two panzer groups: that of the XXIV Panzer Corps from the north and that of the XXXXVIII Panzer Corps from the south.

The thrust of the XXIV Panzer Corps to the east

The XXIV Panzer Corps, under the command of Panzer Group 2, had assembled to the south of Brest-Litovsk and had crossed the frontier on 22 June 1941. It was the task of the panzer corps to bypass the Pripet Marshes to the north and advance in the direction of Moscow as quickly as possible. The operations conducted by the panzer group have been described extensively by its former commander, Colonel-General Guderian, in his book *Erinnerungen eines Soldaten*.[9] Because of this, only a few specific details will be discussed here.

---

[9] Translator's note: Heinz Guderian's memoirs appeared in German as *Erinnerungen eines Soldaten* (Heidelberg: Vowinckel, 1951), and in English as *Panzer Leader*, tr. Constantine FitzGibbon (New York: Dutton, 1952). The sixth chapter of Guderian's book deals with the operations of Panzer Group 2 in Russia in 1941.

As early as the second day of the campaign, the 3rd Panzer Division (Lieutenant-General Walter Model) had circled around the southern outskirts of the well-defended city of Brest-Litovsk and advanced 150 kilometres into enemy territory. At the end of the third day, this spearhead formation of the panzer group had already overcome a fifth of the distance to Moscow. The battle group at the head of the panzer division was changed on an almost daily basis so that the drive along the road of advance could continue with the utmost vigour.

On the seventh day, the 3rd Panzer Division had covered 400 kilometres and was standing in Bobruisk. The city lay on the Berezina, and the panzer division had to stay there for two days, as the bridge over the river had been destroyed. The enemy was fully aware of the danger presented by the deep penetration of the panzer group. He therefore committed strong elements of his air force against this point. Although shot down in large numbers by the German fighter squadrons, Russian aircraft fearlessly took to the skies again and again in order to hinder the construction of a new bridge and prevent the panzer forces from crossing the river. But his efforts were in vain. By 2 July, the panzer division had entered the western part of Rogachev (on the Dnieper), although an immediate attempt to punch through the Stalin Line failed. A few tanks of the III Battalion of the 6th Panzer Regiment that had been equipped for driving through water were able to advance over the Pruth, yet the muddy banks and enemy resistance made further progress impossible. The enemy wanted to hold this sector with all the means at his disposal. He even sought to conduct an armoured attack a little to the south in the vicinity of Zhlobin. Only a rapid strike by a couple of battalions of the panzer regiment that had been on standby to the west of Rogachev could hurl the enemy back over the Dnieper. Our losses were heavy in carrying out this counter-attack, with 22 German tanks put out of action. To the north, an attempt on our part to take possession of the bridges over the river in Mogilev came to grief after we had lost 17 tanks. In Bykhov, though, there was success in gaining a foothold on the opposite bank of the Dnieper. Without delay, the advance resumed in the direction of Roslavl, and the town was taken on 1 August.

Once it had crossed the Dnieper, the deep flanks of the panzer group were increasingly exposed to danger, especially from the south. It required determined fighting in the vicinity of Gomel to eliminate this danger.

The thrust of the XXIV Panzer Corps to the south

The high command had in the meantime decided to change its plans in view of the presence of strong enemy forces near and to the east of Kiev. Standing between the inner wings of Army Groups South and Centre, these forces comprised elements of the 5th, 13th, 21st, and 37th Armies – a total of approximately one million soldiers. They needed to be annihilated. On 22 August, the directive was issued to the effect that this task would be carried out by the Sixth Army and Panzer Group 1 from the south and by the Second Army and Panzer Group 2 from the north.

The northern wing rolled forward on 25 August. The Second Army and the bulk of Panzer Group 2 advanced to the south from the Gomel–Starodub line towards the Desna. Spearheading the panzer group was the XXIV Panzer Corps, whose commander was General of Panzer Troops Leo Freiherr Geyr von Schweppenburg. The first objective of the panzer corps was the city of Konotop, which lay deep in the enemy rear area.

Although subjected to a multitude of enemy counter-thrusts, most of them from the east, the 3rd Panzer Division succeeded, thanks to the bold advance of a reinforced panzer company, in seizing intact the long wooden bridge over the Desna near Novgorod-Seversky as early as 26 August. Covered by the fire of the first tanks that had driven across the river, Pioneer Lieutenant Stöck managed to remove the demolition block on the bridge at the last moment. This was the first step in establishing a bridgehead on the other side of the Desna, whose valley was approximately 500–1,000 metres in width. Amidst fierce fighting, it was possible to expand the bridgehead and cut through the double-track railway line that connected Kiev and Moscow. Konotop was taken not long afterwards, and the advance continued southwards towards the Sula. Our movements had slowed dramatically by then, for heavy rainfalls had caused the state of the narrow roads to deteriorate indescribably.

An advance detachment to be led by Major Frank was put together by the 3rd Panzer Division on 7 September for the purpose of driving to the south as quickly as possible. It took Romny on 11 September and Lokhvitsa on 13 September. The bridges in both cities fell into German hands. There now existed a gap of only 50 kilometres to the spearhead of Panzer Group 1, which was approaching from the south.

Nevertheless, some of the enemy forces succeeded in evading the German pincers as they fell back to the east. And whenever the enemy clashed with our troops, the situation was frequently critical due to the fact that our vehicles could barely manoeuvre on the still muddy roads. There was one occasion on which the II Battalion of the 6th Panzer Regiment had to rush back 20 kilometres to save the command post of the XXIV Panzer Corps from destruction. Elements of the Russian forces had broken through in the vicinity of the command post and were causing problems for the commander of the panzer corps and his staff.

In order to establish direct contact with the German forces approaching from the south, a reconnaissance patrol of tanks, personnel carriers, and anti-tank guns was assembled on 14 September under the command of Lieutenant Wartmann of the 6th Panzer Regiment. The charge carried out by the patrol very much resembled an old hussar attack. It left Lokhvitsa at about noon and was escorted for a short time by Stukas returning from a mission. Retreating enemy columns were encountered as soon as the patrol entered the first village. The enemy troops scattered in wild haste as our tanks charged towards them. They sought cover in woods, near houses, in gardens, and by the road. The Russian artillery, cavalry, truck, and fuel transportation columns were blown to pieces in one swift action so that the dash to the south could continue. There was no time to lose, although there was a temporary loss of radio communication when the patrol entered terrain filled with woods and ravines. The noise of battle could be heard in the distance. Before we knew it, the day had drawn to a close. A German reconnaissance aircraft flew overhead at that moment. It had been sent by the headquarters of Panzer Group 1 to ascertain the location of Wartmann's patrol. The patrol signalled its location with flares. The machine landed in a large empty field, and its pilot shook hands with the panzer troops. The aircraft took off again shortly afterwards and returned to the combat zone of Panzer Group 1, whose spearhead was fighting at that time in the vicinity of Lubny. The patrol pushed further in the direction of where the noise of battle emanated from. It came across another ravine, but soon met up with a pioneer company of Panzer Group 1 that was repairing a blown-up bridge. The pocket had thus been sealed. It was only symbolic at that stage, but it was not long before larger elements of both pincers linked up.

The reconnaissance patrol had conducted a 50-kilometre thrust and had, by 1820 hours on 14 September, sealed the pocket at a point approximately 200 kilometres to the east of Kiev. The great battle of annihilation could begin, and the XXIV Panzer Corps would play an important part in it.

The drive of the XXXXVIII Panzer Corps

The formation that closed the Kiev pocket from the south was the XXXXVIII Panzer Corps. It was given the order to break through the enemy defensive front on either side of the Kremenchug–Pirogi road and to advance past Khorol towards the area east of Lubny. After that, it was to seize the bridge in Lubny itself and set up an obstacle line along the Sula between Lubny and Lokhvitsa so as to prevent the withdrawal of enemy forces to the east.

It was clear, then, that the task of the panzer corps would be a decisive one. Its command post was located in Onufriyevka (south of Kremenchug) on the evening of 10 September, and it was shifted to Kremenchug on the afternoon of 11 September.

(a) The thrust of the 16th Panzer Division to the Sula (10–13 September 1941)

Thundery showers had turned the roads into mud. This delayed the assembly of the 16th Panzer Division, the unit that had been earmarked for the advance on Lubny. Many of the elements of the panzer division had nevertheless managed to reach the area to the south of Kremenchug by the evening of 10 September, and, on 11 September at 1300 hours, they started to roll forward over the recently completed military bridge. This bridge was narrow and became difficult to traverse after nightfall, but it was still possible, by the early hours of 12 September, for the forces of the panzer division to be concentrated in the bridgehead. Only the 64th Rifle Regiment trailed further behind and had yet to enter the bridgehead.

The panzer division started its attack at 0900 hours. It broke through the enemy positions, advanced rapidly to the north, and took Pogreby and Pirogi towards noon. Enemy resistance was light, albeit constant. The panzer division pushed further and reached Semenovka in the afternoon and Karpikha (south of Khorol) at nightfall. A distance of 70 kilometres had been covered on that first day, and the materiel captured was considerable. There were over 30 guns, approximately 100 trucks, and more than 400 horse-drawn vehicles. On top of that, the panzer division occupied an airfield with three undamaged Rata fighters.

In the early hours of 13 September, the panzer division resumed its advance, bypassing the strongly defended Khorol and reaching Lubny. After combat against anti-tank, anti-aircraft, and construction forces, the city was taken towards noon. Yet the fighting in the middle of the city continued into the evening. Even the civil population was involved in preparing barricades and in attacking our tanks with Molotov cocktails. In the meantime, the 64th Rifle Regiment had been following behind the rest of the panzer division, and it took Khorol at 1400 hours.

On 14 September, after clearing Lubny of enemy forces, the panzer division established a bridgehead over the Sula and extended it as far as the railway line. Several entrained Russian tanks opened fire, and the fight against them lasted the rest of the day. Further south, in the evening hours, the reconnaissance battalion of the panzer division took possession of the important crossing over the river near Lukomye.

The enemy had obviously recognised the danger in the meantime, as our aerial reconnaissance spotted long columns of his troops fleeing from Priluki to the east and south-east. He still had available to him a route of retreat that went through Lokhvitsa and Mirgorod (30 kilometres north-east of Khorol). It was necessary to capture Mirgorod so that the enemy would be denied this final route of retreat. This task was assigned to the 9th Panzer Division at 1700 hours on 13 September.

(b) The 9th Panzer Division closes the pocket to the south of Lokhvitsa (13–15 September 1941)

The advance of the 9th Panzer Division, which was supposed to have followed in the wake of the 16th Panzer Division, had been considerably delayed as a result of the unbelievably terrible state of the roads to the south of the Dnieper. There was also a severe shortage of fuel. The

9th Panzer Division had departed Aleksandriya on 12 September, but only a few weak elements had managed to enter the bridgehead by the morning of 13 September. Even so, the panzer regiment set off at 0700 hours. It drove through Globino and arrived at Semenovka towards noon. The remaining elements of the panzer division were still spread out along the road all the way back to Aleksandriya. On the night of 13/14 September, non-stop waves of enemy bombers targeted the military bridge in Kremenchug. Fortunately, they failed to score a direct hit. Two weak battle groups of the panzer division pushed towards Mirgorod and Romodanovka overnight, but they got stuck in marshy terrain. By 0500 hours on 14 September, all the combat elements of the panzer division had crossed the military bridge. A renewed advance that day managed to push through Romodanovka and led to the seizure of Mirgorod at noon. A battle group of the panzer division reached a position close to Snyatin in the evening, and, on the morning of 15 September, it engaged in heavy fighting and took the bridge in Sencha intact. A bridgehead over the Sula was established there shortly afterwards. Contact was established later that day with the 3rd Panzer Division, which had approached from the north and had taken Lokhvitsa.

In the space of two days, the 9th Panzer Division had covered 150 kilometres.

The largest encirclement of the war up to that point had been completed. The enemy had been cut off from his route of retreat to the east. It was now necessary that the westward-facing front be held against attempts by the enemy to break out and that it start to move forward so as to tighten the ring of encirclement.

Aftermath

The fighting was particularly fierce as the pocket was constricted and mopped up between 17 and 24 September. The numerous break-out attempts from the pocket and the similarly numerous relief attacks from the east all had to be repelled. But after that, the colossal battle of encirclement had come to an end, and the XXIV and XXXXVIII Panzer Corps would be required immediately for operations elsewhere.

CHAPTER 8

The XXIV Panzer Corps Drives Towards the Zusha and in the Direction of Tula

The operational situation

After the battle of Kiev, it was the task of Army Group Centre to resume the offensive in the direction of Moscow. Any enemy forces that stood in its way were to be eliminated. The Russian capital was the major objective of the campaign, and it was intended that it be captured before the end of the year. The fierce fighting in the battle of Kiev had delayed the advance on Moscow, and time was running out. The reassembly of the German forces would not be complete before the end of September, and the autumn mud season would set in as early as October. Although the enemy had been severely battered as a result of his heavy casualties over the course of the preceding few weeks, he had proven himself still capable of repeatedly conducting isolated and powerful attacks. Yet we had also suffered heavy losses, especially in materiel, and were lacking replacement parts for our tanks. It was possible for the number of operational tanks in the combat zone of Panzer Group 2 to be brought up to 400, but this figure represented only 40 per cent of the original strength of the formation. Furthermore, most of these tanks had covered up to 2,000 kilometres in predominantly unfriendly terrain and were in urgent need of new motors.

The new operational directive foresaw the immediate concentration of the main attack forces of Panzer Group 2 and the Second Army in the area to the west of the bend in the Oka near Kaluga. Depending on the development of the situation, the panzer group would either intervene in the fighting on the central sector of the army group or it would be placed on the right wing for an approach on Moscow from the south. The destruction of strong enemy forces standing to the south of Bryansk was regarded as a secondary task for the panzer group. This industrial area would only be occupied by the panzer group if it were easy enough to do so; otherwise, the area would only be enveloped to begin with. It was more important that the advance to the east be executed as quickly as possible, for it was bound to come to a halt once the roads became impassable.

The advance towards the Zusha

The panzer divisions were supplied with enough fuel, ammunition, and rations so that they would be able to reach their intermediate objective, the Orel–Bryansk road, without resupply. The point of main effort would lie in the sector of the XXIV Panzer Corps, led by General of Panzer Troops Freiherr Geyr von Schweppenburg. With the 3rd Panzer Division, the 4th Panzer Division, and the 10th Motorised Infantry Division under its command, the panzer corps managed to break through the weak enemy front and, in a period of two days, reach Dmitrovsk. The spearhead formation was the 4th Panzer Division. It had conducted a 130-kilometre thrust on 1 October and had entered the town before nightfall. As the other corps remained far behind, the XXIV Panzer Corps was given the order to carry out a task that had at first been envisioned for its southern neighbour, the XXXXVIII Panzer Corps. That task was the capture of Orel and the seizure of the crossings over the Oka. The 4th Panzer Division therefore lunged to the north-east and, on 3 October, took the bridges over the river intact. It then remained there for a short time while the other divisions caught up.

In the meantime, the XXXXVIII Panzer Corps suffered a severe setback when the enemy launched a surprise counter-attack against the eastern flank of the advancing German forces. Such was the loss in materiel that even one of the regiments of the 25th Motorised Infantry Division found itself in a position in which all its vehicles had been put out of action. Although the 9th Panzer Division had recently been pulled out of the combat zone of the panzer corps for employment elsewhere, it had to be sent back there so as to help regain control of the situation.

Our aerial reconnaissance on 3 October reported that Russian trains and motorised columns were heading westwards. The enemy had in his sights the breakthrough that had been achieved by the panzer group. The depth of penetration of the XXIV Panzer Corps was impressive, but it was narrow and vulnerable. Before any further advance could be contemplated, it was necessary that the German forces take possession of the Orel–Bryansk road and that the widely scattered elements of the panzer corps be concentrated once more.

Given the state of the weather and the nature of the terrain, the panzer group decided that the only possible route for approaching Moscow from the south would be along the paved Orel–Tula road. The headquarters of the XXIV Panzer Corps had come to the same conclusion. Nevertheless, an advance along this road would require sufficient flank and fighter protection as well as plenty of fuel.

The army group ordered that the panzer group initially gain control over the Orel–Bryansk road so that the supply route for the planned advance would be secure. After that, the crossing over the Zusha near Mtsensk (48 kilometres north-east of Orel) and, provided there were sufficient forces available, that over the Oka near Belyov (95 kilometres north of Orel) were to be taken as swiftly as possible so as to create the preconditions for further operations, be they towards Tula or along the Oka.

The 4th Panzer Division, reinforced with a panzer battalion of the 3rd Panzer Division, resumed the advance on 5 October. It smashed through a Russian air landing battalion that had parachuted into the area north-east of Orel and, on the next day, clashed with a large formation of T-34 tanks. The firepower of those enemy tanks was overwhelming. Only by fighting hard and by manoeuvring overnight was the panzer division able to bypass the enemy formation. The small town of Mtsensk was taken a short time later, but the panzer division did not manage to establish a bridgehead across the Zusha. The high ground on the other side of the river was stubbornly defended by the enemy. He had even dug tanks into the ground to serve as fixed fortifications. Wet weather prevented any attempt to envelop the enemy. Meanwhile, as far as the idea of a push towards Belyov was concerned, the panzer corps had no forces to spare.

To the rear right of the XXIV Panzer Corps was the XXXXVIII Panzer Corps, which, on 5 October, had managed to capture Rylsk. However, fuel shortages and muddy roads slowed the continued advance in the direction of Dmitriyev.

To the left of the XXIV Panzer Corps, an advance detachment of the XXXXVII Panzer Corps infiltrated Bryansk in a surprise attack on 6 October. The bridges over the Desna were seized intact. The XXXXVII Panzer Corps then pivoted to the west, towards the approaching Second Army, in order to close the ring of encirclement around the Russian 3rd and 50th Armies.

It was clear that the enemy had been completely taken by surprise by the rapid and deep thrust of the German panzer forces. He defended fiercely wherever possible, but he had barely anything with which to oppose the eastern flank of the panzer group. Only in the vicinity of Orel did the XXIV Panzer Corps encounter well-led enemy forces which, in our estimate, were composed of one cavalry division, one rifle division, and one or two tank brigades. Although the enemy had been compelled to relinquish control of Orel, he had been able to bring the advance of the XXIV Panzer Corps to a standstill when it reached the Zusha.

With the seizure of the Orel–Bryansk road, the first intermediary objective of Panzer Group 2, now renamed the Second Panzer Army, had been reached. Nevertheless, there remained strong pockets of enemy resistance that had to be wiped out.

The advance on Tula

The Fourth Army had in the meantime encircled a large group of Russian forces near Vyazma. On 7 October, the spearhead of the German offensive stood only 50 kilometres to the west of Kaluga, which itself lay 180 kilometres distant from Moscow. Despite the ever-worsening weather, the commander of Army Group Centre, Field-Marshal Fedor von Bock, planned to exploit the successes that had been achieved thus far by penetrating the final defensive line outside Moscow (Kashira–Serpukhov–Borodino) before the enemy forces had a chance to retreat to that line. Colonel-General Guderian had reservations about this plan. He was concerned about the deep flanks of the panzer army and the condition of the vehicles at its disposal. Even so, the panzer army was given the order to thrust towards Tula and seize the crossings over the Upa, thereby preparing for a further advance in the direction of Kolomna, Kashira, or Serpukhov.

The panzer army had thus been set an objective which lay quite some distance away. All three corps under its command would need to push forward alongside one another. Yet, at that moment, only the XXIV Panzer Corps was ready to proceed. The date on which this new thrust would commence was dependent not only on an improvement in the weather but also on the security of the supply lines. Unfortunately, the state of the weather, the condition of the roads, and the security of our supply were all looking bad. The original plan of awaiting the assembly of the other corps would have to be given up under such circumstances. The only remaining possibility was the execution of a narrow thrust by the XXIV Panzer Corps on its own towards Tula. From there, the panzer corps could try to spread out and establish a defensive line immediately to the south of Moscow. There would only be two infantry corps, recently subordinated to the panzer army, that would follow the panzer corps to the right and left.

In order to fully comprehend the difficulties of the subsequent drive that was carried out through mud and winter, it is first necessary to describe the nature of the terrain and the state of the units so far as this has not already been done by Guderian in *Erinnerungen eines Soldaten.*

The Zusha is an approximately 40-metre-wide and 2-metre-deep tributary of the Oka. The former flows into the latter at a point 50 kilometres to the north of Mtsensk. Fertile ground lies between and to the east of these two rivers, and it becomes terribly muddy when it rains. The terrain is much more open than that through which German forces had fought up to that moment. Very few of the woods in this terrain cover a large area. All the riverbanks are steep. Even in the middle of open terrain, there are deep and extensive ravines, the so-called balkas, which were an obstacle for tracked vehicles in any kind of weather. The only paved road at that time was the one that led from Orel to Tula via Mtsensk. Any of the other roads that were available could only be used by tracked vehicles, but their progress was slow. They had to help tow wheeled vehicles and were therefore overburdened. The best vehicles on such roads were the 18-tonne tractors, and they were invaluable in rescuing and bringing further forward the other countless vehicles that had become bogged down in the mud along the long road of advance. There was one panzer regiment whose 60 trucks and 15 tanks were scattered as far back as 200 kilometres. Each artillery piece had to be hauled by 10–24 horses, and the heavy artillery in particular lay a long way to the rear. German tactical superiority had been almost completely negated by the fact that our forces were now restricted to a small number of roads. Furthermore, the appearance of T-34s on the battlefield meant that it was now the enemy who possessed superior armour. We had barely any winter clothing. The only hope for the troops was for the war to come to an end that very year of 1941. The men therefore exerted the utmost effort.

On 10 October, the XXIV Panzer Corps was given the order to top up the fuel levels of its combat-capable mobile units and to launch them towards the objective that had been assigned. Elements of the 17th Panzer Division, 18th Panzer Division, and Infantry Regiment Großdeutschland, as well as the corps artillery of the XXXXVIII Panzer Corps, were to be allocated to the XXIV Panzer Corps for this thrust. Support from the Luftwaffe was also promised.

The first fuel supply columns arrived in Bryansk via Roslavl on 11 October. Everything now hanged on an improvement in the weather.

The battle of Bryansk drew to a close on 17 October. The enemy forces to the south of Sevsk were annihilated, as were those in the forest to the south of Bryansk. Only a few small elements of the Russian 3rd Army were able to escape. 108,000 enemy troops were taken prisoner, while 257 tanks and 763 guns were captured.

There was little joy in the combat zone of the XXXXVIII Panzer Corps. The 9th Panzer Division had advanced in the direction of Fatezh, but it had become hopelessly stuck in mud by 16 October. It was in urgent need of relief, so the 18th Panzer Division (of the XXXXVII Panzer Corps) was sent from Bryansk through Orel and Kromy to Fatezh, where it established contact with the 9th Panzer Division.

In preparation for its advance on Tula, the XXIV Panzer Corps moved the 3rd Panzer Division from the Orel–Mtsensk–Bolkhov area to the Zusha at a point a little to the north of Mtsensk. According to our aerial reconnaissance, fresh Russian forces were approaching the German front from the Tula area. The Fourth Army, which stood to the north of the Second Panzer Army, reported that enemy pressure was intensifying against its right wing. It was high time that the advance began. After multiple postponements, the date chosen for the commencement of Operation *Schlussjagd*, without any regard for the state of the weather, was 23 October.

For the first crossing of the Zusha, the point of main effort would lie in the sector of the 3rd Panzer Division. This sector was reinforced with tracked vehicles from the 18th Panzer Division and with artillery pieces from other units. According to the order for the attack, the 4th Panzer Division would maintain its position near Mtsensk while two groups of the 3rd Panzer Division, placed further to the north, would thrust over the Zusha and roll up the enemy line on the east bank towards the south-east, thereby taking control of the decisive Mtsensk–Tula road. The southern group of the 3rd Panzer Division would be a rifle assault formation; the northern, near Rozhenets and Kakurenkova, an armoured formation under the leadership of Colonel Heinrich Eberbach, the panzer brigade commander of the 4th Panzer Division.

What followed was a real mud battle. The tactical decisions of our commanders were more influenced by the mud than they were by the enemy. Difficulties arose very quickly. Although Group Eberbach managed to create two small bridgeheads, night-time bridge construction was delayed by several hours due to the wet soil of the riverbanks. This eventually led to the abandonment of any attempt to build bridges. Only an emergency bridge would be used. Unfortunately, a tank-drawn 8.8-centimetre anti-aircraft gun slipped down the steep bank after crossing the emergency bridge, causing chaos and further delay. It took so long for the remaining tanks of Group Eberbach to cross the river that the I Battalion of the 6th Panzer Regiment, which had originally been foreseen as a second wave that would expand the bridgehead, had to be given a different task. The battalion would instead follow the rifle assault group over the river. It would have to do so quickly so that it could be of use to the rifle assault group before nightfall. Only on the morning of the second day, when all the tanks had made it to the opposite bank, could an attack be launched from the expanded bridgehead. The II and

III Battalions of the 6th Panzer Regiment, each with approximately 20–25 vehicles and reinforced with armoured personnel carriers and 8.8-centimetre guns, initially set off for the east so as to eliminate the danger to the flank of the rifle assault group. Meanwhile, a weak rifle battalion took over responsibility for the protection of the northern flank of the bridgehead.

The II Battalion of the 6th Panzer Regiment, which was the spearhead unit of Group Eberbach, soon got caught in a minefield. Fortunately, so ineffective were the mines in the muddy ground that only two of our tanks were damaged. Although the battalion clashed with a numerically superior group of enemy tanks, it emerged victorious and achieved its first objective thanks to the temporary improvement in weather conditions and the support of German dive bombers. Only in first or second gear could our tanks advance through the mud, but it meant that the consumption of fuel was considerable. Refuelling would be necessary before the attack could continue. This was managed shortly before nightfall, for the 18th Panzer Regiment had arrived with additional supplies of fuel. Yet neither Group Eberbach nor the rifle assault group had achieved the objective of gaining control of the Mtsensk–Tula road. Colonel Eberbach therefore decided to conduct a deep thrust during the night along a forest path with the idea of reaching the road at a point further to the north-east.

The III Battalion of the 6th Panzer Regiment rolled forward at 1800 hours together with the brigade and regimental command echelons. After a slow drive through the pitch-black night, the battalion encountered a group of enemy tanks shortly before arriving at the road. It was later ascertained that our forces had come across a tank maintenance unit. Several Russian tanks were destroyed in the fire fight that broke out, although many disappeared in the darkness. It was now possible for the road to be occupied, thereby cutting through the supply line and retreat route of the enemy forces that stood immediately to the east of Mtsensk. Seventeen T-34s were later captured without a fight by the rifle assault group in the forest to the north of the road. These Russian tanks had run out of fuel and ammunition and had therefore been abandoned by their crews. The rifle assault group soon reached the road behind the enemy defensive line on the east bank of the Zusha, thereby facilitating the advance of the reinforced 4th Panzer Division over the river.

After this decisive success, the XXIV Panzer Corps continued its drive along the Mtsensk–Tula road through Chern and Plavsk. The road had been so damaged by mines and tracked vehicles that only the armoured elements of the panzer corps, supplied from the air, could advance to begin with. As early as 29 October, the spearhead of the reinforced 3rd Panzer Division stood before the gates of Tula, 150 kilometres to the north-east of Mtsensk. An immediate thrust into the large city was impossible. It was strongly defended with anti-tank and anti-aircraft guns, and we were in any case lacking in forces and fuel. Subsequent attempts to enter the city also failed, for the enemy continued to send reinforcements there. With that, the assault on Moscow had practically come to a halt.

Aftermath

Winter had set in. Our forces struggled over the course of the next few weeks to take Tula, albeit in vain. Although extra ground was gained by bypassing the city to the north-east, the desired objective could no longer be achieved, especially as new Russian units arrived from Siberia and threatened the south-eastern and eastern flanks of the weak German formations. We were finally compelled to withdraw the entire front to a not yet fully prepared winter defensive position.

The major thrust towards Moscow failed due to our overestimation of the capabilities of our forces and our underestimation of the difficulties associated with the climate and the terrain. The campaign in the East had reached its climax.

CHAPTER 9

The First Panzer Army Advances into the Caucasus

The operational situation

The severe setback in the winter of 1941–42 before Moscow induced the leadership of the German Army to focus its subsequent efforts on the southern sector of the Eastern Front. Despite our negative experiences in 1941, Hitler's goals remained utopian and politically motivated. In the sector of Army Group North, an offensive was to be conducted through Leningrad so as to establish contact with the Finns. In the sectors of Army Groups South and Centre, a thrust would be executed as far as the Volga in the vicinity of Stalingrad. However, it was first necessary to create the preconditions for such a thrust. In three successful battles to the south and east of Kharkov, the German front was pushed forward beyond the bend in the Donets to a position along the Oskol. After that, the First and Fourth Panzer Armies set off on their drive in the direction of Stalingrad. But then there was a sudden change in plan. Two simultaneous objectives on the southern sector of the Eastern Front were now set: Stalingrad and the Caucasus. This was a fatal decision that violated the fundamental principle of carrying out one task before moving on to the next. Moreover, these objectives lay on different axes of advance. The German forces would be drawn ever further away from one another the deeper into enemy territory they pushed. The operation in the direction of the Caucasus could only succeed if the northern flank could be covered satisfactorily. Not only would our forces need to reach the Volga; they would also need to eliminate any danger that might arise to their rear in the vicinity of the lower Don.

Army Group A was formed for the advance into the Caucasus. Its first task would be the encirclement and annihilation of the enemy forces in and to the south of Rostov. Only after that could the thrust towards Maykop and Armavir be ventured. Nevertheless, further objectives were already set at that early stage: light infantry and mountain divisions were to advance to the western part of the Caucasus, mobile forces were to seize the Grozny area at the same time, and additional forces were to take possession of the Baku oil region along the Caspian Sea whilst also interdicting the Ossetian and Georgian Military Roads.[10] These were extremely ambitious objectives!

The army group focused on the preliminary operation to begin with, i.e. in the direction of Rostov. It would be necessary to carry out a rapid thrust and to keep the enemy on the back foot. The attacks conducted by two of the corps of the First Panzer Army into the Caucasus in the summer of 1942 will be described here.

The drive of the III Panzer Corps towards Maykop

Between 17 and 26 June 1942, the III Panzer Corps had partaken in the fighting in the vicinity of Izyum and Kupyansk and had soon occupied a position along the Oskol. Elements of the panzer corps pushed further and entered Rostov, where the fighting continued until 24 July. It would thereafter be the task of the panzer corps to stay hard on the heels of the enemy forces retreating to the south and to reach the bend in the Kuban as quickly as possible. Before that, though, it was necessary that all the forces of the army group reach the lower Don, with the First Panzer Army on the central sector, the Fourth Panzer Army on the northern, and the Seventeenth Army on the southern.

In the meantime, on 26 July, the III Panzer Corps was shifted from the battlefield near Rostov and Novocherkassk to a position further to the north-east, where it took over responsibility for the command of the 16th Motorised Infantry Division and Infantry Division Großdeutschland. Although the 14th Panzer Division initially accompanied the III Panzer Corps to the area near Shakhty, it was detached from the panzer corps

---

[10] Translator's note: Both military roads were major routes through the Caucasus.

as early as 27 July so that it could be committed to the advance on Stalingrad. This panzer division would later be destroyed in the tragic battle that took place there.

By crossing the Don, the First Panzer Army finally retook the ground that had been lost in the heavy defensive fighting of the winter of 1941–42. The countryside looked quite different in the summer. The Russian steppes were vast and seemed to extend endlessly to the south.

Both motorised divisions of the panzer corps swiftly established a large bridgehead over the Don to the south of Razdorskaya and a smaller one over the same river to the south of Melikhovskaya. A 24-tonne bridge was soon built near Razdorskaya. On 26 July, while Infantry Division Großdeutschland covered the flanks along the Podpolnaya and the Sal, the 16th Motorised Infantry Division overcame stubborn enemy resistance near Solenyy and created a bridgehead over the Manych near Svoboda.

On 27 July, the north bank of the Manych was cleared of Russian forces, after which another bridgehead was created to the south of Novoselovka. Unfortunately, the enemy had sufficient time to blow up the dam immediately to the south of Spornyy. The consequences of the ensuing flood were severe. The otherwise only 40-metre-wide and slow-flowing river downstream from the dam rapidly widened to approximately 3 kilometres. Any idea of building a military bridge there had to be abandoned. On 28 July and on the days that followed, our heavy infantry weaponry and artillery pieces were ferried across the river near Svoboda and Novoselovka. It was a laborious process, with each ferry trip lasting several hours. Although there was success in expanding the bridgehead, our weak attack forces were unable to dislodge the determined enemy from his field fortifications.

The pioneer troops worked admirably, and, by 30 July, an emergency bridge over the 100-metre-wide dam breach had been completed. This enabled German forces to cross the river on the night of 30/31 July and, immediately after that, to continue with the advance.

On 31 July, the 16th Motorised Infantry Division leapt forward a considerable distance despite the fierce resistance of the enemy. Infantry Division Großdeutschland helped to expand the bridgehead, but it was soon detached from the panzer corps for employment elsewhere. Because of this, the 13th Panzer Division was once more placed under the command of the panzer corps early on 1 August. The panzer division had already advanced from Rostov, overcome enemy resistance, reached the town of Salsk, and established a bridgehead over the Sandata near Nikolayevka. The 16th Motorised Infantry Division arrived in the area on 1 August and established its own bridgehead over the Rassypnaya.

There was some skirmishing with enemy stragglers on 2 August, but, in general, the advance continued non-stop, with the spearhead of the 13th Panzer Division covering 100 kilometres and reaching the Kropotkin–Voroshilovsk railway line immediately to the east of Novo Alexandrovka.

The enemy fled towards Armavir, which lay on the Kuban, and our forces set off in pursuit on 3 August. In one swift motion, the spearhead of the panzer division pierced a defensive front that had been hastily set up by the enemy that morning between the Kuban and the Yegorlyk, and then rushed towards the road bridge to the north of Armavir. The first few German tanks had already driven over the bridge when the enemy detonated it.

Only gradually could the tiny bridgehead be expanded on 4 August. The fighting was hard and our casualties heavy due to the strength of the enemy's defensive forces along the riverbank. Despite the forceful current and our shortage of equipment, we commenced work on a new bridge. It was completed by the early hours of 5 August, and the 13th Panzer Division rolled forward across it without delay. The enemy's defences, which included a number of anti-tank ditches, were quickly overcome. While the 16th Motorised Infantry Division assumed responsibility for the security of the bridgehead, the 13th Panzer Division drove on ahead and, by the end of the day, it had managed to cover a distance of 15 kilometres.

On 6 August, the panzer division crossed the raging torrent that was the Laba River near Kurgannaya. The motorised infantry division had also reached the river and stood near Labinskaya, but the bridges there had been blown up by the enemy. There was no choice but to stop for the time being.

The terrain was challenging in the combat zone of the panzer division. Its troops built bridges and corduroy roads over the multiple arms of the

Laba and ensured that the fords were safe to cross.[11] The panzer division pushed further, its reconnaissance units leading the way. Progress was so slow that, by the evening of 8 August, the bulk of the panzer division had only managed to reach a position to the west of Dondukovskaya. The reconnaissance units had pressed a little further and were standing just outside Maykop.

The 16th Motorised Infantry Division discovered an intact railway bridge near Zassovskaya, which lay to the south of the route of advance that had originally been planned. It was decided that the vehicles of the motorised infantry division would be sent over this bridge at once, and the result was that they successfully reached the area to the east of Kostromskaya before nightfall on 8 August.

On the evening of 9 August, the 13th Panzer Division stormed Maykop, the administrative centre of the surrounding oil-producing region. This meant that the first intermediary operational objective had been reached. Fifty Russian aircraft were captured in perfect condition, but, unfortunately, all the oil installations had been destroyed. A particularly daring raid by a unit of Regiment Brandenburg secured the road bridge, made of iron, that led over the Belaya shortly before the enemy had a chance to blow it up. A bridgehead was quickly established on the opposite bank of the river, although the fighting in the streets of Maykop continued into the night. Even the rear elements of both the 13th Panzer Division and the 16th Motorised Infantry Division fought hard and suffered heavy losses as they prevented the attempts by the enemy to break through to the south and south-east.

On 10 August, elements of the 13th Panzer Division expanded the Maykop bridgehead while the remaining units, together with a battle group of the 16th Motorised Infantry Division from Zassovskaya, advanced deeper into the Caucasus and reached Abadzekhskaya in the evening.

In the course of the subsequent fighting, the panzer corps succeeded in gaining more ground in the western part of the Caucasus. On the

---

[11] Translator's note: Corduroy roads were made of tree trunks and laid across swampy or muddy areas.

whole, though, it had already achieved what was required of it and was soon relieved by mountain infantry troops, who were better suited for the terrain which lay ahead. The panzer corps pivoted to the east on 15 August so that it could be employed on the northern side of the mountain range in terrain that could be traversed by mobile units.

Seven hundred kilometres had been covered in 16 days. Casualties were relatively few: 350 killed in action (including 20 officers), 24 missing, and 1,327 wounded (including 57 officers).

The drive of the XXXX Panzer Corps towards the Terek

The Fourth Panzer Army had initially set off on the northern side of and in the same direction as the First Panzer Army, but as the routes of advance of the two formations gradually diverged, it was decided that the XXXX Panzer Corps would be transferred from the former to the latter. Under the command of the panzer corps were the 3rd and 23rd Panzer Divisions, and its first task would be to cover the eastern flank of the First Panzer Army. This was because the gap between the two panzer armies was becoming ever greater and therefore increasingly vulnerable.

The XXXX Panzer Corps was placed to the north of the III Panzer Corps, and both advanced through the steppes of southern Russia. The 3rd Panzer Division charged forward rapidly and established a bridgehead over the Don in the vicinity of Nikolayevskaya on 23 July. Reconnaissance troops of the panzer division felt their way forward to the Sal. The rest of the panzer division followed quickly, and it succeeded in crossing the Manych in a bold strike. Whilst a panzer battalion thwarted an enemy attack from the north-west, a panzer grenadier battalion crossed the river in assault boats after one hour of artillery preparation. The panzer division subsequently made further progress, with Battle Group von Liebenstein reaching Iku Tuktum on the morning of 2 August and Battle Group Pape establishing a bridgehead over the Yegorlyk near Pregradnoye at roughly the same time.

At 1345 hours on 3 August, the 3rd Panzer Division launched an attack towards Voroshilovsk. By 1600 hours, the city was in German hands.

Nevinnomysskaya, with its railway station and stretch of Baku–Rostov oil pipeline, was taken on 5 August. The XXXX Panzer Corps soon created a bridgehead over the Kuma and approached the Caucasian mountain range. In the blazing sun, temperatures reached 55 degrees Celsius, and the dust that was kicked up by our vehicles was almost unbearable. Neither trees nor shrubs were to be seen anywhere. But it was not long before the appearance of the landscape changed. Battle Group Westhoven reached the beautiful spa town of Pyatigorsk and fought hard against Red officer candidates, NKVD troops, and a women's battalion for the bridge over the Podkumok and for the southern part of the town. On that day, Mount Elbrus, the highest peak in the Caucasus (5,629 metres), was sighted for the first time. In the meantime, the 23rd Panzer Division had taken possession of Mineralnye Vody.

Due to a shortage of fuel, the panzer corps was compelled to remain stationary for several days. Once a few elements of the formation were topped up with fuel, they continued the advance and reached the town of Baksan and the river of the same name a short time afterwards. Remaining in the favourable terrain to the north of the Terek, the XXXX Panzer Corps launched an attack towards Mozdok in conjunction with the LII Army Corps, which had been diverted from its area of operations in the steppes of Kalmykia. The plan was to capture the bridges over the Terek in the vicinity of Mozdok so that the XXXX Panzer Corps could reach towards and facilitate the advance of the III Panzer Corps, which was at that moment struggling forward along the south bank of the Terek. Two battle groups of the 3rd Panzer Division attacked Mozdok on 2 September, putting the skilfully installed Russian anti-tank artillery out of action and infiltrating the town. However, the enemy defensive fire proved to be so powerful that our rifle troops were unable to follow our tanks into the centre of the town. Without adequate support, the German tanks had to disengage. The attack was renewed the next day. It was possible for the northern part of the town to be cleared of enemy forces, but our troops did not manage to capture any bridges. It was because of this that the advance of the XXXX Panzer Corps came to a premature end. In just under six weeks, more than 1,000 kilometres had been covered.

The reverse thrust of the First Panzer Army

By executing a multitude of vigorous thrusts, the First Panzer Army had advanced deep into enemy territory. However, it had now become difficult to make progress. The panzer army, still striving to reach its final objective, had to struggle hard for every single kilometre of ground.

The mountain troops fought against snow and ice in the high mountains of the Caucasus.[12] The point of main effort of the fighting in the combat zone of the panzer army lay in the foothills to the south of the Terek. The III Panzer Corps managed to take Nalchik and was able to approach Grozny, but its striking power was by that time diminishing dramatically. The situation was similar on the north bank of the river, on the southern boundary of the desert-like steppes of Kalmykia. Elements of the 3rd, 13th, and 23rd Panzer Divisions were initially successful in pushing forward, but enemy resistance became so strong that the entire reinforced 3rd Panzer Division eventually had to adopt a mobile defensive position near and to the north of Ishcherskaya. There remained a large gap between the First Panzer Army in the Caucasus and the Sixth Army in Stalingrad. The struggle in Stalingrad was becoming increasingly desperate, so it was there that most supplies were sent. Nevertheless, it was by then apparent that neither Stalingrad nor the Caucasus would be secured. The German forces were lacking in sufficient strength.

Given the hopelessness of the situation, the headquarters of the First Panzer Army repeatedly requested that it be allowed to conduct a gradual withdrawal. Permission was granted at the latest possible moment. From January 1943, the panzer army would fight its way back along the very route it had used for rushing forward. It was engaged in constant combat as it retreated through snow and ice. This was especially the case for the rearguard and security forces that covered the deep eastern flank of the panzer army. Eventually, having lost only about 700 men, the entire panzer army had withdrawn behind the Donets. This reverse thrust helped to stabilise the situation on the southern sector of the Eastern Front, for there had existed the very real danger of a complete collapse after the destruction of the Sixth Army at Stalingrad. Even so, a shortage

---

[12] See Adolf von Ernsthausen, *Wende im Kaukasus: Ein Bericht der 97. Jägerdivision* (Heidelberg: Vowinckel, 1958).

of fuel had made it necessary for the panzer army to abandon and blow up several of its tanks and almost all its heavy artillery pieces. Much valuable equipment had to be ditched and burned so that the vehicles of the panzer army would have enough room to transport the infantry, who otherwise would have been overtaken by the enemy counter-offensive.

Valuable lessons were learnt during the campaign in the Caucasus. A rapid advance can take its toll on the vehicles of the advancing force. Many of those vehicles must be left behind if they are somehow damaged or suffer technical issues. Not only does this reduce the striking power of the leading formations; it also slows down the rear formations in situations where there is just one road of advance, for it is that one road that becomes cluttered with broken-down vehicles. What is worse, the route of retreat becomes blocked, which means that any withdrawal must be conducted gradually. Fortunately, the enemy did not fully recognise and exploit this situation during our withdrawal from the Caucasus. He probably also suffered from a shortage of fuel. It was thus the lack of initiative of the enemy combined with the discipline of the German troops that enabled the First Panzer Army and the other elements of Army Group A to carry out a successful withdrawal.

CHAPTER 10

Experiences with Panzer Attacks

An evaluation of combat reports and of our own experiences always entails the risk of drawing conclusions that are general, biased, or possibly even irrelevant. The reason for any success or setback is usually to be found in the specific conditions that prevailed at the time. The nature of combat constantly changed throughout the course of the war. There were always new insights to be gained. Many of our technical and tactical developments, though good in themselves, had to be abandoned or modified quickly.

It can therefore be said that while it is easy, in the study of past warfare, to identify what went wrong or what did not work, it is far more difficult to ascertain what is useful or valid for the future. Nevertheless, it is perhaps possible to draw a few tentative conclusions.

'Panzer tactics' arose out of our efforts to fully exploit the power of the motor so that the enemy would not have time to take counter-measures or to reorganise his forces. In the orders issued by the German military leadership, motorised units were always committed in the direction of the main operational or tactical objectives. This approach put into practice the idea of Field-Marshal Alfred von Schlieffen that mobility leads to victory. It was employed to great effect during the campaigns in Poland and France. Right up until the moment the enemy leadership had been eliminated, the German troops conducted a form of warfare that was relentless, mobile, and sharply focused on the point of main effort. Although the strong advance of the panzer wedge might have occasionally been held up by enemy resistance, the flexibility of our military leadership ensured that our forces could get going again. As Clausewitz wrote: 'So in war, through the influence of an infinity of petty circumstances, which cannot properly be described on paper, things disappoint us, and we fall short of the mark. A powerful iron will overcomes this friction, it crushes the obstacles, but certainly the machine along with them.'[13] A particularly topical principle in the age of the atom!

Despite our significant victories on the Western Front in 1940 and on the Eastern Front in 1941 and 1942, not even we could avoid being crushed in the end. The obstacles were too great and the objectives too distant. No longer was our sword sharp. No longer could we fulfil so many tasks on so many fronts.

Armoured warfare can be compared with cruiser warfare. Panzer units, like naval units, require secure and well-equipped strongpoints where they can be serviced and resupplied before being able to continue fighting. The enemy should be struck repeatedly so that he is denied the ability to act and deprived of any feeling of superiority. The weak points of his front should be identified and hit hard. Even if the strength of our forces is inferior to that of the enemy, the maintenance of mobility requires that we always attack. By concentrating our forces, it is possible to punch through the enemy front at the most decisive location. If this is not possible, then he should at least be held in check and caused a lot of damage with one panzer strike after another, rather in the manner of the tactics employed in the old cavalry raids. The result is that the strength of the enemy gradually ebbs away, and then a moment arrives when he can be annihilated completely.

The most crucial factor in the conduct of armoured warfare by a nation is the character of its people. The psychological state of a nation at war and the courage and intelligence of its soldiers play an important role in how operations unfold. During the campaign on the Eastern Front, our soldiers encountered a formidable enemy. The Russian soldier was quite different to the German, but he possessed the same will for victory. Both sides achieved incredible feats, albeit at different times and in different ways.

---

[13] Translator's note: this is from Book 1, Chapter 7, of *On War* by Carl von Clausewitz, and I have referred to the 1873 translation by J. J. Graham.

In preparing an attack, the strength of the forces to be employed must correspond to what is needed for the task to be carried out successfully. It is necessary to consider how far away an objective lies and how difficult it might be to reach. The enthusiastic desire of the German troops to press forward, which arose not from a thirst for glory but rather from their awareness of military necessities, brought about a multitude of surprisingly major tactical victories, but the problem was that our operational objectives frequently exceeded what could realistically be achieved. This was a result of the underestimation of the enemy by the supreme command. Consequently, it was often the case that our initial successes were not properly exploited. We also suffered from a shortage of much of what was required for the attainment of our operational objectives, including off-road vehicles and opportunities for supply and repair.

The components of a formation committed to an independent, mobile operation must be assembled correctly and capable of working effectively with one another. Inadequate cooperation, poor communications, and unknown weaknesses of newly allocated units cannot be permitted to add to the difficulties caused by the enemy and the terrain.

As the war progressed, it was often necessary to hastily reorganise or establish units from the remnants of other divisions. Such improvisation, though not ideal, could not be avoided. Our troops were few and the distances vast, so we had to make use of whatever was available. However, these reorganised units usually suffered from poor mobility, technical difficulties, and high casualties. Mobility and rapidity are just as important as firepower, as the last of these can only be fully effective if the units can arrive where they are needed quickly. The components of each German unit in the first few years of the war worked together effectively, rather like a good football team, and were able to cope with all kinds of situations. It was with this in mind that battle groups were always formed. These were unit elements of divisions that could fight independently, often for weeks on end. They were well-supplied and usually given free rein by the divisions. The strikes carried out by these mixed units were often astonishingly successful and can be compared with the hussar attacks of the past.

Ground and air defence have improved dramatically since the end of the war. Strikes by self-sufficient battle groups are less likely to succeed and might only still be possible under certain conditions, e.g. at night, in mist, during bad weather, or against an opponent with inferior weaponry. The penetration of the front would require the concentrated effort of multiple battle groups supported by the air force not only during the assembly phase but also during the attack. These battle groups would need to be well-equipped so that they can cope with the vicissitudes of combat and overcome any difficulties presented by the terrain.

While military principles and good training are of great importance, the personality of the commander can decisively determine the outcome of an attack. The field commander must possess the instinct of the hunter and the ability to comprehend the situation. He must be steadfast and decisive. He must be able to muster all his courage as well as remain calm at critical moments. These are qualities that were able to be maximised during the war thanks to the use of the radio. Our battle group commanders acted in accordance with the maxim of the III Panzer Corps in 1941: 'Think ahead, look ahead, storm ahead!' There were many lower-ranking officers who achieved tremendous results during the war despite the fact that they had never issued a written order prior to the war. As emphasised by Manstein, it is not satisfactory to find solutions that are merely safe and by the book. It is certainly difficult to recognise such qualities in officers during times of peace, as only in an emergency do the most outstanding commanders come to the fore. For this reason, the requirements for promotion were quickly changed during the war. Lower-ranking officers could be swiftly promoted after they had gained experience at the front. Many of them made it to the rank of general.

If an attack was executed correctly, the firefight would mainly be the responsibility of the leading elements of a formation, perhaps even just the reinforced company at the spearhead. The weapons employed at the spearhead needed not only to be powerful but also easily placed in firing position. These weapons were as a general rule the cannons mounted on our tanks, yet they required the help and protection of the other types of weaponry in order to be fully effective. A partnership thus arose in which no arm of the German ground forces felt at a disadvantage and in which each was aware of its special role as a part of the whole. If a unit encountered enemy resistance which could not be bypassed, its thrust would have to be paused briefly so that its forces could be organised to deal the enemy a hard blow. If this was not possible, then the unit would ideally be repositioned to exploit the success of another unit.

In the conduct of offensive operations during the war, it was usually the case that we advanced for roughly three-quarters of the time and fought for the remaining quarter. The most significant challenge was overcoming the many sectors through which marshy streams or rivers flowed. This was an advantage for the Russian. His love of nature meant that all his soldiers could be effective as pioneer troops. The German soldier, on the other hand, could only learn gradually how to navigate the terrain. Any unit assigned the task of carrying out an attack needed to have pioneer troops at its disposal. We found that special detachments of pioneers were necessary for conducting reconnaissance, clearing routes of advance, and controlling and rerouting traffic.

The nature of the terrain greatly influences the planning and execution of an advance. Distant objectives can never be reached in a straight line, as there will always be natural obstacles that lie in the way. Detours are often better and can lead to the objective more quickly. Just as a water channel meanders and takes the path of least resistance, a battle group must manoeuvre with agility if an insurmountable obstacle lies before it. The focus must always remain on reaching the objective as quickly as possible. If a formation, even partially, is confined to the roads, the possibilities for manoeuvre become limited. This can lead to defeat on the battlefield. It is therefore particularly important that the combat and supply units of a formation possess the ability to operate on and off roads. A small, completely off-road unit is always preferable to a large group with different types of vehicles which, due to varying levels of performance, might interfere with one another. During the campaign in the East, the most favourable terrain for carrying out an advance was the steppes between the Don and the Caucasus, especially because there was barely any Russian aerial activity. Although overgrown or populated areas offer good opportunities for cover and manoeuvre, they require that thorough reconnaissance be conducted, that reinforcements in the form of mechanised infantry be allocated, and that high-angle weaponry be committed if any significant advantage is to be gained. It became apparent during the war that splitting up battle groups and sending elements along secondary roads was not a good idea, especially if those secondary roads led through unfriendly terrain. A battle group must maintain cohesion and should advance on a narrow rather than wide front, no matter how inviting the terrain might appear to be.

A considerable challenge is the need to supply the combat troops without sacrificing mobility. Tanks, more than any other vehicle, are dependent on the supply of large quantities of fuel and replacement parts. The more ground that is gained in an advance, the more difficult is the supply of sufficient fuel. The greater the distance becomes between a rapidly advancing unit and the rest of the front, the greater the danger becomes for the supply. The supply units must be protected whenever possible, but they must also be capable of defending themselves. It was discovered during the war that it was best, when faced with a threatening enemy or with difficult terrain, for supply elements to accompany advancing units and even individual companies. Only through the flexible and concentrated incorporation of supply elements into the battle groups could the many challenges be overcome. Aerial supply became important during the war, and it will continue to increase in importance in the future. It is a question of further technological developments whether helicopters, rockets, or something else will become the means by which supplies are transported.

The offensive in the East placed great demands on the supply of fuel. Even if the terrain was reasonably good, our vehicles still consumed fuel quickly if sudden rainfalls turned the roads into mud or if detours were necessary as a result of bridges being blown up or being inadequate in terms of load-bearing capacity. It was always a mistake to pursue the enemy with the last drop of fuel, for it entailed the risk of becoming immobile in what could be a vulnerable position. The enemy in the East enjoyed considerable advantages in this regard, for those of his tanks that were powered by diesel motors could operate at far greater range than our vehicles. A satisfactory solution to this problem might perhaps one day be provided by the nuclear motor.

While the question of ammunition became ever more critical the longer the fighting lasted, the supply of rations was less so, as it was easy to compensate for any shortage of food.[14]

The weather significantly influenced the way in which operations unfolded in the East. In any example of combat on the Eastern Front that might be examined, the weather always plays a role. General of Panzer Troops Werner Kempf wrote down his assessment in this regard:

> The attempt to achieve our final objective before the end of 1941 led to the most severe mistake that can be made with motorised units. Every vehicle – whether motorcycle, car, or tracked vehicle – pursued the enemy so far through muddy roads until the point where they could advance no further. The elements of entire divisions became scattered and immobile. Even our platoon commanders did not always know where all their vehicles were, as they were often separated by several kilometres. Machines, gearboxes, and suspensions were seriously damaged or even destroyed by the senseless slog through mud. Mice even gnawed through the wiring in tanks that were stuck in mud for days and weeks. Such damage could not always be found right away and was in any case not easy to repair on the spot. The soldiers often abandoned their vehicles, usually because they felt as if they had fallen behind and needed to catch up to their comrades. The transmission of orders from the headquarters of a division to all its elements was similarly difficult and could sometimes take a few days. The damage to and loss of so many vehicles could never be remedied, as we were lacking in sufficient replacement parts and maintenance units. In situations like this, it was completely pointless for the divisions to keep driving ahead. The challenges to be overcome had become too great. We ought to have recognised this and come to a halt. We would have then been able to concentrate our forces once more. The troops would have had a chance to catch their breath, and our vehicles could have been serviced and repaired. Our units would have thereby been fully recovered and ready for action. But instead, they remained in a ruined state.

There were similar experiences when offensive operations were carried out in winter. Frost and snow forced us to change our tactics. Vehicles and weapons needed to be serviced more regularly. Only small units with great firepower and off-road capability could maintain mobility.

---

14 Translator's note: Munzel does not go into detail on how it was possible to compensate for a shortage of food. German policy in the East was to feed its soldiers and civilians by starving the Russian population. It was envisioned that this Hunger Plan would result in the deaths of tens of millions of people. See Timothy Snyder, *Bloodlands: Europe between Hitler and Stalin* (London: Vintage, 2011), 162–63.

While battle groups require weaponry of all sorts to be able to fight independently, the vehicles at their disposal, if possible, ought to be of the same type. The chaotic variety of vehicle types during the war made the conduct of operations extraordinarily difficult. Wheeled vehicles could not travel off-road with tracked vehicles, yet the latter could not keep pace with the former on good roads. Although often unavoidable in those days, the mixture of armoured and unarmoured tracked and wheeled vehicles caused considerable difficulties. It is astonishing to realise that the daily distances covered by our panzer thrusts rarely exceeded 150 kilometres. This was a result of the time consumed in maintaining and repairing vehicles, the difficulties in supplying sufficient fuel, the increasing defensive strength of the enemy, and the weather and road conditions in the East.

The regimental headquarters of our formations were generally unable to cope with the demands of leading such composite units. They very much needed to have their own means of conducting reconnaissance and of communicating with superior and subordinate headquarters. Although variety in terms of weaponry was good, the way in which the units were put together depended too much on what was available rather than on what would have been ideal. We needed mechanised infantry for the support of our tanks, but we generally had a shortage of such troops. In order to provide effective close support, mechanised infantry, as well as other units, had to be adequately equipped with anti-tank weapons and armoured vehicles. Nevertheless, it must be emphasised that any unit ought to be capable of defending itself, at least initially, against a surprise armoured attack, as it is of no use if that unit is destroyed before the arrival of friendly tanks. While the entire operation in 1941 might at a glance be regarded as a success, our forces were so weakened that they would never be able to recover. Our panzer formations became ever more fragmentary in their composition towards the end of the war. In emergency situations, of which there were many, the troops did not pay any attention to principles regarding the correct assembly and commitment of forces. They had to make use of what was available. Even our senior military commanders fell prey to the survival instinct, living a hand-to-mouth existence.

Reconnaissance and security are particularly important in offensive operations. Aerial reports and any other sources of information form the basis for decisions on the way in which forces are employed. For a battle group to remain in the picture during an advance, not only must it listen in on radio traffic; it must also maintain direct contact with reconnaissance aircraft via forward air control units. After all, it must be borne in mind that both friendly and enemy troops are always on the move during combat and that the situation therefore changes constantly. Nevertheless, it would be wrong to await reconnaissance reports for too long. Only direct contact with and combat against the enemy can truly clarify the situation. As stated by Guderian, a panzer commander must 'have the courage to fight in the unknown'. The military commander, provided the unit under his command is strong and mobile, ought to be capable of mastering even the most challenging situations by being organised and flexible in the commitment of his forces.

Reconnaissance troops should be a part of any attack. Like hornets, they must swarm around and protect an independent combat unit. Just as we were short of mechanised infantry during the war, we were also lacking in reconnaissance troops. Even if reconnaissance units make constant contact with the enemy and are thereby unable to push ahead, they are still of great value for covering gaps in the front or for securing open flanks and rest areas. Indeed, the best form of security can be provided by a good reconnaissance unit whose strength and means are based on the task to be carried out. Even so, it is by no means beyond the realms of possibility for a reconnaissance unit to be pushed back by a stronger enemy force. This unit must therefore keep moving or at least change position frequently. It is best if it can do so to the rear of the enemy force, as this disrupts the attempts by the enemy to send reinforcements to the front. The point here, as emphasised by Manstein, is to maintain mobility: 'If the battle group comes to a halt, it will soon be attacked by enemy reserves from all sides.'

In conclusion, it can be said that the following preconditions are of the utmost importance for the preparation and conduct of panzer attacks:

(a) Appropriate commanders must be selected. They must have the courage to consider alternative solutions and must also have a firm grasp of the task they are to carry out. Furthermore, they should lead their troops from the front. An affinity with nature and a nose for the correct measures to be taken are qualities they should possess. Particularly important too is the ability to improvise.

(b) Units must be led decisively and with conviction, while orders must be brief and to the point. The commander of an attack must have a clear understanding of the task to be carried out and must be given the means to act independently. The maxim of the III Panzer Corps, 'He who starts early wins the day!', and that of the XXIV Panzer Corps, 'He who moves at night is spared much blood', should be put into practice.

(c) The troops should be suitably equipped for their assigned task. Any materiel that exceeds what is required and that might become a burden should be left behind. There must be no element of a unit that hinders the remaining elements.

(d) A unit committed to an attack must possess a strong sense of community and must be flexible in terms of organisation. This enables the unit to be led easily and efficiently.

(e) Such a unit must also have good training, and its commander should be able to think quickly and be capable of taking the initiative. He should possess a good understanding of the various arms of the ground forces so that, if necessary, he can immediately take command of other units on the battlefield.

(f) An attacking unit must have its own supply elements. These elements should be capable of manoeuvring, driving off-road, and protecting themselves. They should also, if necessary, be able to meet the needs of the combat troops for days on end without being replenished.

It is difficult to establish regulations for and to learn how to conduct an attack. As stated by Rommel: 'The best results of a field commander are achieved when ideas develop not in accordance with some predetermined scheme but rather freely and in relation to the given surroundings.' Any overreliance on a plan, any hesitation in making a bold decision, or any unnecessary delay in leaping into action can result in the death of an attack, be it on a small or large scale.

The loss of time results in the loss of the battle!

APPENDIX I

Headquarters Staff

XXXXVIII Panzer Corps (1941)

Commander: General of Panzer Troops Kempf
Chief of staff: Lieutenant-Colonel Friebe
First general staff officer: Major Berlin

57th Infantry Division

Commander: Lieutenant-General Blümm
First general staff officer: Lieutenant-Colonel Schmidt (Hans)

75th Infantry Division

Commander: Lieutenant-General Hammer
First general staff officer: Major von Einem

16th Motorised Infantry Division

Commander: Major-General Henrici
First general staff officer: Lieutenant-Colonel Gundelach

60th Motorised Infantry Division

Commander: Lieutenant-General Eberhardt
First general staff officer: Lieutenant-Colonel Pohlmann

11th Panzer Division

Commander: Major-General Crüwell
First general staff officer: Major Wolff

16th Panzer Division

Commander: Major-General Hube
First general staff officer: Major Müller (Walter)

SS Motorised Division Leibstandarte Adolf Hitler

Commander: SS-General Dietrich
First general staff officer: SS-Lieutenant-Colonel Keilhaus

Motorised Regiment Hermann Göring

Commander: Colonel Konrad

XXIV Panzer Corps (1941)

Commander: General of Panzer Troops Freiherr Geyr von Schweppenburg
Chief of staff: Colonel Wagener

3rd Panzer Division

Commander: Lieutenant-General Model (later Major-General Breith)
First general staff officer: Lieutenant-Colonel Pontow

4th Panzer Division

Commander: Major-General Freiherr von Langermann
First general staff officer: Lieutenant-Colonel Heidkämper

10th Motorised Infantry Division

Commander: Lieutenant-General von Loeper
First general staff officer: Major von Unold

Infantry Regiment Großdeutschland

Commander: Colonel Hörnlein

III Panzer Corps (1941)

Commander: General of Cavalry von Mackensen
Chief of staff: Colonel Faeckenstedt

13th Panzer Division

Commander: Lieutenant-General von Rothkirch und Panthen
First general staff officer: Major Kraemer

14th Panzer Division

Commander: Major-General Kühn (Major-General Heim from 1 July 1942)
First general staff officer: Lieutenant-Colonel Hörst

XXXX Panzer Corps (1942)

Commander: General of Panzer Troops Freiherr Geyr von Schweppenburg (later Lieutenant-General Henrici)
Chief of staff: Colonel Wagener

3rd Panzer Division

Commander: Major-General Westhofen
First general staff officer: Lieutenant-Colonel Voß

23rd Panzer Division

Commander: Lieutenant-General Mack (killed in action near Mozdok and replaced by Lieutenant-General von Boineburg und Lengsfeld)[15]

---

[15] Translator's note: There is no mention in the text of the first general staff officer for the 23rd Panzer Division, and the name is not known.

APPENDIX 2

Excerpts from the War Diary of the Commander of the 8th Company of the 6th Panzer Regiment

12 July 1942

Uneventful advance behind the 23rd Panzer Division, which we must follow at top speed.
(115 kilometres)

13 July 1942

Near Ternoskaya. Attack against Russians who have broken through. The 8th Company alone takes 600 prisoners.
(40 kilometres)

14 July 1942

Cooperation with the 3rd Motorcycle Battalion. A marching column is routed. 7 anti-tank guns and 2 Stalin Organs are destroyed. The motorcycle battalion is securing a sector 10 kilometres in width.
(30 kilometres)

15 July 1942

Tank battle near Nizovki. 9 tanks are put out of action. A column of trucks is routed.

16 July 1942

Armoured personnel carriers of the 8th Company carry out reconnaissance as far as the sector of the 22nd Panzer Division.

18 July 1942

Emergency assistance required by the 394th Infantry Division. Completely quiet by the time we got there. A Romanian division approaching from the north-west.
(20 kilometres)

20 July 1942

The company returns to its sector. Two days of rest are planned. Maintenance work to be undertaken.

21 July 1942

The company must depart quickly and sets off over the steppes in multiple columns alongside one another.
(85 kilometres)

22 July 1942

Pivot to the south towards Kameno Brodsky via Tatsinskaya.
(80 kilometres)

23–24 July 1942

Quiet in the sector of the company. Baking cakes and eating sausages. Many of our tanks had to be handed over.

25 July 1942

Continuation of the advance at 0800 hours. Crossed the Don on a pontoon bridge at 2000 hours. Muddy roads. Trucks bogged down despite our attempts to tow them.
(30 kilometres)

26 July 1942

Completely muddy roads on the way to Karov and Ninov. Advancing to the south. The task of the panzer battalion is to take the bridge over the Sal in the vicinity of Nesmeyanovka. The 8th Company must remain behind to provide security.
(55 kilometres)

27 July 1942

Over the Sal in the late afternoon. Air raid at the same time by low-flying enemy warplanes.
(30 kilometres)

28 July 1942

0230 hours. Overnight advance across the terrain. The 8th Company is the spearhead unit. Large quantities of foodstuffs requisitioned.
(85 kilometres)

29 July 1942

Advance to the east and then to the south. The 1st and 4th Companies attack towards Proletarskaya. The 8th Company is to detonate the Stalingrad–Krasnograd railway line. The task is carried out and we capture five trucks, nine locomotives, a hospital train, and trains loaded with grain and electrical equipment.
(90 kilometres)

30 July 1942

Establishment of a line of security in Gundaroff. Emergency departure in the evening. A platoon of the 7th Company caused an armoured train to burst into flames on the night of 30/31 July. Withdrawal after midnight.
(45 kilometres)

31 July 1942

Return to Proletarskaya.
(28 kilometres)

1 August 1942

Russian attack from the east against Petrovskaya. The 8th Company counter-attacks. A Russian battalion is annihilated. Continuation of the advance over the Manych.
(65 kilometres)

2 August 1942

Battle Group von Liebenstein departs for the south at 0700 hours. The 8th Company is the spearhead unit. Rapid progress. Pregradnoye reached

at 1700 hours. Sixty prisoners taken and 4 heavy mortars captured. The Russians are fleeing. Fuel levels are depleted.
(105 kilometres)

3 August 1942

We have come to a halt. No fuel. Our squads take more Russians prisoner. The I Battalion seizes Voroshilovsk.

4 August 1942

Further advance to the south at noon through desolate steppes. No trees. No bushes.
(45 kilometres)

5 August 1942

Advance towards Voroshilovsk across hills and then over terrain that is vast and without any trees. The 4th Company takes Nevinnomysskaya.
(40 kilometres)

6 August 1942

The appearance of the terrain has changed. It resembles Thuringia, although it is rather unfavourable for military operations.
(35 kilometres)

7 August 1942

Sudden continuation of the advance through foothills and on roads that are in poor condition towards Boronkovskaya, which lies on the Kuban.
(57 kilometres)

8 August 1942

Destruction of an enemy tank battalion near Svorovka. Approaching Mozdok from the north.
(130 kilometres)

23 August 1942

Destruction of two enemy tank platoons. The bulk of the 6th Panzer Regiment, including the 8th Company, enters Mozdok.

24 August 1942

The 5th and 8th Companies assist mechanised infantry units in the seizure of Mozdok.

September 1942

Advance in the direction of Ishcherskaya.
(40 kilometres)

Until December 1942

Several mobile defensive battles take place.

Total distance covered = 1,250 kilometres

APPENDIX 3

A Selection of Orders Issued by the Units of the 11th Panzer Division

The following selection of orders demonstrates how important it was to have available a variety of units so that the correct weaponry could be brought into action quickly and precisely where it was needed. It took too much time to draw upon units from other sectors of the front, something that was frequently impossible anyway due to the difficulties of the terrain in Russia.

15th Panzer Regiment, Operations Section, 21 June 1941

Order for the attack

1. The enemy before the XXXXVIII Panzer Corps is the 46th Rifle Division. He occupies a fortified position, not particularly deep, along the frontier in the hills on the opposite bank of the Western Bug. It appears as if he has neither reserves nor emplacements further back.
2. The infantry of the XXXXVIII Panzer Corps will attack on B Day at Y Hour. With the 57th Infantry Division on the right and the 75th Infantry Division on the left, the attack will proceed over the Western Bug and will penetrate the enemy position. This will enable the mobile formations to advance quickly to the east in the direction of the Dnieper. The neighbouring unit to the right of the XXXXVIII Panzer Corps will be the 297th Infantry Division (of the XXXXIV Army Corps), while that to the left will be the 14th Panzer Division (of the III Panzer Corps). The latter is to advance from Hrubieszow towards Kiev via Lutsk and Rovno.

3. Once the infantry divisions prise open the front, the 11th Panzer Division will thrust through the gap and will lead the advance along the main road through Sokal, Tartakov, Stoyanev, Radekhov, and Lopatyn. It will then force the crossing of the Styr at Szczurowjce and will drive relentlessly through Dubno, Ostrog, Polonne, Berdichev, and Bialacerkiew as far as the Dnieper. The various battle groups are to attack swiftly and are to support one another in their efforts so that any Russian resistance will be broken immediately. All forces will be committed to overcoming any difficulties that might arise due to the condition of the roads or the nature of the terrain. It will be the task of the infantry formations to deal with any elements of the enemy forces that are bypassed by the panzer formations. Attacks by enemy tanks are to be counter-attacked and destroyed at once by exploiting our superiority in armour-piercing weaponry.
4. Battle Group A, led by the divisional commander, is to be composed of the 231st Panzer Reconnaissance Battalion, the reinforced 15th Panzer Regiment, and the 61st Motorcycle Battalion. The battle group will be ready for action by 0600 hours on 22 June 1941 so that, once the order is given, it can set off without delay from its assembly area along the road through Witkow, Dolhobyczow, Oszczow, Warez, Opulsko, and Zabuze towards Sokal, where it is then to cross the Western Bug in a concentrated attack.
5. The task of the 15th Panzer Regiment is to advance along the main road towards the Styr and seize Szczurowjce in a single stroke. It will secure the village and keep it open for the rest of the 11th Panzer Division.
6. Order of battle:
    (a) Sub-Group Schimmelmann: staff of the 15th Panzer Regiment, II Battalion of the 15th Panzer Regiment, 6th Company of the 15th Panzer Regiment, 2nd Company of the 110th Rifle Regiment, an 8.8-centimetre flak battery, two platoons of the 1st Battery of the 71st Light Flak Battalion, one platoon of the 2nd Company of the 209th Panzer Pioneer Battalion, one battery of the I Battalion of the 119th Artillery Regiment.
    (b) Sub-Group Schmahl: I Battalion of the 15th Panzer Regiment (without two light platoons), 2nd Company of

the 209th Panzer Pioneer Battalion (without one platoon), half a bridge column, I Battalion of the 119th Artillery Regiment (without two batteries).

(c) Sub-Group Körtge: two combat trains, two light panzer platoons of the I Battalion of the 15th Panzer Regiment, one column of the 231st Reconnaissance Battalion, one platoon of the 1st Battery of the 71st Light Flak Battalion.

7. It is necessary to ensure the security of the flanks during the advance, especially to the south. Reconnaissance will need to be carried out near Kamianka Strumilova and Brody!

8. Lines of attack: twist in the road in central Sokal – church in southern Stoyanov – bridge over the Styr in Szczurowjce (see map of scale 1:100,000); road fork in southern Sokal – Leshnev (see map of scale 1:300,000).

9. Enemy paratroopers, wherever they appear, are to be attacked and annihilated immediately. Do not await orders to do so.

10. The swastika flag will no longer be flown at all times. Once we cross the Western Bug, the flag is only to be flown as a recognition signal when friendly aircraft fly overhead. It is important on such occasions that this recognition signal be shown as quickly as possible.

11. So that the ground troops will be able to identify them, German combat aircraft have not only nationality markings but also bright yellow paint. Specifically:
    (a) one third of the underside of the aerofoils, extending from the wingtips, are painted in yellow; and
    (b) a yellow ring, about half a metre in width, is painted around the fuselage.

12. Radio communications will exist between the divisional commander and the 15th Panzer Regiment. Nevertheless, radio silence is to be strictly maintained until contact has been made with the enemy!

13. It is to be reported:
    (a) when the Stoyanov–Druzkopol line has been crossed,
    (b) when Lopatyn has been reached, and
    (c) when the Styr has been reached.

14. The regimental command post is to be based in Telatyn until the commencement of the advance.

Riebel

11th Panzer Division, Operations Section, Divisional Command Post, 6 July 1941

The following is the way in which the troops are to be organised for the advance on 6 July 1941, which is expected to begin at around noon.

For the divisional headquarters.
Signed by the first general staff officer.

(a) Battle Group Bohlmann
- Advance guard (Lieutenant-Colonel von Stockhausen): 61st Construction Detachment, 2nd Company of the 110th Rifle Regiment, Panzer Company Kaphengst, 1st Panzer Reconnaissance Platoon of the 231st Panzer Reconnaissance Battalion, one platoon of the 3rd Battery of the 71st Light Flak Battalion (four-barrelled guns).
- Main body: 111th Rifle Regiment, II Battalion of the 15th Panzer Regiment, II Battalion of the 119th Artillery Regiment (without the 6th Battery), 7th Battery of the 110th Artillery Regiment, one flash ranging platoon of the 334th Observation Battalion, 1st Company of the 209th Panzer Pioneer Battalion, 2nd Company of the 61st Anti-Tank Battalion (one medium platoon and two light platoons), 3rd Battery of the 71st Light Flak Battalion (without one platoon), one platoon of the 1st Battery of the 71st Light Flak Battalion, one platoon of the 1st Company of the 61st Medical Battalion.

(b) Battle Group Riebel: 15th Panzer Regiment (without the II Battalion), I Battalion of the 110th Rifle Regiment (without the 2nd Company), 231st Panzer Reconnaissance Battalion, I Battalion of the 119th Artillery Regiment, 844th Heavy Artillery Battalion, headquarters battery of the 119th Artillery Regiment, 334th Observation Battalion (without one flash ranging platoon), 1st Battery of the 71st Light Flak Battalion (without one platoon), 13th and 14th Companies of the 61st Heavy Motor Transport Column, 2nd Platoon of the 1st Company of the 61st Medical Battalion.

(c) 341st Panzer Signal Battalion (aside from the elements with the command section), staff and signal communication platoons of the

61st Anti-Tank Battalion (without the command echelon), staff and signal communication platoons of the 71st Light Flak Battalion (without the command echelon), staff and signal communication platoons of the I Battalion of Motorised Regiment Hermann Göring, 2nd Battery of the 71st Light Flak Battalion (without one platoon), 3rd Platoon of the 1st Company of the 61st Medical Battalion, staff of the 11th Rifle Brigade (without the motorcycle section).
(d) Battle Group Lutz: 110th Rifle Regiment (without the I Battalion), III Battalion of the 119th Artillery Regiment (without the 7th Battery), 5th Battery of the 119th Artillery Regiment, one platoon of the 2nd Battery of the 71st Light Flak Battalion, 1st Company of the 61st Anti-Tank Battalion (two medium platoons and one light platoon), fuel and lubricants supply elements with the 8th, 9th, and 10th Heavy Motor Transport Columns.
(e) March Group Neureiter: 61st Divisional Supply Service, quartermaster section and the rest of the divisional staff, noncommitted elements of the 341st Panzer Signal Battalion, supply troops according to the orders of the quartermaster section.
(f) Aside from the march units: command section of the 11th Panzer Division with the command echelons, 1st Battery (8.8-centimetre guns) of the flak battalion of Motorised Regiment Hermann Göring, 5th Light Battery of Motorised Regiment Hermann Göring (based in Kamionka), 209th Panzer Pioneer Battalion (based in Polonne, without one company).

The commanders of recently subordinated units are to report to the leader of the march group, who will decide upon the allocation of those new units.

11th Rifle Brigade, Operations Section, Brigade Headquarters, 10 July 1941, 0205 hours

Order for the advance of Battle Group Angern on 10 July 1941

1. On 9 July, elements of the 16th Motorised Infantry Division fought in the area to the south-east of Chudnov against strong enemy forces that had approached from the south.
2. Battle Group Angern annihilated this enemy on 10 July in conjunction with the 16th Motorised Infantry Division.

3. Order of march in appendix.
4. The situation at 0415 hours is as follows:
   - The I Battalion of the 15th Panzer Regiment is standing along the Berdichev–Chudnov road. Its spearhead is in the high ground of the Malaya–Tatarinovka area, while a line of security has been established to the west and north-west.
   - Behind the leading company, enough room (approximately 500 metres) is to be left for the command, orderly, communications, and radio echelons of the 11th Rifle Brigade as well as for the command echelon of the III Battalion of the 119th Artillery Regiment.
   - The 2nd Company of the 110th Rifle Regiment is at the railway crossing in Holodki.
   - Behind the I Battalion of the 15th Panzer Regiment are a platoon of the 71st Light Flak Battalion, the command echelon with the 61st Construction Detachment, the 1st Company of the 61st Anti-Tank Battalion, and flak units with 8.8-centimetre guns.
   - The 61st Construction Detachment is about 1,500 metres to the south-east of the aforementioned railway crossing.
   - The 2nd Company of the 209th Panzer Pioneer Battalion stands approximately 2,500 metres to the south-east of the railway crossing.
   - The flak units with 8.8-centimetre guns are further to the sout-heast.
   - Standing to the north-west and ready to set off is the III Battalion of the 119th Artillery Regiment. Also in the area are two platoons of the 71st Light Flak Battalion and one company of the 61st Anti-Tank Battalion (to the west of Berdichev), the precise placement of which shall be determined by the commander of the III Battalion of the 119th Artillery Regiment.
5. On 10 July 1941 at 0320 hours, the commander of the I Battalion of the 15th Panzer Regiment reported to the command post of the rifle brigade on the road to the north-west of Berdichev.

11th Rifle Brigade, Operations Section, 10 July 1941

Order of march of Battle Group Angern

- Advance guard: 1st Company of the 15th Panzer Regiment; one pioneer reconnaissance squad of the 2nd Company of the 209th Panzer Pioneer Battalion.
- Command echelon: command, orderly, signals, and radio sections of the 11th Rifle Brigade; command elements of the III Battalion of the 119th Artillery Regiment.
- Main body: I Battalion of the 15th Panzer Regiment (without one company); 2nd Company of the 110th Rifle Regiment; three platoons of the 71st Light Flak Battalion; Command Echelon 2; 61st Construction Detachment; two companies of the 61st Anti-Tank Battalion; flak units with 8.8-centimetre guns; 2nd Company of the 209th Panzer Pioneer Battalion; one flak battery (8.8-centimetre guns) of Motorised Regiment Hermann Göring; III Battalion of the 119th Artillery Regiment (without the 9th Battery).

15th Panzer Regiment, Operations Section, Regimental Command Post, 16 July 1941

Organisation of the forces for the march on 16–17 July 1941

1. The panzer regiment will take up a new position in the vicinity of Molchanovka.
2. Route of march: Voytovka, Rozyn, Molchanovka.
3. Time of march: Yet to be decided.
4. Order of march:
    - Reconnaissance platoons of the I and II Battalions, staff of the II Battalion, regimental staff, II Battalion (without one company), 2nd Company of the 110th Rifle Regiment, I Battalion (without one company), 3rd Company of the 61st Anti-Tank Battalion, 13th and 14th Companies of the 61st Heavy Motor Transport Column, rifle echelons, Combat Train II.
    - The 1st Battery of the 71st Light Flak Battalion will be distributed as before. Combat Train I to be divided amongst the units.

The wheeled vehicles of Combat Train I are to be pulled by tanks should the roads be in poor condition.
5. Voytovka will be the point at which units will join the march column. Traffic at this point will be managed by an officer from the II Battalion.

Draft: Riebel

Verified by: First Lieutenant Löstmann (Adjutant)

11th Rifle Brigade, Operations Section, Brigade Headquarters, 8 August 1941, 2245 hours

Order for the advance of Battle Group Angern on 9 August 1941

1. Battle Group Angern is to reach Novo Mirgorod on 9 August 1941 and is then to be placed at the disposal of Panzer Group 1.
2. Route of advance: Tyishchovka, Lipnyazhka, Dobrovelichkovka, Glodosy, Khmelyevoye, and further in a direction to be determined by the results of reconnaissance. Road reconnaissance to be conducted by the 231st Panzer Reconnaissance Battalion, and it is to report to the 11th Rifle Brigade.
3. Disposition and order of march: 231st Panzer Reconnaissance Battalion (with a platoon of the 1st Battery of the 71st Light Flak Battalion placed under its command), staff of the 11th Rifle Brigade, 209th Panzer Pioneer Battalion, 15th Panzer Regiment (with one platoon of the 1st Battery of the 71st Light Flak Battalion and the 2nd Company of the 110th Rifle Regiment placed under its command, but without the I Battalion and without the bulk of the troops), 111th Rifle Regiment (without its I Battalion), I Battalion of the 119th Artillery Regiment, 61st Anti-Tank Battalion (without one company).
4. Assembly:
   (a) Departure point: Northern part of Tyishchovka.
   (b) Departure traffic to be managed to the north of Tyishchovka by an officer of the II Battalion of the 111th Rifle Regiment

and to the south-east of Tyishchovka by an officer of the 209th Panzer Pioneer Battalion.

(c) Times of departure: 231st Panzer Reconnaissance Battalion (with a flak platoon under its command) at 0335 hours, staff of the 11th Rifle Brigade (with a signal communications platoon) at 0405 hours, 15th Panzer Regiment (with a flak platoon and the 2nd Company of the 110th Rifle Regiment under its command) at 0420 hours, II Battalion of the 111th Rifle Regiment at 0510 hours.

The staff of the 111th Rifle Regiment and one company of the 209th Panzer Pioneer Battalion will set off in accordance with the order of march in Tyishchovka. The I Battalion of the 119th Artillery Regiment, the 61st Anti-Tank Battalion (without one company), and the rest of the 209th Panzer Pioneer Battalion shall follow behind the II Battalion of the 111th Rifle Regiment.

5. Each unit will determine the precise movement of its subordinate elements.
6. From 0600 hours, the units of the 11th Panzer Division shall no longer be advancing along the Novo Arkhangelsk–Tyishchovka–Dobryanka road.
7. Radio communications are to be maintained with the 11th Panzer Division, the 15th Panzer Regiment, the 231st Panzer Reconnaissance Battalion, the 111th Rifle Regiment, the 209th Panzer Pioneer Battalion, and the 61st Anti-Tank Battalion.

Code signals for the advance: Lipuyasha (8 g 8), Dobrovelichkovka (8 t 8), Glodosy (8 a 8), Khmelyevoye (8 z 8), Bolshaya Viska (8 y 8), Novo Mirgorod (8 L 8).

Reports are to be made when these locations are reached by the leading elements of the 231st Panzer Reconnaissance Battalion and the 209th Panzer Pioneer Battalion.

8. I will march at the head of the brigade staff echelon.

Angern

References

Grams, Rolf. *Die 14. Panzer-Division 1940–1945.* Bad Nauheim: Podzun, 1957.
Guderian, Heinz. *Erinnerungen eines Soldaten.* Heidelberg: Vowinckel, 1951.
Lucke, Fritz. *Panzerkeil im Osten: Gedenkbuch der Berlin-Märkischen 3. Panzer-Division.* Berlin: Die Wehrmacht, 1942.
Mackensen, Eberhard von. 'Mit Kleist durch die Ukraine: Die Operationen der 1. Panzerarmee im Ostfeldzug'. Report (1941).
Mackensen, Eberhard von. 'Mit Kleist in den Kaukasus: Die Operationen der 1. Panzerarmee im zweiten Kriegsjahr gegen Russland'. Report (1942).
Mackensen, Eberhard von. *Vom Bug zum Kaukasus: Das III. Panzerkorps im Feldzug gegen Sowjetrußland 1941–1942.* Neckargemünd: Vowinckel, 1967.
Manstein, Erich von. *Verlorene Siege.* Bonn: Athenäum, 1955.
Philippi, Alfred. 'Das Pripjetproblem'. *Wehrwissenschaftliche Rundschau*, supplementary issue no. 2 (1956).
Röhricht, Edgar. *Probleme der Kesselschlacht: Dargestellt an Einkreisungs-Operationen im Zweiten Weltkrieg.* Karlsruhe: Condor, 1958.
Steets, Hans. *Gebirgsjäger bei Uman: Die Korpsschlacht des XXXXIX. Gebirgs-Armeekorps bei Podwyssokoye 1941.* Heidelberg: Vowinckel, 1955.
War diary of the 6th Panzer Regiment of the 3rd Panzer Division (1941).
Several private sources have also been used.

Index

Armavir, 126, 128

Babuszki, 38–39, 41
Badovka, 21, 25
Baku, 126, 131
Balabanovka, 64, 70
Berdichev, xxv, 2, 34, 36–54, 94, 104, 154, 158
Beresteczko, 6–7, 9–11, 13–14, 17
Bialacerkiew, 38, 40, 53, 57, 62, 67, 79, 154
Bialolowka, 53–56, 58
Bialopol, 38, 51–52
Black Sea, xi, xxxi, 89–91, 101
Bolshaya Viska, 84, 161
Borszczahowka, 54, 56
Brauchitsch, Walther von, 3, 92
Brest-Litovsk, 108–109
Brodov, 21, 25
Brody, 9, 11, 13–16, 18, 155
Bryansk, 116–118, 120
Buraki, 43–45, 48
Buzovka, 59, 66

Cherkassy, 91, 101, 106
Chudnov, 31–32, 34, 37–40, 42–43, 157–158
Crüwell, Ludwig, 46, 66, 69, 154–155
Czerniawka, 53–54

Dobra, 74, 76
Dobrovelichkovka, 160–161
Dobryanka, 78, 161
Dubno, xx, xxii, 8–9, 11–20, 24–26, 154

Eberbach, Heinrich, 121–122

Frantovka, 60, 72

Gaysin, 60, 71
German armed forces
  Anti-Tank Battalions
    61st, 156–161
    670th, 13, 24–25, 35, 68, 81
  Armies
    Second, 107–108, 110, 115, 118
    Fourth, 118, 121
    Sixth, 2–3, 91–92, 106–107, 110, 132
    Seventeenth, 2, 75, 78, 92, 108, 126
  Army Corps
    XXIX, 2, 24
    XXXXIV, 6, 8, 13, 34, 55–57, 86, 153
    LV, 8, 15–16, 57
  Army Group A, 126, 133
  Army Group Centre, 107–108, 110, 115, 117–118, 125
  Army Group South, 1–2, 107–108, 110, 125
  Artillery Regiment
    119th, 154–161
  Battle Group Angern, 41–43, 50, 53–54, 157, 159–160
  Battle Group Bohlmann, 22, 156
  Battle Group Kempf, 92, 96, 100
  Battle Group von Liebenstein, 130, 150
  Construction Detachment
    61st, 156, 158–159
  Corps Artillery Command
    108th, 13, 100
  courage and performance of, xii, 6, 14, 22–23, 36, 54, 81, 87, 89, 92, 105

Group Eberbach, 121–122
Group Schwedler, 57, 67, 71–74, 77, 83
impacted by bad roads and supply difficulties, *passim*
Infantry Divisions
 44th, 17–18, 22–23, 103
 57th, 3–11, 13, 18, 45, 58, 61–65, 67, 69, 153
 75th, 3–8, 19, 24, 45, 153
 111th, 15–17, 23, 26, 36, 46, 48, 50, 52
 297th, 8, 77–79, 83, 85, 153
 298th, 103–104
Infantry Division Großdeutschland, 126–127
Infantry Regiment Großdeutschland, 9, 120
Infantry Regiments
 60th, 34–35, 37–39, 43–45, 47, 56, 58, 62, 81, 96–100
 92nd, 46, 50–52
 156th, 33, 41–42, 56–58, 69, 80–81
 179th, 10, 12, 67, 69
 199th, 11–12
Light Flak Battalion
 71st, 154–160
Luftwaffe, 11, 13, 20, 22, 31, 35, 38, 60, 90, 120
Motorcycle Battalion
 61st, 7–8, 154
Motorised Infantry Divisions
 16th, chapters 2–5 *passim*, 126–129, 157
 25th, 24, 84, 104, 116
 60th, 39–40, 42–48, 50–53, 106
Motorised Regiment Hermann Göring, 11, 24, 66, 68, 78–79, 86, 157, 159
Mountain Divisions
 1st, 83, 85
 4th, 79, 83, 85
OKH (High Command of the German Army), 105, 110
Panzer Armies
 First, xii, xxxix, 125–127, 130, 132–133

Second, xxxvi, 118–119, 121
 Fourth, 125–126, 130
Panzer Corps
 III, xii, xxxiii, 2, 4, 18, 24, 32–33, 36, 38, 44, 46, 49, 53, 85, 103–106, 126–132, 138, 144, 153
 XIV, 4, 36, 49, 51, 53, 57, 63, 76, 79, 82–83, 85, 105
 XXIV, 107–108, 110–112, 114–120, 123, 144
 XXXX, 130–131
 XXXXVII, 118, 120
 XXXXVIII, xi–xii, xxxiv, chapters 1–6 *passim*, 107–108, 112, 114, 116, 118, 120, 153
Panzer Divisions
 3rd, v, 109–110, 114, 116–117, 120–121, 123, 130–132
 4th, 116–117, 121–122
 9th, 46, 51, 65, 70, 78, 80, 83–84, 113–114, 116, 120
 11th, xxiv, xxvi, 4, chapters 2–4 *passim*, 89, 153–154, 156–157, 161
 13th, 24, 32, 36, 38, 44, 103–104, 106, 127–129, 132
 14th, 84, 103–104, 106, 126–127, 153
 16th, chapters 2–5 *passim*, 112–113
 18th, 3, 120–121
 23rd, 130–132, 148
Panzer Group 1, chapters 1–5 *passim*, 105–108, 110–111, 160
Panzer Group 2, 107–110, 115–118
Panzer Pioneer Battalion
 209th, 154, 156–161
Panzer Reconnaissance Battalion
 231st, 154, 156, 160–161
Panzer Regiments
 6th, v, 109, 111, 121–122, 148–152
 15th, 7, 153–156, 158–161
Rifle Brigade
 11th, 157–161
Rifle Regiments
 64th, 64, 66–67, 69, 95, 112–113
 79th, 94–95, 97
 110th, 7–9, 28, 154, 156–161

111th, 156, 160–161
SS Division Wiking, 54, 77, 106
SS Motorised Division Leibstandarte
    Adolf Hitler, 25, 35, 37–40,
    chapters 4–5 *passim*
SS Regiment Westland, 77, 81, 86
Stuka raids by, 48, 50–52, 56, 68, 71,
    81, 111
Glodosy, 160–161
Golovanevsk, 75, 78, 85
Gomel, 108–110
Greiga, 93–95, 97–98
Grozny, 126, 132
Guderian, Heinz, 107–108, 118–119, 143

Hitler, Adolf, 107, 125
Holodki, 42, 45, 158
Hopczycia, 58, 61
Horbkov, 5, 9
Hrubieszow, 103, 153
Hube, Hans-Valentin, 8, 14–15, 99
Hungarian armed forces
    cavalry units, 97–98
    Mobile Corps, 78, 83, 91–94, 96, 98,
        100
    Motorised Brigades
        1st, 91, 93, 98
        2nd, 93, 98

Ishcherskaya, 132, 152
Italian 9th Infantry Division Pasubio, 91,
    106
Ivakhny, 64, 71
Ivanki, 74, 77–78
Iwankowce, 48, 50–51

Januszpol, 37, 41–44, 52

Kaluga, 115, 118
Kamyaneche, 76, 78, 80–81, 83–84
Kashira, 118–119
Kempf, Werner, xii, 2–4, 6, 11, 15, 17,
    21, 26, 32–33, 36, 43, 66, 80, 86–87,
    141
Khazhyn, 38–39, 41, 50
Kherson, 94–96, 99–101
Khizhnya, 70, 73

Khmelyevoye, 160–161
Khorol, 112–113
Kiev, v, xxxiii, 1–2, 41, 49, 53, 55, 59,
    103–105, 110, 153
    Battle of, xxxiv–xxxv, 1, 107–108,
        112–115
Kirovograd, 74, 85
Kiszczynce, 69, 72
Kleist, Ewald von, 2–3, 26, 36, 41, 53, 68
Kniaza Krynycia, 62, 64, 66, 73
Konela, 65–66, 68, 72–73
Konstantinovka (east of Ternovka), 84, 97
Konstantinovka (on the Southern Bug),
    85, 90–92, 97
Konstantinovka (east of Nikolayev), 97–98
Koziatyn, 41, 52–53, 55, 57
Kozyn, 9, 15–16
Krasnopol, 37, 39–41, 45
Krasnovolka, 37–38
Kremenchug, 106, 108, 112, 114
Kremenets, 10–12, 14–17, 19, 24, 26
Krupets, 18, 26
Krystynopol, 6, 8
Kuniow, 21, 25

Labun, 33, 35
Lachowce, 27, 29, 32–33
Lashchova, 77–78
Legezino, 76, 78–79, 81
Leshnev, 9–13, 18, 155
Lezhelov, 50, 52
Lipnyazhka, 78, 86, 91, 160
Lisicze, 25–26
Lokhvitsa, 110–114
Lopatyn, 7–10, 154–155
Lubar, xxv, 29, 32–40, 43
Lubny, 108, 111–113
Lukaszowka, 62, 66, 71
Lutsk, 24–25, 103–104, 153

Makhnovka, 37–38, 40–41, 44, 47–48, 50,
    52–53
Mankovka, 72, 74–75
Manstein, Erich von, ix, xiv, 138, 143
Mashurov, 78–79
Maykop, 126, 129
Merva, 7, 10

Mirgorod, 113–114
Miropol, xxv, 29, 31–35, 37–40, 42, 49
Mlynov, 9, 15, 17, 24
Monastyryshche, 60, 62, 64–66, 69, 72–74
Moscow, v, 1, 107–110
  assault on, xxxviii, 101, 115–119, 123, 125
Moszkow, 24–25
Mozdok, 131, 151–152
Mtsensk, 117, 119–123

Nesterovka, 66, 70, 74–75
Nevinnomysskaya, 131, 151
Nikolayev, xxxi–xxxii, 89–101
Nizgorce, 50–51
Novo Arkhangelsk, 75–86, 161
Novo Danzig, 94–98
Novo Grigoryevka, 82–83
Novo Mirgorod, 89, 160–161
Novo Petrovka, 96, 100
Novo Poltavka, 93, 95–96, 98
Novyi Bug, 93, 95

offensive operations and mobile warfare
  history of, xiii–xiv
  principles of, 125, 135–140, 142–144
  lessons from, 133, 135, 137–142
Olgopol, 92–93
Oratov, 56, 58, 60, 62–64, 66–67
Orel, 116–120
Osiczna, 63–64
Ostrog, xxi–xxiii, 12–16, 18–22, 24–25, 27–28, 35, 154
Ostrov, 8–11
Ozerna, 54, 56

Panskij List, 73–74
Peresadovka, 98–99
Perespa, 5–6, 8
Pervomaisk, 75, 83, 91
Peski, 93, 98
Piatyhorka, 47–48, 50
Pirogi, 112–113
Plaszowa, 8, 10
Podobna, 65, 75
Podorozna, 43–45
Podvysokoye, 83, 85

Pohrebyszcze, 56, 60–62
Polonne, 18, 28, 31–32, 34, 37, 39–40, 154, 157
Pomoynik, 75–76
Poryck, 7, 9
Potash, 78–79
Pregradnoye, 130, 150
Pripet Marshes, 1–2, 101, 107–108
Ptycza, 9, 19–20, 22–23
Pyatki, 41–43

Radekhov, 7–11, 154
  first tank battle near, xx, 6–7
Rajgrodek, 41, 45, 47–48, 50, 52
Rawszczynia, 6, 8
Riebel, Gustav-Adolf, 7, 155, 160
Rivers
  Desna, 108, 110, 118
  Dnieper, 2, 53, 85, 90, 92, 101, 105–107, 109, 113, 153–154
  Don, 125–127, 130, 139, 149
  Donets, 2, 125, 132
  Horyn, 13, 16, 21, 29, 33, 104
  Ikva, 12, 15–16, 23
  Ingul, 92–95, 97–99
  Kuban, 126, 128, 151
  Laba, 128–129
  Manych, 127, 130, 150
  Oka, 115–117, 119
  Oskol, 125–126
  Sal, 127, 130, 149–150
  Sinyukha, 80, 82–84
  Slucz, 29, 31–33, 35, 37–39, 42, 104
  Southern Bug, 85, 89–92, 99
  Styr, xx, 6–8, 10–11, 17, 104, 154–155
  Sula, 108, 110, 112–114
  Terek, 130–132
  Viliya, 19, 21, 25, 27
  Western Bug, xix, 2, 5–6, 153–155
  Yegorlyk, 128, 130
  Zusha, xxxvii, 115–122
Rogi, 75–77, 79, 81
Romanian armed forces, 91, 93, 101
Romanov, 28, 37, 39
Rommel, Erwin, xiv, 144
Romny, 108, 110
Roslavl, 109, 120

INDEX • 167

Rostov, 126, 128, 131
Rovno, 24–25, 103–104, 153
Rozyn, 51–54, 159
Rundstedt, Gerd von, 1, 4

Saselye, 95, 97–98
Schweppenburg, Leo Freiherr Geyr von, 110–111, 116
Semenovka, 113–114
Serpukhov, 118–119
Sitkowce, 66, 71
Sitno, 11–12, 19
Skvira, 49, 51, 54–55, 67
Slavuta, 27–28
Sokal, 3–6, 9, 154–155
Sokolovka, 59–60, 62, 66, 68–70, 72, 74–75
Soviet Armies
  3rd, 118, 120
  5th, 105, 110
  6th, 75, 80, 86
  12th, 75, 80, 86
  26th, 57, 59
Stadnitsa, 67, 69, 71
Stalingrad, 125, 127, 132, 150
Stalin Line, xxiv, 5, 29, 31–34, 36, 104, 109
Starodub, 108, 110
Starokonstantinov, 33–36
Starostynce, 58, 62
Stawiszcze, 56–57, 62, 65, 68
Stoyanov, 6–7, 10, 154–155
Stumpfeld, Hans–Joachim von, 16, 18
Sukhoi Yelanets, 90, 93
Sverdlinovo, 80–81, 83, 86
Szczurowjce, 6, 8, 154–155
Szepetowka, 18, 21, 28, 31–33
Szumsk, 24, 27

Talnoye, 75–78, 81–82, 86
Talyanki, 78–79

Tartakov, 5–6, 8–9, 154
Tavkino, 95–96, 100
Ternovka, 79–85
Tetiev, 54, 56, 60, 63–64
Tishkovka, 78, 82–83
Torgovitsy, 84–85
Tula, xxxviii, 115, 117–123
Tyishchovka, 160–161

Uman, xxviii, 55
  battle of, xxx, 59–87, 89–90, 106
  pocket, xxxii, 73, 75, 78, 80, 82–87, 101

Verba, 13–15, 17, 19–20, 26
  tank battle near, xxiii, 22–23
Volodarka, 54, 56–57, 62
Volosovka, 38, 41
Voroshilovsk, 128, 130, 151
Voytovka, 64, 159–160
Voznesensk, 89–91

Warkowicze, 10, 21
Werbowce, 33, 35, 49
Wielbowno, 18–19, 22, 25
Woszjatskoje, 91–92
Wysokie, 63–64

Yampol (west of the Horyn), 27, 29
Yampol (near Novo Arkhangelsk), 82, 90
Yelanets, 90, 92

Zaradynce, 54, 56
Zaslav, 18, 20, 24–25, 27, 29, 32
Zaszkow, 56, 59–60, 62, 74
Zelenkov, 76, 83
Zhitomir, 2, 33, 36, 38, 44, 51, 103–104
Zibermanovka, 65, 68, 73–74, 76
Zvyahel, 32–33, 38, 103–104
Zywotow, 60, 62–64, 67